The SHAPE
of the GOSPEL

The SHAPE of the GOSPEL

New Testament Essays

Robert C. Tannehill

Cascade Books
A division of Wipf & Stock Publishers
199 West 8th Avenue, Suite 3 • Eugene OR 97401

THE SHAPE OF THE GOSPEL
New Testament Essays

Copyright © 2007 Robert C. Tannehill. All rights reserved. Except for brief quotations in critical publications or reviews, no part of this book may be reproduced in any manner without prior written permission from the publisher. Write: Permissions, Wipf & Stock, 199 W. 8th Ave., Eugene, OR 97401.

Cascade Books
A Division of Wipf and Stock Publishers
199 W. 8th Ave., Suite 3
Eugene, OR 97401

ISBN 10: 1-59752-511-1
ISBN 13: 978-1-59752-511-4

Cataloging-in-Publication data

Tannehill, Robert C.
The shape of the gospel : New Testament essays / Robert C. Tannehill.

xvi + 238 p.; 23 cm.

ISBN 10: 1-59752-511-1 (alk. paper)
ISBN 13: 978-1-59752-511-4

1. Bible. N.T. Gospels—Criticism, interpretation, etc. 2. Bible. N.T. Mark—Criticism, interpretation, etc. 3. Bible. N.T. Matthew—Criticism, interpretation, etc. 4. Narration in the Bible. 5. Paul, the Apostle—Saint. I. Title.

BS2395 T26 2007

Manufactured in the U.S.A.

Contents

Preface vii
Acknowledgments xi
Abbreviations xiii

PART I: Gospel Sayings and Stories 1

1. Tension in Synoptic Sayings and Stories 3
2. The Pronouncement Story and Its Types 19
3. Varieties of Synoptic Pronouncement Stories 35
4. Types and Functions of Apophthegms in the Synoptic Gospels 57
5. The Gospels and Narrative Literature 99
6. "You Shall Be Complete"—
   If Your Love Includes All (Matthew 5:48) 127

PART II: The Gospel of Mark 133

7. The Disciples in Mark:
   The Function of a Narrative Role 135
8. The Gospel of Mark as Narrative Christology 161
9. Reading It Whole:
   The Function of Mark 8:34–35 in Mark's Story 189

PART III: Paul's Gospel 201

10. Paul as Liberator and Oppressor:
    Evaluating Diverse Views of 1 Corinthians 203
11. Participation in Christ:
    A Central Theme in Pauline Soteriology 223

Preface

AFTER THE PUBLICATION OF my collected essays on Luke–Acts,[1] K. C. Hanson, Editor in Chief of Wipf and Stock Publishers, suggested a companion volume of my New Testament essays on topics other than Luke–Acts. The result is the book you have in hand. It contains essays previously published in a variety of places, except for the last essay ("Participation in Christ: A Central Theme in Pauline Soteriology"), which was written for this volume. As in the first volume, I have added introductory paragraphs to orient the reader to the contents of each essay and to briefly explain its significance.

Most of the following essays reveal my interest in the significance of literary forms—both the short literary forms in the Gospels, such as pronouncement stories, and an entire Gospel as a formed narrative. I am interested in the significance of these forms, not just in literary classification systems (although I develop my own typology of pronouncement stories). I am interested in literary form as a clue to how the text may engage hearers and readers—impact their thought and life—if they are sensitive respondents. The Gospel stories have been shaped in ways that give them particular potentials for significant engagement. Study of literary form can help us recognize these potentials.

The first essay, "Tension in Synoptic Sayings and Stories," serves as a brief introduction to my interest in literary form by suggesting applications to three types of material: synoptic sayings (with attention to their forceful and imaginative language),[2] pronouncement stories, and the Gospel of Mark as a narrative. Essays 2–5 and 7–9 expand on this beginning. The first focus is pronouncement stories, those brief scenes in which Jesus responds to something said to him or observed by him (essays 2–4). Rudolf Bultmann, in his work on form criticism, discussed these stories under the title "apophthegms."[3] His classifications of these stories

---

1. Tannehill, *The Shape of Luke's Story: Essays on Luke–Acts* (Eugene, OR: Cascade, 2005).

2. See Tannehill: *The Sword of His Mouth* (1975; reprinted, Eugene, OR: Wipf & Stock, 2003).

3. *The History of the Synoptic Tradition*, trans. John Marsh. Rev. ed. (New York: Harper

do not do what I want to do, namely, clarify the dynamics in these stories so that we can understand how they engage people with certain commitments and presuppositions. Therefore, I developed my own typology designed to clarify these dynamics. In an essay not included in the present volume, I summarized the potential effect of many synoptic pronouncement stories with the term "attitudinal shift."[4] The way that the stories have been shaped gives them the power to produce significant shifts in basic attitudes of hearers and readers. I investigate the literary forms that contribute to this power.

The essay on "The Gospels and Narrative Literature" is broader in scope, discussing a variety of short narrative forms in the Gospels and, briefly, the Gospels as longer narratives.

I got my start in what later came to be called narrative criticism as a member of the Mark Seminar of the Society of Biblical Literature. In that seminar a small group of scholars was beginning to experiment with methods borrowed from literary studies, applying them to the Gospel of Mark. A significant change was taking place in Gospel studies. The Gospel of Mark was being approached as a totality with plot development and character portrayal, shaped by a narrator with points of view. "The Disciples in Mark" originated as a paper presented to the Mark Seminar. Perspectives developed in this essay are still important to me. This essay on the disciples follows their story line from its beginning to the end of Mark's Gospel and highlights a significant shift in their relation to Jesus. Since I also wanted to comment on the central story line in Mark, the story of Jesus, the essay on the disciples was followed by "The Gospel of Mark as Narrative Christology." The third Markan essay, "Reading It Whole," demonstrates how study of a whole Gospel as narrative can enrich our understanding of a particular part by clarifying its function within the larger story. These investigations of Mark contributed to my work when I changed my focus to Luke–Acts as a narrative.

All of these investigations represent a significant shift from the area of my Ph.D. dissertation, which was on dying and rising with Christ as a theme in Pauline theology.[5] This shift does not mean that I lost interest in

& Row, 1976) 11–69.

4. Tannehill, "Attitudinal Shift in Synoptic Pronouncement Stories," in *Orientation by Disorientation: Studies in Literary Criticism and Biblical Literary Criticism Presented in Honor of William A. Beardslee*, ed. Richard A. Spencer, PittsTMS 35 (Pittsburgh: Pickwick, 1980) 183–97.

5. A revision of the dissertation was published as *Dying and Rising with Christ: A Study in Pauline Theology*, BZNW 32 (1967; reprinted, Eugene, OR: Wipf & Stock, 2006).

Paul. My retirement as Academic Dean of Methodist Theological School in Ohio in 2000 has allowed me to address certain issues in the interpretation of Paul, resulting in two essays that are included in this volume. The essay on "Paul as Liberator and Oppressor" reflects on the seeming conflict between two recent lines of interpretation of 1 Corinthians. I am interested in hermeneutical issues raised by the debate, especially because of limits to our knowledge of the situation Paul faced, resulting in uncertainties about the purpose behind Paul's words and the possible consequences of them. The essay on "Participation in Christ" is a new effort to deal with some of the issues raised by my early work on dying and rising with Christ. Discussions of Pauline theology in recent decades enable me to look at these issues from a broader perspective and to propose some ideas that will, I hope, contribute to current conversations about Pauline soteriology.

Acknowledgments

1. "Tension in Synoptic Sayings and Stories" was first published in *Interpretation* 34 (1980) 138–50. ©1980 Union Theological Seminary in Virginia. Used by permission.

2. "The Pronouncement Story and Its Types" was first published in *Semeia* 20 (1981) 1–13. Used by permission.

3. "Varieties of Synoptic Pronouncement Stories" was first published in *Semeia* 20 (1981) 101–19. Used by permission.

4. "Types and Functions of Apophthegms in the Synoptic Gospels" was first published in *Aufstieg und Niedergang der römischen Welt* II.25.2, edited by Wolfgang Haase (Berlin: de Gruyter, 1984) 1792–829. Used by permission.

5. "The Gospels and Narrative Literature" was first published in *The New Interpreter's Bible*, edited by Leander E. Keck et al. (Nashville: Abingdon, 1995) 8:56–70. Used by permission.

6. "'You Shall Be Complete'—If Your Love Includes All (Matthew 5:48)" was first published in *Journal of Theology* 108 (2004) 29–34. Used by permission.

7. "The Disciples in Mark: The Function of a Narrative Role" was first published in *Journal of Religion* 57 (1977) 386–405. ©1977 University of Chicago. All rights reserved. Used by permission.

8. "The Gospel of Mark as Narrative Christology" was first published in *Semeia* 16 (1979) 57–95. ©1980 Society of Biblical Literature. Used by permission.

9. "Reading It Whole: The Function of Mark 8:34–35 in Mark's Story" was first published in *Quarterly Review* 2/2 (Summer 1982) 67–78. Used by permission.

10. "Paul as Liberator and Oppressor: How Should We Evaluate Diverse Views of 1 Corinthians?" was first published in *The Meanings*

We Choose: Hermeneutical Ethics, Indeterminacy and the Conflict of Interpretations, edited by Charles H. Cosgrove, Journal for the Study of the Old Testament Supplement Series 411 (London: T. & T. Clark, 2004) 122–37. Copyright © 2004 T. & T. Clark International. Reprinted by permission of the Continuum International Publishing Group.

11. "Participation in Christ: A Central Theme in Pauline Theology" has not previously been published.

Abbreviations

AB	Anchor Bible
ABD	*Anchor Bible Dictionary*, 6 vols., edited by David Noel Freedman (New York: Doubleday, 1992)
ABRL	Anchor Bible Reference Library
ANRW	*Aufstieg und Niedergang der römischen Welt*, edited by Hildegard Temporini and Wolfgang Haase (Berlin: Walter de Gruyter)
ANTC	Abingdon New Testament Commentary
BDAG	*A Greek-English Lexicon of the New Testament and other Early Christian Literature*, 3d ed., revised and edited by Frederick William Danker (Chicago: University of Chicago, 2000)
BETL	Bibliotheca ephemeridum theologicarum lovaniensium
BJRL	*Bulletin of the John Rylands Library of Manchester*
BWANT	Beiträge zur Wissenschaft vom Alten und Neuen Testament
BZNW	Beihefte zur Zeitschrift für die neutestamentliche Wissenschaft
CBQ	*Catholic Biblical Quarterly*
CC	Continental Commentaries
EKKNT	Evangelisch-Katholischer Kommentar zum Neuen Testament
ESEC	Emory Studies in Early Christianity
FCBS	Fortress Classics in Biblical Studies
FF	Foundations and Facets
FRLANT	Forschungen zur Religion und Literatur des Alten und Neuen Testaments
GBS	Guides to Biblical Scholarship
HR	*History of Religion*
HTR	*Harvard Theological Review*
ILCK	International Library of Christian Knowledge
Int	*Interpretation*
JAAR	*Journal of the American Academy of Religion*
JBL	*Journal of Biblical Literature*

JR	*Journal of Religion*
JSNTSS	Journal for the Study of the New Testament Supplement Series
LB	*Linguistica biblica*
LCL	Loeb Classical Library
LEC	Library of Early Christianity
LXX	Septuagint
NIB	*New Interpreter's Bible,* 12 vols. (Nashville: Abingdon, 1994–2004)
NICNT	New International Commentary on the New Testament
NIGTC	New International Greek Testament Commentary
NIV	New International Version of the Bible
NovT	*Novum Testamentum*
NRSV	New Revised Standard Version of the Bible
NT	New Testament
NTAbh	Neutestamentliche Abhandlungen
NTR	New Testament Readings
NTS	*New Testament Studies*
OT	Old Testament
par.	parallel passages
PittsTMS	Pittsburgh Theological Monograph Series
PTMS	Princeton Theological Monograph Series
QR	*Quarterly Review*
RSV	Revised Standard Version of the Bible
SBLDS	Society of Biblical Literature Dissertation Series
SBLMS	Society of Biblical Literature Monograph Series
SBLSP	*Society of Biblical Literature Seminar Papers*
SBLSymS	Society of Biblical Literature Symposium Series
SBLTT	Society of Biblical Literature Texts and Translations
SBM	Stuttgarter Biblische Monographien
SBT	Studies in Biblical Theology
SE	*Studia evangelica*
SemSup	Semeia Supplements
SNT	Studien zum Neuen Testament
SNTSMS	Society for New Testament Studies Monograph Series
TDNT	*Theological Dictionary of the New Testament,* 10 vols., edited by Gerhard Kittel and Gerhard Friedrich, translated by Geoffrey W. Bromiley (Grand Rapids: Eerdmans, 1964–76)
TRu	*Theologische Rundschau*
TToday	*Theology Today*

TTS	Trierer theologische Studien
TWNT	*Theologisches Wörterbuch zum Neuen Testament,* 10 vols., edited by Gerhard Kittel and Gerhard Friedrich (Stuttgart: Kohlhammer, 1932–)
TZ	*Theologische Zeitschrift*
UNT	Untersuchungen zum Neuen Testament
WBC	Word Biblical Commentary
ZSNT	Zacchaeus Studies New Testament

PART I

Gospel Sayings *and* Stories

I

TENSION
in SYNOPTIC SAYINGS
and STORIES

The following short essay provides a useful introduction to essays that follow because it suggests some of the reasons why I am interested in studying the literary and rhetorical features of synoptic sayings and stories. The study of formal features is not an end in itself. Literary observations can provide clues to understanding the appropriate functions of the texts as human communication. In particular, the tensive language of the texts enables them to do more than inform. This feature of synoptic texts helps them to move their hearers through the impact of forceful and imaginative language, inviting a change in fundamental values and commitments.

The introductory section of this essay summarizes a longer argument in The Sword of His Mouth (1975; reprinted, Eugene, Ore.: Wipf & Stock, 2003; 1–31), and the following section on synoptic sayings receives further support and illustration in that book. The last two sections of this essay draw on more extensive work on pronouncement stories (or apophthegms) and on the Gospel of Mark. Further essays on these topics in the present volume develop and support my brief comments here.

Text as Message

SCHOLARSHIP SHOULD PROTECT THE independence of the biblical text. Historical scholarship has helped to do this by showing us that biblical texts are not the mirror image of the modern reader's theology, piety, and social world, for they speak from and to a world that in many ways is strange to us. Nevertheless, modern scholarship often muffles the independent voice of the text. We insert the text into our own pre-established world in a way that will cause the least disturbance. Where the church's influence is strong, this may mean domesticating the text to a conventional Christian piety and morality. Where the academy's interests are dominant, another kind of domestication may take place. We cease listening to the text as a *message* in which someone writes to readers (including, finally, to us) about matters of human seriousness and treat the text as *evidence* for the production and defense of a theory of our own devising. The production and testing of theories need not be an idle pastime. At their best, theories can be new ways of seeing that open up new dimensions of understanding of texts and human life. But treating the text as evidence rather than as message allows us to subordinate it to our interests. The text is domesticated to the academic enterprise. The interests and concerns of the original speaker or writer are forgotten so that the text may serve our interests, the production and defense of a theory, which may be useful for professional advancement and may even disclose some truth but may also lack the ultimate concern of the original speaker.

There is a kind of scholarship that can help us to focus on the text as message. It is still young and, contrary to my hopes, it may not prove to be the wave of the future. It can be placed among the "literary" approaches to the Bible. However, interest in the Bible as literature conceals a variety of competing purposes. Not all of these new approaches will help us to read the text as message. If, however, we focus on the text as an act of communication between writer and reader, a communication that may not only convey information but also seek to influence, to challenge, to change, we are recognizing the text as a message. Literary analysis can help us explore the nature and dimensions of this message. This analysis should be guided by awareness that, in literary art and wherever the personal impact of language is important, content cannot be separated from form. The contrary assumption leads to abstracting an idea or information from the text, ignoring the fact that the text may be intended to fascinate, entice, or present a personal challenge.

I have been impressed with the large amount of forceful and imaginative language in the synoptic Gospels. The shapers of these words evidently wished to speak with strong personal impact. They wished not merely to inform but to challenge. They called for change in basic commitments, values, and attitudes. We as persons are defined not only by what we assume to be true but also by what interests and concerns us. The forceful and imaginative language of the Gospels seeks to change those assumptions, interests, and concerns.

If the speakers and writers of the Gospels, through their use of forceful and imaginative language, are calling for change in the lives of their hearers and readers, it is the task of the interpreter to clarify the dimensions of this change by careful study of the language of the call. The movement sought is often reflected in the language used. We encounter "tensive language,"[1] language that embodies a tension and expresses a conflict with ordinary ways of thinking and acting. Careful study of the language can help the interpreter to locate the primary point of tension and explore the linguistic strategies used to encourage change. Not only the explicit commands are a call and challenge, for statements and stories may also contain hidden imperatives and invitations to change.

This concern with the literary form of the text as message does not mean ignoring its social and historical setting. Communication is seldom fully explicit. It rests upon assumptions shared by a social group at a particular time in history. The interpreter may aid our understanding by clarifying the implicit background of what is expressed. Furthermore, study of the literary and rhetorical features of the Gospels, leading to clarification of the points of tension mentioned above, can help us to be precise about speakers' and writers' perceptions of value conflicts in their historical settings, thus contributing to historical and sociological study of the Gospels.

The following reflections may suggest what is at stake for us as human beings in this approach to the Gospels:[2] Our ordinary language fits and serves us like a house in which we have long lived. Everything is in place for our use. Our language reflects our daily interests and activities; the words run along paths as clearly marked as the threadbare trails in an old carpet. But, just as the walls of our house limit our sight, so our ordinary language limits our perception of truth and value. Primarily it allows us to speak of our work and household duties. Beyond this house of routine language is the un-remark-able (what cannot be said and therefore escapes our notice).

This house of routine language defines our routine world. It implies an interpretation of ourselves as part of meaningful space. Because the house is small, we are also small. There are potential dimensions of our being unrealized in this little world. If these are essential to our full humanness, our humanness is distorted or lost. To speak theologically, our little world becomes the world of sin and death in which God's purpose for humanity is negated since our house has no windows to what transcends it.

---

1. This phrase is used by Philip Wheelwright, *Metaphor & Reality* (Bloomington: Indiana University Press, 1962) 45–69.

2. Compare the longer statement in Tannehill, *The Sword of His Mouth* (1975; reprinted, Eugene, Ore.: Wipf & Stock, 2003) 11–31.

The house in which we live is the product of imaginative interpretation. We (guided by our families and culture) have created it by our interpretive perception, memory, and intention.[3] Our perception is selective; it is determined by what we care to see, by what is important to us according to some interpretation of the world. Our memory is also selective. Furthermore, the past is always present to us in some interpretation and can change its meaning by new interpretation. Our intentions are also imaginative products; we set up images of what is good for us to be and do. But our memory, our intentions, our special way of perceiving are aspects of our very being. To a large extent they determine who we are. We are cripples if they reveal an interpretation of self and world that is false and crippling.

We can only escape such "evil imaginations of the heart" when the imagination is reawakened to new interpretive work. While routine language provides the walls and fixtures of our house, locking us into its cramped space, language can also be the key to freedom. Language that breaks with the routine world, speaking from and to the imagination, can change the routine ways in which we interpret and can mediate a new vision of self and world. Language escapes its ordinary limits by meaningful distortions of ordinary speech. Since ordinary language directs our attention to the superficial, blinding us to the unique, the beautiful, and the mysterious, poets do strange things with language. For instance, metaphor is important in poetry. Metaphor is a strange way of speaking in which the poet uses a word in a context foreign to it. There is deliberate tension with the ordinary use of the word, and this meaningful distortion can deepen our perception. Such distortion is necessary because of the medium in which the poet works. The poet is less like a sculptor who begins with an amorphous block of stone than like a sculptor who begins with auto bumpers from a junkyard. The material has already been shaped to another purpose, and the artist must twist it away from its original shape and meaning, challenging the routine of language and our routine world. A similar challenge may come through the creation of alternative worlds in story.

The Gospel stories offer us worlds in which we may share imaginatively. At key points these worlds are structured in ways that differ sharply from the assumptions that control our lives. This difference appears both in the turn of events and in the forceful words of Jesus within the story.

---

3. On the relation of the imagination to memory and intention, see Ray L. Hart, *Unfinished Man and the Imagination: Toward an Ontology and a Rhetoric of Revelation* (New York: Herder & Herder, 1968) 138–53, 188–227.

But the points of tension of which the original speakers and writers were sharply aware have been lost to us, for we have learned to incorporate the Gospels into a familiar and comfortable world. This is facilitated by interpreting the forceful and imaginative language of the Gospels as if it were language of another kind. We assume that we should distill a clear religious idea or doctrine from this language, an idea stripped of imaginative power and of the tensive expression that challenges the routine world. Then it may be accepted as true, but it does not stir the imagination nor disturb the old assumptions shaping our lives, and life does not change. Or it may be accepted as a rule of behavior, but it does not affect our basic goals and values. Thus the words of religion promote a hidden hypocrisy, an intellectual acceptance and a legalistic obedience that do not transform. Jesus and the Evangelists were seeking something more, as careful study of their language shows.

What I have said will, I hope, suggest the significance of my previous probing of the synoptic Gospels. This has taken place at three levels: (1) the sayings attributed to Jesus, (2) the pronouncement stories, (3) the Gospel of Mark as a unitary narrative. The remainder of this essay will illustrate and summarize some of the results of this probing.

Tensive Language in Sayings

First let us consider the tensive language in the sayings attributed to Jesus.[4] At this point we will study these sayings apart from their narrative setting. This can be done with least loss when the saying is part of a larger sayings collection like the major blocks of teaching found in Matthew. When presented in this way, the narrative setting of the teaching fades, the teaching appears to be teaching for all times, and the Evangelist is suggesting that the "you" addressed by Jesus includes the readers, not just a limited group gathered on a particular occasion of Jesus' past ministry.

Many of the sayings attributed to Jesus contain commands. We are tempted to interpret these as rules of behavior, instructions on how we are to act. Such an interpretation reveals a fateful short circuit in our response to the text. Those concerned primarily with external behavior attempt to speak with clarity, describing the required behavior in precise and literal language. We would find good rules of behavior in a clear set of instructions for assembling a bicycle or in clearly written legislation. Neither the instructions nor the legislation is likely to resemble poetry. The words about the birds and the lilies in Matt 6:25–33 (par. Luke 12:22–31) are

---

4. For studies of this material see Tannehill, *Sword*.

quite different.[5] The command "Do not be anxious" could be taken as a rule of behavior. However, anxiety is remarkably difficult to control by the conscious will. It is important that the teaching does not stop with this simple command but continues with language that is similar to poetry. Something profoundly meaningful for humanity is discovered in concrete experiences of nature (the simplicity and directness with which birds gather food; the beauty of the field flowers), which thereby become images of something greater, and the power of this perception is reinforced by repetitive pattern with climax, by emphatic diction, and by contrast with human patterns of life. Freedom from anxiety comes not through attempting to follow a rule of behavior but only through an insight into a reality often hidden from us, an insight akin to the insights that poets seek to engender with their poems. Attempting to escape anxiety without this insight produces either frustration or hypocrisy. Careful attention to the form of expression can warn us against this mistake.

There is a large amount of tensive language in the sayings attributed to Jesus. The position of Jesus stands in tension with another position, expressed or assumed, and this tension is emphasized. There are, for example, a group of sayings that I have called "antithetical aphorisms," sayings that are brief and pointed but make strong, unqualified assertions containing a sharp contrast. The contrast is expressed by a sort of word-play, using the same words in negative and positive form or using antithetical terms.[6] We also find in the Jesus tradition a group of sayings that can be called "focal instances."[7] A focal instance may begin with an "if . . ." or "whoever . . ." clause and seem to resemble casuistic law. But the situation described is so specific that the focal instance does not provide a very useful general rule when confined to its literal sense. For instance, we are told what to do when slapped on the right cheek (Matt 5:39) but are left without explicit instructions about many other situations that may be partially similar. The situation is so specific because the speaker intends to shock his hearers with an extreme command. The command is not a clear and useful rule of behavior but immediately clear is its shocking variance with the way that people usually behave in such a situation. The discovery that Jesus expects such surprising behavior in a specific instance leads the hearer or reader to think beyond the literal meaning of the words. For the command stands in tension not only with expected behavior in that

---

5. On this passage see Tannehill, *Sword*, 60–67.
6. On the antithetical aphorism see Tannehill, *Sword*, 88–101.
7. See Tannehill, *Sword*, 67–77.

particular situation but with a whole pattern of behavior that dominates life. We have an instance that does not fit the dominant pattern. It calls that pattern into question and suggests a different pattern to replace it. Thus the specific command has a wide range of implications, but it is left to the creative disciple to determine what these implications are. The focal instance speaks only indirectly to situations beyond the specific one described and makes no attempt to mediate complicated conflicts of values. It is not a rule of behavior that can be followed mechanically but rightly works through the imagination. It is formed to create tension with accepted patterns of behavior by exemplifying the unconsidered possibility that breaks out of the old patterns and by stimulating hearers to imagine similar daring action in the situations that they face. When the moral imagination is awakened in this way, these words have had their intended effect.

Consider the following focal instance (Matt 5:23–24):

> So if you are offering your gift on the altar and there you remember that your brother has something against you, leave there your gift before the altar and go; first be reconciled to your brother and then come and continue offering your gift.

Why would the speaker wish to give instructions concerning this particular situation? The situation is very specific, resulting from the unusual conjunction of two activities: A cultic offering is in progress and at that same time the one who brings the offering remembers that his brother has something against him. This is not a general instruction to examine one's conscience and relationships so that one can approach God. If the speaker were seeking to establish a regular and practical self-examination or act of reconciliation, he would certainly have required that it take place before the offering was under way so that it would not be interrupted. These words do not establish a rule for orderly worship but insist on disruption. The adverbs of place and time ("there . . . there . . . first . . . then . . ."), placed in emphatic position at or near the beginning of the clauses, serve to exclude the more easily acceptable ways of behaving: taking care of the matter before going to the temple or after the offering is concluded. When some churches incorporate a gesture of reconciliation into their order of worship, perhaps using this text as a rubric, it does not have the same effect. Only with a keen sense of irony can these words become part of an order of worship, for they make their point through insisting on the disruption of the expected and orderly. Thereby they imply a surprising shift in values. The worship of God is made to wait upon reconciliation with a fellow human being. Through this extreme instance the cruciality of reconciliation is presented with an imaginative force that can affect our thinking in many other situations. These words have power in spite of the fact that they rarely, if ever, were a useful guide to behavior. Evidently the author of Matthew recognized that the importance of these words does not reside in their literal meaning, for they were retained after the destruction of the temple, when the literal sense could no longer apply.

Tensive Language in Pronouncement Stories

In the previous section I mentioned the antithetical aphorism as one form of tensive language in the sayings of Jesus. The statement in Mark 2:27, "The Sabbath came for the sake of humanity, not humanity for the sake of the Sabbath," is an example of an antithetical aphorism. It sharply contrasts two different attitudes toward the Sabbath, affirming the one and negating the other. In this case the aphorism is part of a pronouncement story or apophthegm. We must now consider the literary effect of presenting sayings of Jesus as the climactic element in pronouncement stories.[8] At this point we must begin to recognize the importance of narrative, confining ourselves, however, to individual episodes that are unified by a single set of characters and a single place and time.

A pronouncement story is a brief narrative that relates how someone responded to something said or observed on a particular occasion. The response is a pronouncement (sometimes combined with action), and this pronouncement is the climactic element in the story. The story is told for the sake of the pronouncement, and the impact of Jesus' words is heightened by presenting him in interaction with other persons. The tension present in many of Jesus' sayings, such as the antithetical aphorism quoted above, becomes dramatic tension between persons in these brief scenes. Whether the climactic saying is antithetical or not, many of these narratives convey a sense of antithesis by presenting persons with contrasting attitudes in a situation of conflict.

These stories have been shaped by an author or storyteller, that is, they have been shaped as literature. They fit into a literary genre of

---

8. Additional discussion of pronouncement stories may be found in Tannehill, "Types and Functions of Apophthegms in the Synoptic Gospels," in *ANRW* II.25.2, 1792–829; and in idem, "Introduction: The Pronouncement Story and Its Types" and "Varieties of Synoptic Pronouncement Stories," *Semeia* 20 (1981) 1–13, 101–19. (These three essays are included in the present volume.)

which we have many examples in Greek writings of the Roman period.[9] Furthermore, pronouncement stories are highly selective in what they present. While actual conversations often go on at some length with unclear results, the exchange in a pronouncement story is succinct and pointed. Details that might distract from the climactic pronouncement are omitted, including the reply of the other party. And the pronouncement is often in language that is rhetorically striking. Thus the pronouncement story is shaped to have a particular impact upon the reader. It is meant to affect the reader's attitudes and actions, moving them into line with those expressed in the climactic response. Nevertheless, there is some artful indirectness in these stories. The author does not present Jesus speaking directly to the reader of the Gospel but tells a story about the past. Readers must participate indirectly, imaginatively, in a situation that is not their own, but this may be the means by which attitudes are changed.

The pronouncement is made in response to something said or observed. Thus there are two necessary parts to a pronouncement story: the story setting that indicates the provocation for the pronouncement, and the response to this provocation in the pronouncement (and sometimes in action). When we study synoptic pronouncement stories with this in mind, we discover that provocation and response may be related in a number of different ways, giving rise to different types of pronouncement stories.[10] Distinguishing these types will help us to see that tension appears in different ways within these stories. This tension may correspond to a shift in attitude that the teller of such a story wishes to bring about in the listener. Therefore, clarification of the story type and of the particular tension in an individual story will help to clarify the attitudinal shift that such a story encourages.[11] A basic attitude involves value commitments, emotional attachments, the orientation of the will, and evaluative thought. Such attitudes shape personal life at a deep level, and a shift in basic attitudes can deeply affect the self. The interpreter of pronouncement stories should be alert to the shift from one attitude to another invited by many of these stories, for this shift is a major part of their function.

---

9. Especially rich collections of pronouncement stories are found in Plutarch's *Moralia*, vol. 3, LCL; in Book VI of Diogenes Laertius' *Lives and Opinions of Eminent Philosophers*; and in Lucian's *Demonax*.

10. See the essays listed in note 8.

11. See Tannehill, "Attitudinal Shift in Synoptic Pronouncement Stories," in *Orientation by Disorientation: Studies in Literary Criticism and Biblical Literary Criticism Presented in Honor of William A. Beardslee*, ed. Richard A. Spencer, PittsTMS 26 (Pittsburgh: Pickwick Publications, 1980) 183–97.

In Mark 2:23–28, the story containing the antithetical aphorism concerning the Sabbath, the tension in the story arises from the objection of the Pharisees against the behavior of the disciples and, implicitly, against Jesus. This is an example of a type that I call objection stories.[12] In an objection story the provocation is an objection to something already said or done, and the response is an answer to that objection. Since the provoker takes a critical stance toward the responder, the central tension in the story is defined by the conflict between these characters. This tension appears as soon as the objection is disclosed and centers on the responder, who is being attacked. Suspense is high until we discover whether an effective response is possible.

The conflicts between the early church and Jewish neighbors are mirrored in the objection stories, which may at times serve to strengthen already strong walls. However, the response in such stories often expresses a perception of God's will with challenging power not only for the opponents of the Jesus movement but also for its members. Few of Jesus' followers would see the issue clearly or be fully committed to his radical position. Thus objection stories may not only require new thought from opponents but move some of Jesus' followers to new or renewed attitudes.

Another type of story, the correction story, contains no criticism of Jesus, and yet Jesus responds to what he hears or sees by correcting it. To a disciple who wishes to go and bury his father, Jesus responds, "Leave the dead to bury their own dead!" (Matt 8:21–22 par.). He replies to the laudatory blessing of his mother (and, by implication, of himself) by saying, "Rather, blessed are those who hear the word of God and keep it" (Luke 11:27–28). To Peter's magnanimous suggestion that he forgive as many as seven times, Jesus replies, "I do not say to you as many as seven times but as many as seventy times seven" (Matt 18:21–22).[13] In these stories also there is tension between Jesus and the one to whom he is responding, but here the tension appears as a surprise. The position corrected may appear to be reasonable or laudable, but Jesus does not praise or accept it. The corrective response of Jesus opens up a gap between himself and the initial position taken by another. The two positions define a decision for hearers

---

12. This type corresponds closely to Rudolf Bultmann's controversy dialogues; see *The History of the Synoptic Tradition*, rev. ed., trans. John Marsh (New York: Harper & Row, 1963) 11–21, 39–54. The other types that I will discuss do not correspond to types used by Bultmann.

13. Or "as many as seventy-seven times."

and readers of such stories. They are faced with the question of whether they can negotiate this shift in position.

The complement of correction stories is commendation stories, in which Jesus responds by commending rather than correcting another person. It might seem that commendation stories would be lacking in tension, since Jesus and the person commended agree. However, tension is also prominent in these stories, as two observations show: Jesus may commend someone or something not commendable by another standard of judgment, and the majority of synoptic commendation stories are hybrids, combining (in most cases) correction and commendation. In these hybrids Jesus' commendation is balanced by the negative judgment of someone else, or the action or attitude commended is balanced by a negative action or attitude. Jesus' response commends one person or group and corrects another. In Mark 10:13–16 par. Jesus corrects the disciples who have rebuked the children and commends the children because they represent those to whom the Kingdom belongs. The difference between Jesus and the children, on the one hand, and the disciples, on the other, is the central tension in the story. In Luke 17:12–19 the contrast is not between two ways of judging (as in the story of the children) but between two ways of acting: one healed leper shows gratitude and nine do not. However, this in itself does not disclose the tension in the story that calls for attitudinal shift on the part of readers. Few would argue with the judgment that gratitude is commendable. Tension arises when readers are belatedly told that the grateful leper was a Samaritan. This combination of qualities, grateful and Samaritan, found in one whom Jesus commends, calls in question prejudice against Samaritans. It is evidently this prejudice that the story seeks to change. This story and the story of the children also illustrate the tendency in commendation stories for Jesus to commend those who are judged to be bad or unimportant when another standard of judgment is employed.

A similar observation can be made about quest stories, for in them people who would be judged negatively by many (e.g., sinners and Gentiles) are presented as successful questers (see Mark 7:24–30 par.; Matt 8:5–13; Luke 7:36–50; 19:1–10). In the quest story, a type of pronouncement story that appears to be rare outside the Gospels, a person approaches Jesus in quest of something of great importance, and the story tells us whether he or she succeeds in obtaining what is sought. Jesus remains the figure of authority in the story, and a pronouncement of Jesus near the end of the story will determine its outcome. However, unlike Jesus' dialogue partners in other pronouncement stories, the quester is placed in the center of our attention. Narrative suspense arises from the quester's need and extends until we discover whether the quester succeeds or fails in meeting that need with the help of Jesus. Thus we read the story from the viewpoint of the quester's need, which promotes sympathy with the quester. There may be additional features in the story that promote such sympathy, and when Jesus declares the success of the quest with a commendatory statement, a favorable reaction by the reader seems to be required. However, tension for the reader arises when questers have characteristics that seem to disqualify them in the eyes of many. Within the story these characteristics may give rise to obstacles that must be overcome before the quests can be successful. The major obstacle to a quest will probably define the issue on which the storyteller wishes to change attitudes. Thus in the story of Zacchaeus (Luke 19:1–10), the obstacle is the religious community's exclusion of this quester, prefigured in the crowd blocking Zacchaeus's access to Jesus and expressed in the crowd's objection to Jesus staying with him. Their rejection is countered by Jesus' declaration of Zacchaeus's share in salvation and his right to belong to the religious community. ("He also is a son of Abraham.") The tension between these two attitudes defines the decision with which the story confronts its readers.

Tension in the Gospel of Mark

There is increasing recognition that the Gospel of Mark can and should be read as a unitary narrative and that, when this is done with the aid of perspectives from literary studies, the message and the art of the Evangelist stand out with new clarity.[14] Preoccupation with the pre-Gospel units of tradition and with the editorial modification of those units obscured the fact that Mark is a continuous narrative presenting a meaningful development to a climax and that each episode should be understood in light of its relation to the story as a whole. The unity of the Markan narrative is clearer when we consider this common feature of story structure: a commission or task, accepted by a story character, results in a unified narrative sequence as the narrator tells us how the character fulfills that commission

---

14. See Tannehill, "The Disciples in Mark: The Function of a Narrative Role," *JR* 57 (1977) 386–405, and idem, "The Gospel of Mark as Narrative Christology," *Semeia* 16 (1979) 57–95. These articles expand and substantiate the following discussion of Mark. They are included in the present volume. See also Norman R. Petersen, *Literary Criticism for New Testament Critics* (Philadelphia: Fortress, 1978) 49–80; idem, " 'Point of View' in Mark's Narrative," *Semeia* 12 (1978) 97–121; and Werner H. Kelber, *Mark's Story of Jesus* (Philadelphia: Fortress, 1979).

or fails to fulfill it. The commission provides an overarching purpose or goal, and events of the plot take on meaning because they represent movement toward the goal and obstacles to its realization.[15] The events in Mark form a unitary narrative in relation to the commission that Jesus received from God and the commission that the disciples received from Jesus. The story gradually discloses what these commissions require and shows Jesus accepting these requirements and the disciples rejecting them.

In relation to these commissions the narrative becomes a meaningful plot filled with internal tension, the tension of suspense as we wait to see whether the commissions will be fulfilled and the tension of conflict among characters. A good narrator can guide the readers' reactions to the narrative and can through the narrative present a unique vision of goodness and truth for the readers' consideration. As a result, an external tension may also arise, a tension between the readers' assumptions of goodness and truth and the narrator's vision presented in the story. In various ways the internal tension of the story may contribute to this external tension and provide clues to the message of the author, including clues to the changes required of the readers if they are to share in what the author believes to be good and true. Indications of the author's control of the narrative, if they reveal consistent tendencies, are especially important clues. When we investigate what is emphasized in Mark and how the readers' evaluation of events and characters is guided by the Markan story, we do find a meaningful pattern that clarifies both the internal and the external tension. For instance, the author's emphasis is disclosed by repetitive patterns in the story; certain things are brought to the readers' attention repeatedly. The readers are expected to evaluate these in light of the words and actions of Jesus, the central figure of authority in the story. Particularly the disciples, who have been called to follow Jesus, are to be judged by whether their words and actions are in harmony with Jesus. In his teaching Jesus provides the norms by which the disciples can be judged, and these norms make clear that the two story lines that develop from the commission of Jesus and the commission of the disciples should run parallel. When the disciples do not follow Jesus' teaching or Jesus' way, a negative judgment is required by the norms of the story.

In Mark the story of the disciples is carefully shaped and presents a strong view of the disciples that neither Matthew nor Luke can fully accept. Evidently the author of Mark has a special interest in this aspect of the plot, which suggests that there is a message for the readers in the

---

15. See Tannehill, "Narrative Christology," 60–63 (in the present volume 163–65).

disciples' story. In order to understand the function of this story line in Mark, we cannot simply look at the isolated scenes in which the disciples appear, note that they are sometimes presented positively and sometimes negatively, and add up the results. The picture changes radically when we approach Mark as a developing narrative and note how the author deals with the disciples: he presents them favorably in the early part of the Gospel, making clear the greatness to which they have been called; then he shows that the disciples are unable to understand Jesus because of their anxious self-concern; then he presents the disciples in open conflict with Jesus on issues central to their commission. Finally he shows the disciples breaking faith with Jesus and deserting him at the passion. The author emphasizes each aspect of this changing relationship by repetition, placing similar scenes at regular intervals in a section of the Gospel and making the desertion of Jesus by the disciples in chapter 14 the emphatic climax of a long development. The purpose of this remarkably negative story of the disciples is a matter of debate in Markan scholarship. Some see it as indication of the author's rejection of a group of theological opponents or as explanation of the demise of the Jerusalem church.[16] However, the author anticipated, I believe, that his readers would identify with the disciples and encouraged this identification by his positive portrait of the disciples early in the Gospel so that the negative turn in the disciples' story would lead the readers to reexamine their own discipleship. Thus the purpose of the author of Mark was not merely to present certain ideas about Jesus or to warn his readers against some group distinct from themselves but to lead his readers through a particular story in which they could discover themselves and thereby change. If this is true, the tension between Jesus and the disciples, internal to the story, mirrors an external tension between the church as the author perceives it and the discipleship to which it is called.

This tension receives its greatest power and depth in the half of the Gospel dominated by the passion. The coming passion of Jesus is suddenly announced to the disciples in Mark 8:31. To this point readers have been allowed to form a view of Jesus and the disciples in which suffering and death were not major factors. Now suffering and death are central not only to the commission of Jesus but also the commission of the dis-

---

16. See Theodore J. Weeden, *Mark: Traditions in Conflict* (Philadelphia: Fortress, 1971); Werner H. Kelber, *The Kingdom in Mark* (Philadelphia: Fortress, 1974); idem, *Mark's Story of Jesus* (Philadelphia: Fortress, 1979). For points in the debate, see Tannehill, "Disciples in Mark," 393–94, 403–4; idem, "Narrative Christology," 82–84 (in the present volume 145–46, 157–58, 181–83).

ciples (8:34—9:1). Each of the three passion announcements (8:31; 9:31; 10:33–34) is followed by teaching that includes an antithetical aphorism (8:35; 9:35; 10:42–45). In these aphorisms the way of Jesus and the disciple is presented as paradox, sharply underscoring the conflict between this way and reasonable human plans. In the passion story this paradox is turned into drama in the mocking scenes that follow each of the main events in Jesus' way to the cross (the two trials and the crucifixion), for the same words that reject the dying Jesus are ironic confession of him. The dramatic tension of these events is heightened by a series of suggestions of ways in which Jesus might escape. Those inclined to seek such escape from death are enticed to false hope; then hope is crushed as the ways of escape are closed one by one.[17] Mark's readers must face the conflict between the way of Jesus and their own desire for security, a desire that will make them like the faithless disciples. The tension is heightened by presenting Jesus' way as paradox and as triumph by irony.

While the discussion of synoptic sayings, pronouncement stories, and the Gospel of Mark in this article is very sketchy, additional explanation and substantiation can be found in the writings cited in the footnotes. I hope that my discussion suggests possibilities worthy of exploration by those who wish to wrestle seriously with the message of the Gospels. For the varieties of tension that we can observe as literary phenomena in the Gospels can reveal a message coming to us not simply as information but as challenge.

---

17. See Tannehill, "Narrative Christology," 85–87 (in the present volume 184–86).

2

The PRONOUNCEMENT STORY and ITS TYPES

This essay originally appeared as the introduction to a collection of essays by members of the Pronouncement Story Work Group of the Society of Biblical Literature. The essays that followed discussed pronouncement stories in various bodies of ancient literature. My essay on "Varieties of Synoptic Pronouncement Stories" (included in the present volume) is an application of this opening, methodological statement to the synoptic Gospels. After defining pronouncement story, "The Pronouncement Story and Its Types" discusses how such stories are rhetorically shaped to influence their readers or hearers and proposes a typology consisting of six types of pronouncement stories.

Defining the Pronouncement Story

THE NAME "PRONOUNCEMENT STORY," coined by Vincent Taylor,[1] will be used to designate the literary genre discussed in this essay because it is immediately descriptive, indicating the two characteristic parts of the genre, a *pronouncement* that is the climactic element in a brief *story*. As used here, pronouncement story will correspond rather closely with Rudolf Bultmann's "apophthegms,"[2] and less closely with Martin Dibelius's "paradigms."[3] It also overlaps with the *chreia* discussed by some ancient scholars.[4]

---

1. Vincent Taylor, *The Formation of the Gospel Tradition* (London: Macmillan, 1933) 29–30, 63–87.

2. Rudolf Bultmann, *The History of the Synoptic Tradition*, rev. ed., trans. John Marsh (1968; reprinted Peabody, Mass.: Hendrickson, 1994) 11–69.

3. Martin Dibelius, *From Tradition to Gospel*, trans. Bertram Lee Woolf (New York: Scribners, 1934) 26, 37–69.

4. See Heinrich Lausberg, *Handbuch der literarischen Rhetorik: Eine Grundlegung der Literaturwissenschaft*, 2d ed., 2 vols. (Munich: Hueber, 1973) 536–40; Ronald F. Hock and

A pronouncement story is a brief narrative in which the climactic (and often final) element is a pronouncement that is presented as a particular person's response to something said or observed on a particular occasion of the past. There are two main parts of a pronouncement story: the pronouncement and its setting, i.e., the response and the situation provoking that response. The movement from the one to the other is the main development in these brief stories.

Brevity is a relative matter, of course. In some cases a pronouncement story is a single sentence, with the occasion indicated in a subordinate clause and the response in the main clause. However, a pronouncement story can be longer without losing its basic characteristics. Descriptive detail can be added, and several exchanges of dialogue can take place. It remains a pronouncement story so long as the description and dialogue lead on to a climactic utterance that summarizes the responder's response to the situation. This utterance must be the dominant element in the story as a whole. Preceding material will lead up to it, and it will bring the story to a close or, at most, be followed by a brief indication of the effect of the utterance. There are also some stories in which the utterance is accompanied by action, word and action together constituting the response (see below). A longer, more complex story may be a sign that other interests are competing with the final utterance. A number of exchanges between characters in the story may indicate that a number of points are being made about a topic, decreasing the dominance of the final utterance and suggesting that we have a short dialogue rather than a pronouncement story. On the other hand, these exchanges may simply prepare for the climactic utterance. In the synoptic Gospels a pronouncement story up to ten verses in length is not unusual, and there are a few that are longer. There are pronouncement stories of comparable length in non-Christian authors.[5] The test of dominance is important in deciding whether a story is a pronouncement story. Is there an utterance at or near the end of the story that dominates the story as a whole because the rest of the story leads up to it and contributes to the impression that it makes? If so, we probably have a pronouncement story.

Edward N. O'Neil, *The Chreia in Ancient Rhetoric*, Vol. 1: *The Progymnasmata*, SBLTT 27 (Atlanta: Scholars, 1986). For a large collection of ancient pronouncement stories, see Vernon K. Robbins, *Ancient Quotes and Anecdotes* (Sonoma, Calif.: Polebridge, 1989).

5. Plutarch provides examples of medium and long pronouncement stories. See the texts quoted in John E. Alsup, "Type, Place, and Function of the Pronouncement Story in Plutarch's *Moralia*," *Semeia* 20 (1981) 15–27; and Vernon K. Robbins, "Classifying Pronouncement Stories in Plutarch's *Parallel Lives*," *Semeia* 20 (1981) 29–52.

The pronouncement itself is usually short, often a single sentence, and is sometimes strikingly succinct in expression. But a response of three or more sentences is possible, provided that it makes a single major point related to the provoking occasion. On the other hand, a general discourse in a lengthy paragraph or a series of separate sayings roughly equal in importance suggests that we have moved outside the pronouncement story genre.

There are some pronouncement stories in which the response consists of a pronouncement accompanied by an action. The two together constitute the response and indicate the attitude of the responder. Ancient scholars recognized this possibility in discussing the types of *chreia*.[6] They also noted that an expressive action might take the place of an utterance.[7] Such cases are rare, however, and they have not caused me to abandon the convenient designation pronouncement story. In such stories the expressive action is given the role usually reserved for the dominant utterance: it is the climactic disclosure of a significant response for which the rest of the story provides the provoking occasion. As Lausberg says, "The action has semantic purpose like a pronouncement."[8]

A pronouncement story is meaningful in itself and can stand alone. We find collections of them that make no attempt to provide a narrative bridge from one story to the next.[9] A pronouncement story may also be embedded in an essay or speech, or form an episode in a larger narrative. In the latter case, the pronouncement story remains meaningful in itself, even though it may gain added meaning through its function in the larger plot of the narrative. Its relative independence is usually indicated by a shift in some characters and/or a shift in time or place before and after the pronouncement story. This marks the scene as an occasion separate from other occasions.

The pronouncement story is stylized and should not be confused with a complete and neutral report of an actual conversation. Some conversations may be as brief as the average pronouncement story and end with a memorable statement, but most conversations are longer, and even if a striking statement is occasionally made, it seldom ends the matter. The pronouncement story is highly selective in what it presents. In most

---

6. Lausberg, *Handbuch*, 539.
7. Ibid., 538–39.
8. Ibid., 538.
9. See, for example, (pseudo?)-Plutarch, *Sayings of Kings and Commanders*, and Lucian, *Demonax*.

cases we are told only those details of the situation that help to make the response understandable and impressive. This is an indication that the pronouncement story is rhetorically shaped. The storyteller has shaped the story to make an impression on the hearer or reader. The parties in the story are not given an equal hearing. The pronouncement of the one person is placed in climactic position in the story so that it will make the dominant impression. The rest of the story points forward to this pronouncement, which is being recommended by the storyteller for admiration and emulation. The pronouncement itself is often expressed in forceful and memorable language. Since it is usually the end of the story, it makes the final impression on the reader or hearer, without the distraction of statements that qualify or contradict.

To recognize that a pronouncement story is a form of influence exercised by the storyteller upon an audience is, in a sense, to "unmask" the storyteller. It is comparable to moving from a naive reaction to a play to the realization that persons have staged these events with an audience in mind, whether the drama is fiction or represents the dramatic shaping of historical events. Such unmasking should not lead us to reject all such forms of influence as illegitimate. Influence is a pervasive and necessary aspect of human communication. When we communicate with other persons, we not only convey ideas but also exercise influence on those persons. Such influence has its dangers: it may manipulate others for the benefit of the manipulator. But it may also be the way in which one person helps another to grow, gaining new insight into the possibilities of humanness. While the pronouncement story may contain brief arguments, most of these stories are so brief and so shaped to increase the rhetorical impact of the dominant utterance that there is little room for rational argument. Still, the forceful words, made more forceful by their setting, can provoke a new way of seeing things. They can stimulate imaginative thought along lines previously neglected or rejected. Although the appeal may be as much to the imagination and the will as to the reason, reason has a rightful role in assessing a pronouncement and unfolding its implications. But reason itself is impoverished if it is not stimulated by words that work in the imagination. Without such stimulus the past will dictate to the present what it must think. Thus the imaginative impact of these little dramatic scenes, including the rhetorical force of the climactic utterance, can contribute to the value and importance of pronouncement stories.[10]

10. On the significance of forceful and imaginative language together with studies of

The direction of the influence being exercised through the story is clarified if we consider the relation between the setting and the dominant pronouncement, or between the stimulus (the situation provoking the pronouncement) and the response. The climactic response, by its position in the story and often by its forceful expression, is being recommended to the reader (unless we have a pronouncement story parody). Commonly it expresses an attitude that the storyteller regards as admirable and exemplary, though occasionally the pronouncement is valued simply because it is funny. In many cases this attitude contrasts with another attitude, sometimes expressed or represented by another character in the story, sometimes indicated in another way or presupposed from the social setting of the story. The various forms of contrast enable the story to express an attitudinal shift. The reader or hearer is being invited to follow this shift, rejecting one attitude and embracing another.

It is useful to speak of attitudes here in order to indicate that more than the intellect is involved. A basic attitude includes value commitments, emotional attachments, the orientation of the will, and evaluative thought. Such attitudes shape personal life at a deep level, and a shift in basic attitudes can deeply affect the self. The interpreter of pronouncement stories should be alert to the movement from one attitude to another that many of these stories invite. This will help the interpreter to understand the purpose of the rhetorical shaping of the story and the pronouncement. It will also help us to understand more clearly how pronouncement stories reflect the value conflicts of the ancient world.[11]

The discussion of synoptic pronouncement stories has been and continues to be heavily influenced by the work of Rudolf Bultmann and Martin Dibelius. It is unfortunate that the study of the pronouncement story and its types has made little progress since their important work. The discussions that follow will show that a new understanding of the types of pronouncement story is both possible and useful. Dibelius did not attempt to classify paradigms into types. Bultmann did divide his apophthegms into three classes: the controversy dialogues, the scholastic dialogues, and the biographical apophthegms. The last of these appears to be a miscellaneous grouping without clear formal definition, and

---

such language in synoptic sayings, see Tannehill, *The Sword of His Mouth* (1975; reprinted, Eugene, Ore.: Wipf & Stock, 2003).

11. See further Tannehill, "Attitudinal Shift in Synoptic Pronouncement Stories," in *Orientation by Disorientation: Studies in Literary Criticism and Biblical Literary Criticism in Honor of William A. Beardslee,* edited by Richard A. Spencer, PittsTMS 26 (Pittsburgh: Pickwick, 1980) 183–97.

Bultmann overlooked significant similarities and differences among texts in classifying them as he did. Renewed consideration of the types of pronouncement story will allow us to clarify further the functions for which the various types are fitted.

Bultmann was primarily interested in the history of the pre-Gospel tradition. While that is a legitimate interest, it is also important to consider pronouncement stories as we find them in ancient texts, seeking to understand them as acts of communication between writers and readers. This is the controlling interest here. Furthermore, the volume of *Semeia* that this essay originally introduced represents a much broader investigation of pronouncement stories in ancient literature than Bultmann and Dibelius were able to present in their discussion of parallels to synoptic stories. This broad investigation was the result of cooperative research by members of the Pronouncement Story Work Group, sponsored by the Society of Biblical Literature.[12]

The typology developed in the second part of this essay emerges from the definition of pronouncement story with which I started. There are two necessary parts to a pronouncement story, the response and the situation provoking that response. A system of types emerges when we consider the various ways in which the provoking occasion and the response are related to each other in groups of pronouncement stories. These two main parts of a pronouncement story are correlative, i.e., the function of the one part must correlate with the function of the other or the story will be malformed and confusing. Each part must be understood in relation to the other and that relationship can be defined. When large groups of pronouncement stories are examined with this in mind, a useful system of types can be developed. The two main parts of a pronouncement story can be discerned even in stories that are relatively long for the genre. The response begins when the responder (the one who will utter the climactic pronouncement that settles the matter as far as the story is concerned)

---

12. See *Semeia* 20 (1981). This *Semeia* volume on pronouncement stories includes essays on Plutarch's *Moralia* and *Parallel Lives*, Diogenes Laertius's *Lives and Opinions of Eminent Philosophers*, the writings of Philo and Josephus, intertestamental and Tannaitic literature, the *Gospel of Thomas*, and early Christian apocryphal literature. In addition the Work Group examined Philostratus, *Life of Apollonius of Tyana, Lives of the Sophists;* and Lucian, *Demonax*. A grant from the National Endowment for the Humanities for a student research assistant helped me to check, organize, and extend the data furnished by other members of the Pronouncement Story Work Group. I am grateful to the National Endowment for the Humanities for this support, and to the student assistant, David D. Wilson, Jr.

takes charge of the situation and begins to move toward the climactic pronouncement, even if there are some preliminary steps before the climax.

The stimulating occasion may include dialogue addressed to the responder or it may not. The responder may simply respond to something observed. This in itself does not determine the function of the first part of the story. Furthermore, the presence of a question addressed to the responder does not tell us how the question functions in a particular story. The responder may accept it as a legitimate request for instruction and respond accordingly, but the question may also express an objection, announce a quest, or express an assumption which the responder will correct.

Construction of a typology based on the relation of the stimulating occasion and the response has the advantage of focusing on a feature essential to the pronouncement story as such. It directs our attention to the pronouncement story as a whole, rather than defining types on the basis of a part considered in isolation. It focuses on the main development in the story, the movement that makes the story a story. The stimulating occasion creates suspense and expectation in the reader, who will want to know what is going to happen as a result. The response discloses the result. Each of the types listed below corresponds to a particular kind of movement from stimulus to response. Furthermore, this way of defining the types can provide clues to the rhetorical function of the story, the potential for influencing the reader that results from the story's literary shape. The interaction between stimulus and response may reflect or anticipate types of interaction between the reader and the story. Recognizing this will help us to understand the purpose behind the shaping of both setting and pronouncement.

This approach can also contribute to our knowledge of the ancient world. The tension within a story may reflect the interaction of a person or group with the surrounding world, at least as pictured by the group that regards the dominant utterance as valuable and, perhaps, normative. The stories not only disclose the ideals that are being promoted by certain persons and groups but may also mirror the perceived conflict between these ideals and other attitudes in the ancient world. Something of the value conflicts of the time shines through. Definition of the movement from stimulating occasion to response in the story can aid us in understanding how the stories reflect these conflicts. Finally, this typology can increase the value of comparative study of pronouncement stories in various literatures of the ancient world. It allows us to compare the relative frequency of use of the different types in various documents, note unusual variations within the types, and recognize how the interaction basic to each type can be employed to express the special concerns and values of particular religious, philosophical, and cultural perspectives as they interact with the surrounding world.

Types of Pronouncement Stories

The following types of pronouncement stories appear when we study the relation between the stimulating occasion and the response in each story:

1. Correction stories (or simply "corrections")
2. Commendation stories ("commendations")
3. Objection stories ("objections")
4. Quest stories ("quests")
5. Inquiry stories ("inquiries")
6. Description stories ("descriptions").

I cannot claim that these types encompass all of the pronouncement stories in the literature of the ancient Mediterranean world. However, these types, or combinations of them (see below on "hybrids"), fit a large number of these pronouncement stories.

The names of the types appear to relate to one part of the pronouncement story, either the stimulus or the response. However, they actually describe the pronouncement story as a whole, since the parts are correlative. In corrections and commendations it is the response that corrects or commends, but this implies a stimulus in which someone has taken a position by word or action that can be corrected or commended. Objections, quests, and inquiries have names that refer most clearly to the stimulus part of the story, but in each case there must be a response appropriate to the type. Indeed, only the response can make clear how the initial situation is relevant and functional in the story.

I will now describe the types of pronouncement story more carefully and give an example of each type.

Correction Stories

In a correction story the responder corrects someone whose actions or words are presented in the stimulus part of the story. By action, by outright statement, or by implication from something said, someone has taken a position as to what is right or expedient, and the responder corrects that position. Thus two attitudes are contrasted in correction stories. Because of the dominant and final position of the response, as well as its rhetorical force in many cases, the attitude expressed there will make the chief impression on the reader. It is being recommended in contrast to the attitude being corrected.

The responder may respond to something observed without being addressed by the one who is corrected, or the response may be part of a dialogue in which the responder replies to a statement, request, or question from the one corrected. In the case of requests and questions, the responder does not grant the request or answer the question but corrects an assumption on which the request or question was based. The correction causes tension between the corrector and the one being corrected. This tension does not become clear in the story until the response is made. Thus the development differs from objection stories, which may also involve a corrective response. In objection stories an objection is raised against the responder, and this provokes the response. Thus tension appears already in the stimulus part, and the responder has a personal interest in the reply, having to defend previous words or actions. In a correction story, however, the position adopted in the stimulus is not an objection against the responder. The position taken may seem innocent, perhaps even commendable. It may represent common practice and ordinary values. The reader may initially agree with or tolerate such practices and values. But the story opens up distance between such views and the position of the responder. This also opens up a choice for the reader, which can lead to a shift of attitudes and priorities.

Correction stories are the most common type of pronouncement story in Lucian's *Demonax*, Philostratus's *The Life of Apollonius of Tyana*, Diogenes Laertius's *Lives and Opinions of Eminent Philosophers,* and (pseudo?)-Plutarch's *Sayings of Kings and Commanders*. Corrections represent a large share of the pronouncement stories found in non-Christian Greek literature of the Roman period. An example from Lucian:

> When one of his friends said: "Demonax, let's go to the Aesculapium and pray for my son," he replied: "You must think Aesculapius very deaf, that he can't hear our prayers from where we are!"[13]

---

13. Lucian, *Demonax* 27 in *Lucian*, LCL, vol. 1, trans. A. M. Harmon (Cambridge, Mass.: Harvard University, 1953).

Commendation Stories

Commendations are similar to corrections in that the responder responds to a position taken by another person with an evaluative comment. However, in commendations the responder commends rather than corrects the other person. The response will affirm or praise something said, done, or represented by the other person. This tends to make the person commended into a model to be imitated by others. The responder maintains an important position in the story, being the source of the recommended evaluation, but the one commended also represents positive values in these stories.

The shared and stable values of a culture can be reinforced by such stories. However, the response gains in interest when it contains a surprise, i. e., when it is unusual in light of other, common judgments about the matter. In such cases there is an implicit contrast between the commendation and another viewpoint. This contrast may come to expression in the response. It may be strongly expressed, as synoptic commendations often do, through the introduction of a third character into the story who takes a negative view of the one being commended or who acts in a way contrary to the action being commended. In such a case we have a hybrid story, in which two movements typical of pronouncement stories are combined, with the response correcting one person and commending another or replying to an objection from one person and commending another. Thus the commendation story, as well as the correction story, may reveal the competition of values and value judgments at the time and place of its origin. It may disclose a hidden value and importance in a person or attitude that seemed unimportant or contemptible by ordinary standards.

Quest stories may also contain a statement of commendation if the quest is successful. However, in quest stories someone approaches the responder seeking help and the success or failure of this quest is announced at the end of the story. In other words, the suspense created by a quest determines the limits and structure of the story. This is not the case in commendations.

An example of a commendation story from Plutarch:

> Another woman, hearing that her son had fallen on the field of battle, said: "Let the poor cowards be mourned, but, with never a tear do I bury you, my son, who are mine, yea, and are Sparta's as well."[14]

14. Plutarch, *Sayings of Spartan Women* 241A, in Plutarch, *Moralia*, LCL, vol. 3, trans.

Objection Stories

Objection stories, like correction stories, present a situation of conflict. However, in corrections the conflict is first indicated by the response, while in objections it is created by an objection to the behavior or views of the responder or his followers. The objection story has three parts, though the first two are often combined:

1. The cause of the objection.
2. The objection, which is sometimes expressed by a question asking why something was done or said.
3. The response to the objection.

The cause of the objection may either be narrated prior to the objection or reported as part of the objection.

In an objection story the responder is already committed to a position through the words or action causing the objection. The resulting challenge creates tension within the story and puts the responder in a difficult situation. However, an impressive response is all the more impressive because it occurs in a situation of difficulty and risk. The response may correct assumptions on which the objection was based, resembling the response in a correction story in this respect. It may also move the conflict to a basic level, disclosing issues of fundamental priorities and of basic perceptions of truth and value behind the conflict.

In my article on "Varieties of Synoptic Pronouncement Stories" (found later in this volume) I will refer to a group of testing inquiry stories in the Gospels. These stories are similar to objections in that the suspense of the story focuses on the responder, whose authority is being challenged or tested. The two groups of stories differ, however, for in the testing inquiries the responder is not replying to an objection against a position already taken.[15]

The following example of a brief objection story comes from Diogenes Laertius:

F. C. Babbitt (modified) (Cambridge, Mass.: Harvard University, 1968).

15. Objection stories correspond to Bultmann's controversy dialogues, but Bultmann obscures the distinction that I wish to make between objections and testing inquiries. While first distinguishing stories that begin with an objection from stories that begin with a question from opponents concerning Jesus' unknown position, Bultmann later includes texts of the latter type in his discussion of controversy dialogues. Compare Bultmann, *History,* 12–21, 26–27 with 48–49.

> To one reproaching him [Diogenes] for entering unclean places he said, "The sun, too, enters the privies but is not defiled."[16]

Quest Stories

A pronouncement by the responder is found near the end of a quest story, as in other pronouncement stories, and this pronouncement has a crucial role in the story, for it will determine the success or failure of the quest. However, quests are often more elaborate than other pronouncement stories, and the quester has a more prominent role than most persons encountered by a responder in pronouncement stories. The story concerns a person in quest of something important to human well-being. It begins by introducing the quester and the quest; it ends by indicating the success or failure of the quest. This interest in the outcome of events for the person who encounters the responder is not typical of pronouncement stories in general, but it is a necessary part of a quest story. The story attracts the reader's attention not only to the words of the responder but also to the quester, whose need and desire to fulfill that need provide tension in the story and define its central movement. Because the story focuses attention on the quester's need and awakens interest in the possible fulfillment of that need, it tends to awaken the reader's sympathy. This can heighten the effect of the stories on the reader, making failure seem tragic and success satisfying, even if the questers have some attributes that seem to disqualify them.

The responder is the person of authority in the situation, and the quester comes to the responder for help. The responder may pose a difficult condition, or someone may object to the quest. These obstacles are important in the story, for they indicate the issue that is crucial for the outcome of the quest, an issue on which the storyteller may wish to change the audience's attitudes. A quest story will not end until we have been informed whether the quester succeeded or failed. A successful quest may end with a statement of commendation by the responder.

Although there is an important group of quest stories in the synoptic Gospels, it has been difficult to find quest stories elsewhere.[17] Therefore,

---

16. Diogenes Laertius, *Lives and Opinions of Eminent Philosophers* VI.63, LCL, trans. R. D. Hicks (Cambridge, Mass.: Harvard University, 1950, 1958).

17. The Pronouncement Story Work Group discovered only a few examples of quest stories outside the Gospels. In addition to the example that I give, see Diogenes Laertius, *Lives* VI.36, quoted in Paula Nassan Poulos, "Form and Function of the Pronouncement Story in Diogenes Laertius' *Lives*," *Semeia* 20 (1981) 56–57, and Plutarch, *Moralia* V.403F–

some features of the description above, such as the remarks about the reader's sympathy, may reflect aspects of synoptic stories that do not apply to quest stories elsewhere. The following story from Diogenes Laertius appears to be a good example of a quest, except that the final sentence merges the successful outcome with following events.

> She [Hipparchia] fell in love with the discourses and the life of Crates, and would not pay attention to any of her suitors, their wealth, their high birth or their beauty. But to her Crates was everything. She used even to threaten her parents she would make away with herself, unless she were given in marriage to him. Crates therefore was implored by her parents to dissuade the girl, and did all he could, and at last, failing to persuade her, got up, took off his clothes before her face and said, "This is the bridegroom, here are his possessions; make your choice accordingly; for you will be no helpmeet of mine, unless you share my pursuits."
>
> The girl chose and, adopting the same dress, went about with her husband . . .[18]

Inquiry Stories

An inquiry story moves from a question or request for information to the answer to that question or request. Other types of pronouncement stories may contain questions, but inquiries lack the special features of these other types. The responder does not respond by correcting an assumption on which the question is based, as in a correction story. The question is accepted and an answer is supplied. The question does not express an objection to something already said or done by the responder. It is not the announcement of a quest that is shown to succeed or fail at the end of the story. The dramatic conflict and tension between persons characteristic of many of the other stories are largely lacking in the inquiries. What happens to the characters becomes less important, leaving the teaching given by the responder as the remaining matter of importance. The reader's interest focuses almost entirely on the content of the instruction given in the response. Frequently the story setting contributes little to the pronouncement, except that it may introduce the topic being discussed and suggest application of the teaching to a particular group or problem.

404A, quoted in John E. Alsup, "Type, Place, and Function of the Pronouncement Story in Plutarch's *Moralia*," *Semeia* 20 (1981) 25.

18. Diogenes Laertius, *Lives* VI.96–97, trans. R. D. Hicks.

The relative lack of dramatic tension in inquiries does not apply to a subtype that I will call testing inquiries. There is an important group of testing inquiries in the synoptic Gospels. I will describe this subtype in the article on "Varieties of Synoptic Pronouncement Stories" (included in this volume).

Inquiries are fairly common in the literature that I have examined, though not as common as corrections. An example from Philostratus:

> When the king asked him [Apollonius] how he could rule with stability and security, he said, "Honoring many but trusting few."[19]

Description Stories

Description stories begin with a general indication of the situation to which the pronouncement relates. This provides the setting for a comment in which the responder describes the situation, usually in apt and striking language, expressing some remarkable aspect of it. The descriptive comment may be humorous, highlighting something ridiculous or incongruous in the situation. It may also be poignant, highlighting the tragedy of human limitations or the fateful consequences of what has happened. The descriptive response does not answer an inquiry, nor does it positively or negatively evaluate the situation inspiring the comment. Such evaluation would result in a correction or a commendation. The concern for description rather than evaluation is a defining characteristic of the descriptions. While the response may indicate that the situation is incongruous or tragic, it does not imply that it could be otherwise. Rather than saying, "This is not the way it should be; change it," the speaker is saying, "However we may have planned and whatever our desires, this is the way it is." Thus the descriptive response expresses some striking quality of a particular situation. This quality may be unique to the situation, or the situation may manifest a recurrent quality of life.

I offer two examples from (pseudo?)-Plutarch. The first is humorous and applies to a unique situation; the second is poignant and suggests a quality of life in general.

> Of his son, who was pert towards his mother, he [Themistocles] said that the boy wielded more power than anybody else in Greece; for the Athenians ruled the Greeks, he himself ruled the

---

19. Philostratus, *The Life of Apollonius of Tyana* I.37, LCL, trans. F. C. Conybeare (London: Heinemann, 1917, 1921).

> Athenians, the boy's mother ruled himself, and the boy ruled the mother.[20]

> When he [Agesilaus] was about to break camp in haste by night to leave the enemy's country, and saw his favourite youth, owing to illness, being left behind all in tears, he said, "It is hard to be merciful and sensible at the same time."[21]

As already noted above, several of the types may be combined in a single story to form a hybrid story. In this case the developments from stimulus to response characteristic of several types are found within one story, and the response has more than one function. This may occur when there are only two characters in the story, but it is more likely to occur in stories that present three persons or groups in important roles. The responder may correct one party and commend another, respond to the objection of one party and commend another, respond to an objection and to a quest, etc. In the following example from (pseudo?)-Plutarch, Archelaus is both responding to an objection (indicated by the man's astonishment) and commending Euripides.

> When Archelaus, at a convivial gathering, was asked for a golden cup by one of his acquaintances of a type not commendable for character, he bade the servant give it to Euripides; and in answer to the man's look of astonishment, he said, "It is true that you have a right to ask for it, but Euripides has a right to receive it even though he did not ask for it."[22]

In my essay on "Varieties of Synoptic Pronouncement Stories" I apply the typology discussed above to pronouncement stories in the synoptic Gospels and will discuss further the functions of the different types. Most of the other articles published in *Semeia* 20 also employ this typology, showing the frequent or infrequent usage of the story types in various ancient literature. In his article on pronouncement stories in four of Plutarch's *Lives*, Vernon K. Robbins proposes some modifications of the typology, and the reader will want to compare Robbins's system with that proposed here.[23] I find his distinction among first, second, and third per-

---

20. (Pseudo?)-Plutarch, *Sayings of Kings and Commanders* 185D, in Plutarch, *Moralia*, vol. 3, LCL, trans. F. C. Babbitt.
21. Ibid., 191A.
22. Ibid., 177A.
23. Robbins, "Classifying Pronouncement Stories in Plutarch's *Parallel Lives*," *Semeia* 20 (1981) 29–52.

son corrections and commendations to be a helpful refinement. Calling attention to inverted correction and commendation stories, i.e., stories in which the primary character of the writing as a whole is corrected or commended, rather than correcting or commending, is also helpful. Robbins labels these "rebuffs" and "laudations." Continuing study of pronouncement stories may reveal other types or subtypes, helping us to appreciate the complex possibilities of these seemingly simple stories.

3

Varieties *of* Synoptic Pronouncement Stories

This essay applies the typology developed in "The Pronouncement Story and Its Types" to synoptic pronouncement stories. Five of the six types are well represented in the synoptic Gospels. Especially noteworthy are a group of hybrid stories combining commendation with correction or objection, an important group of well-developed quest stories, and a group of testing inquiries that show more dramatic tension than the other inquiries. The stories of each type are listed, sometimes with brief explanation. Differences in usage of the types by the three synoptic Gospels are noted. I also note certain common features of the climactic sayings and preliminary dialogues, and I suggest ways in which the story types may function to change the attitudes and commitments of hearers and readers.

Introduction

THE TYPOLOGY DISCUSSED IN the preceding essay, "The Pronouncement Story and Its Types," provides a useful framework for the study of synoptic pronouncement stories. It highlights the differing relationship between the climactic response in a pronouncement story and the situation provoking that response, and this relationship provides clues to the functions that these stories are shaped to perform in communication between speaker and hearer or writer and reader. I have discussed these matters in two previous articles. The essay on "Types and Functions of Apophthegms in the Synoptic Gospels" supplements this essay by providing more detailed discussion of individual texts and of my reasons for relating them to particular types.[1] This previous article also discusses the functions of the types of pronouncement stories, a discussion that is carried further in my

---

1. Tannehill, "Types and Functions of Apophthegms in the Synoptic Gospels," in *ANRW* II.25.2, edited by Wolfgang Haase (Berlin: de Gruyter, 1984) 1792–829. This essay is included in the present volume.

article on "Attitudinal Shift in Synoptic Pronouncement Stories."[2] Some overlap with these articles is unavoidable. To reduce this to a minimum, I will simply list the texts that I judge to belong to each type, except in some cases where explanation is needed and can be briefly given. I will discuss certain features of composition, especially of the climactic sayings and the preliminary dialogues, that seem to be characteristic of the various types. Some differences among the three synoptic Gospels in the use of the pronouncement story will also be noted. Finally, I will summarize my understanding of the function of each of the pronouncement story types.

I do not assume that each of the texts I discuss is a pre-Gospel unit of oral tradition. It is quite possible that the formation of pronouncement stories continued into the late, redactional stages of the Gospel tradition, as is suggested by the occurrence of parallel sayings in divergent settings. No attempt will be made to separate material of early and late origin, beyond noting that certain scenes (especially inquiries), though marked as separate narrative episodes by a change of setting and/or characters, comment on material in a previous scene, indicating that they did not have an independent origin.

Before dealing with the five types of synoptic pronouncement story, the following general comments can be made: The frequency with which Greek authors of the Roman period use one sentence pronouncement stories, with the occasion for the pronouncement reduced to a subordinate clause (often a participial clause),[3] makes the rarity of this construction in the synoptic Gospels noteworthy. The Gospels tend to use several sentences in paratactic relation, resulting in a somewhat longer story. Longer stories are not absent from the non-Christian authors,[4] but the lack of use in the Gospels of the common one sentence story is remarkable. Luke is a partial exception. There we do find some tendency to describe the occasion for a pronouncement in a participial clause (see Luke 3:15, 17:20, 21:5).

---

2. Tannehill, "Attitudinal Shift in Synoptic Pronouncement Stories," in *Orientation by Disorientation: Studies in Literary Criticism and Biblical Literary Criticism Presented in Honor of William A. Beardslee,* edited by Richard A. Spencer. PittsTMS 26. (Pittsburgh: Pickwick, 1980) 183–97.

3 See Diogenes Laertius, *Lives and Opinions of Eminent Philosophers* VI.4 (five pronouncement stories in the first five Greek sentences), VI.5 (two pronouncement stories in the first two Greek sentences; a third in the last sentence).

4. They seem to be especially common in Plutarch (and works attributed to him).

It is also characteristic of Luke to place a parable in a pronouncement story setting, where the parable becomes the response to some situation that is briefly described. Luke 7:36–50, 10:25–37, 12:13–21, 15:1–32, 18:9–14, and 19:11–27 are examples.[5] There is some overlap here with the tendency, discussed below under "Objection Stories," to reply to critics by pointing to an analogy for the criticized behavior. This tendency is found in all three synoptic Gospels.

Correction Stories

The following correction stories are found in Mark:

- Mark 1:35–38 par. Luke—Jesus departs from Capernaum
- Mark 9:33–37 par. Matt, Luke—who is greatest?[6]
- Mark 9:38–40 par. Luke—the strange exorcist
- Mark 10:35–45 par. Matt—request of James and John
- Mark 11:15–17 par. Matt, Luke—casting out the traders
- Mark 12:18–27 par. Matt, Luke—question about the resurrection
- Mark 13:1–2 par. Matt, Luke—the great temple buildings

Possibly 8:11–12 (refusal of a sign) and 12:35–37 par. Matt, Luke (David's son) should also be included.[7]

In addition, Matthew has the following correction stories:

- Matt 4:1–11 par. Luke—the temptations
- Matt 8:19–20 par. Luke—the homeless Son of Man
- Matt 8:21–22 par. Luke—let the dead bury the dead
- Matt 11:20–24—woes on Galilean towns
- Matt 17:24–27—the temple tax
- Matt 18:21–22—forgive seven times?

Luke alone has the following correction stories:

---

5. See also Luke 14:15–24, where the relation of the parable to the introductory statement by the dinner companion is not very clear.

6. In Matthew's version Jesus' response introduces a long discourse. Also, Matt 18:1–5 lacks Mark's reference to the disciples arguing about greatness, weakening the correction. Nevertheless, the phrase "unless you turn and become . . ." seems to imply correction.

7. Mark 12:35–37 par. is a correction if Jesus is rejecting the view that the Christ is David's son.

- Luke 3:15–17—the people suspect that John is the Christ
- Luke 9:61–62—plowing and looking back
- Luke 11:27–28—blessing of Jesus' mother
- Luke 12:13–21—request to divide an inheritance
- Luke 13:1–5—repentance or destruction
- Luke 14:7–11—places at table
- Luke 14:12–14—inviting guests to dinner
- Luke 17:20–21—the kingdom among you
- Luke 18:9–14—the Pharisee and the tax collector
- Luke 19:11–27—the pounds
- Luke 19:41–44—weeping over Jerusalem
- Luke 22:24–27—dispute about greatness at the Last Supper
- Luke 23:27–31—the weeping women

Possibly Luke 9:52–56 (rejection at a Samaritan village) and 13:31–33 (warning against Herod) should also be included.

There are also hybrid pronouncement stories that combine correction with another type of development. The following stories combine correction and commendation:

- Mark 3:31–35 par. Matt, Luke—Jesus' true family
- Mark 10:13–16 par. Matt, Luke—blessing the children
- Mark 12:41–44 par. Luke—the poor widow
- Mark 14:3–9 par. Matt—the anointing

The following stories combine correction with testing inquiry:

- Mark 10:2–9—question about divorce
- Matt 12:38–42—request for a sign
- Matt 16:1–4—second request for a sign

The large number of correction stories found only in Luke is noteworthy. While only five correction stories are unique to Matthew (including hybrids), there are thirteen to fifteen correction stories unique to Luke. This observation should be considered along side the fact that the correction story is the most common type of pronouncement story in a number of non-Christian authors.[8]

8. The correction story is the most common type of pronouncement story in Diogenes

Matthew 12:38–42 and 16:1–4, scenes in which Jesus responds to a request for a sign, contain a strong corrective element. A generation that seeks a sign is "evil and adulterous"; the men of Nineveh and the queen of the south will condemn it. Nevertheless, Jesus is also being tested and a response is made to the request: Jesus points to the sign of Jonah. Since Jesus both corrects and responds to a testing request by supplying an answer, these stories are hybrid, combining correction and testing inquiry. Mark 8:11–12, the refusal of a sign; Mark 12:18–27, the question about the resurrection; and Matt 4:1–11, the temptations, are somewhat different. In all these stories Jesus is being tested. This is explicit in Mark 8:11–12 and Matt 4:1–11, and is indicated in Mark 12:18–27 by the fact that the question is based on a premise that the questioners reject. It does not arise from a search for truth but is a trick question designed to embarrass Jesus. However, in these stories Jesus does not answer the question or respond to the requests, except by correcting them. These stories are simply corrections, not hybrids, though the tension in the stories is heightened by the indications that Jesus is being tested.

In a correction story the responder takes a position that contrasts with and corrects the position assumed through word or action by some other party. It is not surprising, then, that the climactic saying in a correction story often contains a negation and a contrast. In a number of cases the response is formulated by using a negation followed by a strong "but" (ἀλλά or πλήν), as in Mark 10:43–45; 12:25, 27; Matt 4:4; 18:22; Luke 23:28. In other cases we find a negation followed directly by the reason for the negative response (often expressed in a γάρ or ὅτι clause), as in Mark 9:39, 10:14, Luke 17:20–21. A corrective response may also be expressed in an antithetical aphorism, a brief saying in which the corrected attitude is paradoxically tied to its opposite, as in Mark 9:35, 10:43–44, Luke 18:14.[9]

The usefulness of these speech patterns in corrective responses can help us to recognize correction stories where there might otherwise be some doubt. When a position as to what is right or expedient is clearly expressed in the provoking setting by an action or statement, or is clearly assumed by a question or request, and then is corrected in the response,

---

Laertius' *Lives*; see Paula Nassen Poulos, "Form and Function of the Pronouncement Story in Diogenes Laertius' *Lives*," *Semeia* 20 (1981) 59–60; the same is true of Lucian's *Demonax*, Philostratus' *Life of Apollonius of Tyana*, and (pseudo?)-Plutarch's *Sayings of Kings and Commanders*, among other works.

9. On antithetical aphorisms see Tannehill, *The Sword of His Mouth* (1975, reprinted Eugene, Ore.: Wipf & Stock, 2003) 88–107.

the corrective movement in the story is clear. There are cases, however, in which the position being corrected is only made clear in the response. In Luke 13:1–5 certain people tell Jesus about the Galileans killed by Pilate. They do not express an opinion about this. However, Jesus begins by suggesting, in a question, what they may think about these Galileans. Although this is only a possible opinion, the story is designed to correct it, and Jesus expresses this with the common negation followed by "but." The words of Jesus in Luke 14:12–14 are introduced only by an indication that they were addressed to the host who had invited Jesus to dinner. The words, however, are typical of a corrective response (negation followed by "but"), and, since the practice being corrected is the ordinary one, the author of Luke can assume that the host followed it and is being corrected. Similarly, the negations with which the response in Luke 17:20–21 begins lead us to believe that the Pharisees hold the rejected views, even though this is not clearly expressed in their introductory question.

Correction stories are little dramatic scenes in which tension is disclosed between the corrector and the person or group corrected. This tension may come as a surprise. Unlike the objection stories, the response is not provoked by criticism of the responder. We do not know how the story is going to develop until the response is made, for the position corrected may appear at first to be harmless or even praiseworthy. But the corrective response challenges the common and accepted, or it takes the bad but tolerable and makes it appear very bad indeed. Thus the correction story opens up distance between a position accepted by some important group, perhaps by almost everyone, and the position of the responder, thereby placing a choice before the hearer or reader. Common practice is often on the side of the initial position, but the story is on the side of the responder's challenge. For the pronouncement story is not value-neutral. The response is placed in climactic position and is often phrased with rhetorical power. The responder's view is being recommended; the story is an invitation to readers to change their attitude and actions in line with the challenge of the responder. This challenge involves an appeal to the will and often to the imagination. Although correction stories contain brief supporting reasons (often introduced by γάρ or ὅτι), a pronouncement story is quite different than an extensive dialogue in which positions are thoroughly discussed. Reasons must strike like lightning; there is no room for lumbering argument. On the other hand, the rhetorical impact of words is important, for strong words can provoke new thought, awaken the imagination, and open new perspectives that can lead to change in values and commitments. The dramatic tension between persons, inherent to a correction story, contributes to this rhetorical impact.

The typology I am using calls attention to this important group of correction stories, a type of story not previously recognized. This should increase awareness of their challenging function. Rather than isolating historical facts or religious ideas from their tensive setting, interpreters of these stories should become aware that the stories embody a movement from one value stance to another and that the reader is being invited to follow that movement.

Commendation Stories

Most synoptic commendation stories are hybrid. However, this is not the case with three scenes concerned with the privileges and authority of one or more of the disciples:

- Matt 13:51–52—treasures new and old
- Matt 16:13–20—the blessing of Peter
- Luke 10:17–20—the return of the seventy

The first of these refers back to the preceding parables and so is not a fully independent scene.

The frequency of hybrid pronouncement stories in the synoptic Gospels is significant. Most of the commendation stories not only commend but also correct or answer an objection. In these stories the commending judgment of Jesus contrasts with the judgment of someone else. The hybrid commendation stories are developed for the sake of this contrast. Thus there is tension in these stories, as well as in the corrections, and both types are designed to move the reader away from one attitude toward the attitude that Jesus represents.

Four stories combine correction and commendation. In Mark 10:13–16 par. Matt, Luke (the blessing of the children) Jesus not only commends the children for what they represent but also corrects the disciples. In Mark 14:3–9 par. Matt (the anointing) Jesus both commends the woman and corrects those who have criticized her. Both of these stories contain three characters (individuals or groups), one of whom is judged by the other two. The story begins with a negative judgment, which is corrected by Jesus' positive judgment. In Mark 3:31–35 par. Matt, Luke (Jesus' true family) Jesus commends those sitting around him by calling them his mother and brothers and also corrects the previous application of these terms to his natural family. In this case the correction applies not only to the messengers in 3:32 but also to the narrator in 3:31, both of whom have used mother and brothers in the usual way. The initial use of these terms in their normal meaning emphasizes the sudden shift introduced by Jesus. Instead of the expected consistency of viewpoint, the story juxtaposes two different meanings of the same phrase.[10] Mark 12:41–44 par. Luke (the poor widow) is similar, although the correction is not as emphatic. In commending the widow Jesus contrasts her with all the others who contributed to the temple; she put in "more than all." Previously, however, the narrator told us that "many rich were putting in much," while the widow put in only two *lepta*. This reading of the situation, based on ordinary economic values, is corrected by Jesus.

The relationships among the characters in Luke 10:38–42 (Mary and Martha) are similar to those in the blessing of the children and the anointing, but there are also new developments. Martha and Jesus not only make contrasting judgments about Mary, but Mary and Martha also act in contrasting ways. Furthermore, Martha not only criticizes her sister but also Jesus. When Jesus' behavior provokes an objection, to which he must reply, we have an objection story. Hence, this is a hybrid objection-commendation. The two objection-commendation stories in Matt 21:14–16 (out of the mouth of babes) and Luke 19:37–40 (entry into Jerusalem) are similar to each other. In both cases praise of Jesus causes an objection. Jesus' response to the objection also shows his approval of the initial praise, which is explicitly Christological.

In Matt 16:13–20 the authority of a particular individual (Peter) is being affirmed. In most cases, however, a commendation story commends not so much the person as the values and attitudes represented by the person. In this way the commended person becomes a model for others. The values of the Jesus movement are represented not only by Jesus but also by those whom he commends. Commendation stories recommend these values to the reader. The hybrid stories make us aware that these values are in competition with others. In these stories Jesus not only affirms but also negates. His way of thinking is a challenge to other ways of thinking. The story recommends Jesus' attitude, but it also displays the tension between this and other attitudes, which may have a firm hold on ordinary life. So in these stories also a choice is clarified, and change in personal attitudes becomes a possibility.

---

10. On Mark 3:31–35 see further Tannehill, *Sword*, 165–71.

Varieties of Synoptic Pronouncement Stories   43

The tendency in commendation stories to present people as models will be developed further in quest stories. In some commendations conflict with ordinary social values is indicated by the commendation of people who are socially inferior (children, the poor widow). This will be a strong tendency in synoptic quest stories.

Objection Stories

The following objection stories are found in Mark:

- Mark 2:15–17 par. Matt, Luke—meal with tax collectors
- Mark 2:18–22 par. Matt, Luke—fasting
- Mark 2:23–28 par. Matt, Luke—plucking grain on the Sabbath
- Mark 3:1–6 par. Matt, Luke—Sabbath healing of withered hand
- Mark 3:22–30 par. Matt, Luke—Beelzebul controversy
- Mark 6:1–6 par. Matt—the prophet in his home town
- Mark 7:1–15 par. Matt—eating with defiled hands
- Mark 8:31–33 par. Matt—Peter's rejection of the passion announcement
- Mark 9:9–13 par. Matt—the resurrection and Elijah
- Mark 10:23–27 par. Matt, Luke—the rich and the Kingdom

In addition, the following objection stories are found in Matthew and Luke:

- Matt 3:13–15—John's objection to baptizing Jesus
- Luke 2:41–51—the boy Jesus in the temple
- Luke 11:37–52—against the Pharisees and lawyers
- Luke 13:10–17—Sabbath healing of a woman
- Luke 14:1–6—Sabbath healing of man with dropsy
- Luke 15:1–32—Jesus is accused of eating with sinners and responds with parables

Luke 16:14–15 and 20:16–18 are not independent stories. The objections in these passages refer back to the preceding teaching of Jesus. In both cases the brief objection and response is not sufficiently important to turn the larger passage into an objection story. They are dependent objection sequences similar to the dependent inquiry scenes that will be mentioned later. In Matt 19:3–12 (the question about divorce) Jesus responds to a testing inquiry and then to two objections to the position that he has taken. Each of the three responses is roughly equal in importance, which suggests that this story has moved away from the climactic ending typical of a pronouncement story and toward a more diffuse dialogue form.

We should also consider those stories in which an objection sequence is combined with another type of development to form a hybrid story. The following stories combine objection and commendation: Matt 21:14–16 (out of the mouth of babes), Luke 10:38–42 (Mary and Martha), Luke 19:37–40 (entry into Jerusalem). There are also some quest stories in which the climax of the story includes Jesus' response to an objection (Mark 2:1–12 par. Matt, Luke, healing of the paralytic; Luke 7:36–50, the sinful woman in the Pharisee's house; Luke 19:1–10, Zacchaeus) or Jesus' approval of another person's response to an objection (Mark 7:24–30 par. Matt, the gentile woman; Luke 23:39–43, the penitent criminal; perhaps Matt 8:5–13, the centurion).

Although the other types being used in this essay are different from those used by Bultmann, objection stories correspond fairly closely with Bultmann's controversy dialogues. Nevertheless, there are some differences in the texts judged to be examples of the type. Bultmann included Mark 11:27–33, basing his judgment on a shorter, reconstructed version of the story.[11] However, in its present form, this appears to be a testing inquiry. In the first part of his discussion of apophthegms, Bultmann correctly distinguished stories based on an objection to something that has already happened from stories that begin with a question by opponents concerning Jesus' position, which is not known.[12] Later, however, he ignores this distinction and includes Mark 12:13–17, 12:18–27, and 10:2–12 in his general discussion of controversy dialogues.[13] I do not include these passages in the objection stories. On the other hand, I do include a number of passages omitted by Bultmann: Mark 6:1–6 par., 8:31–33 par., 9:9–13 par., 10:23–27 par., Matt 3:13–15, Luke 2:41–51, 11:37–52, 15:1–32, and the hybrid stories Mark 7:24–30 par., Matt 21:14–16, Luke 10:38–42, 19:1–10, 19:37–40, 23:39–43. The difference between Bultmann's interest in the history of the pre-Gospel tradition and my interest in the rhetorical function of the story forms is apparent here, and our typologies

---

11. Rudolf Bultmann, *The History of the Synoptic Tradition*, rev. ed., trans. John Marsh (1976; reprinted, Peabody, Mass.: Hendrickson, 1994) 19–20.

12. Ibid., 12–21, 26–27.

13. Ibid., 48–49.

are quite different when we move beyond objection stories or controversy dialogues.

Although Bultmann designated Mark 6:1-6 (the prophet in his home town) a biographical apophthegm,[14] it appears to me to be a good example of an objection story. To be sure, the questions in 6:2-3 are not clearly negative apart from the comment "And they took offense at him." But this statement clearly indicates that the preceding questions constitute an objection of the townspeople to one of their own claiming or exercising such unusual powers. The saying of Jesus in 6:4 is a relevant response. Jesus describes such an objection as the strange exception to the honor that all others are willing to give a prophet. An attitude so out of step with the judgments of others is dubious.

Martin Dibelius regarded Luke 2:41-51 (the boy Jesus in the temple) as an outstanding example of a legend.[15] I do not deny its legendary features, but careful consideration of the central tension of the plot shows that it follows the pattern of an objection story. After an unusually long narrative introduction, Jesus' mother expresses her objection to her son's behavior, using a question beginning with "why," a style common in objection stories. The climactic pronouncement is a response to this objection.

The order of the story elements in the Sabbath healing stories varies, causing some uncertainty in relating them to the types. In Mark 3:1-6 the opponents do not express an objection. Nevertheless, their negative attitude toward Sabbath healing is indicated in v. 2. Jesus' position on the matter also seems fairly clear. The opponents anticipate what Jesus is going to do, and their negative attitude is an anticipatory objection to the healing that follows. The evangelist also suggests that it is based on past knowledge of Jesus' behavior. The introductory statement "He entered again into the synagogue" recalls to the reader Jesus' previous Sabbath miracle in Mark 1:21-28. Thus the evangelist can view the negative attitude of the opponents as an indication of their objection to behavior previously demonstrated, behavior that they anticipate will be repeated. Jesus responds to this objection with both words (3:4) and action (the healing).

In Luke 14:1-6 the negative attitude of the opponents is indicated by the statement that they were "watching" or "lying in wait" for him (a

---

14. Ibid., 31-32.

15 Martin Dibelius, *From Tradition to Gospel*, trans. Bertram Lee Woolf (New York: Scribner, 1934) 106-9.

reminiscence of the Sabbath healing in Luke 6:6–11) and by the indication in 14:6 that they would have liked to "answer back" but could not. In this story the healing precedes Jesus' principal pronouncement, making clear that his words are a defense of his behavior against the objection implied in the Pharisees' attitude. Matt 12:9–14, although parallel to Mark 3:1–6, has been changed sufficiently to make judgment difficult. This is the first Sabbath healing in Matthew, so we cannot assume that the opponents are acting on the basis of previous knowledge. In contrast to Mark, Jesus is asked a question. This is not an objection but merely asks Jesus to express his opinion about Sabbath healing. Jesus responds to the question with a definite answer before the healing takes place. This suggests that we can understand the story as a testing inquiry, with a healing miracle providing a framework. Nevertheless, the statement that the opponents are asking "in order that they might accuse him" (parallel to Mark) may indicate that they anticipate Jesus' position and implicitly object to it. If so, Jesus responds as expected; the anticipation proves correct and constitutes an objection to a position that Jesus actually holds and must defend.

As with correction stories, there are more uniquely Lukan objection stories than uniquely Matthean. Matthew preserves more of the Markan objection stories and elaborates them, adding arguments to refute the opponents, but has few additional ones.

In non-Christian authors short objection stories are often introduced by a participle of ὀνειδίζω ("reproach, mock").[16] This construction is not used in the Gospels.

A remarkable aspect of the responses in objection stories is the frequent use of rhetorical questions, often combined with an appeal to an analogous situation.[17] A question, even a rhetorical one, seeks a response. The judgment of the objector is asked for. This judgment is guided by the question, which makes a particular conclusion seem inevitable. The question asks the objector to affirm this conclusion, which requires a change of mind. Although the reactions of other people to Jesus' climactic words are seldom indicated in the pronouncement stories, there is a sense in which these objection stories are deliberately incomplete until these questions are answered. Those who overhear what is being said (including the readers of the Gospels) must give their own answers to Jesus' argumentative question. The rhetorical question brings a decision into focus. It

---

16. See Diogenes Laertius, *Lives and Opinions of Eminent Philosophers* VI.4, 6, 56, 58, 66, 67, etc.

17. This was noted by Bultmann, *History*, 41.

puts the matter into a perspective that contrasts with the perspective from which the objectors are judging and asks all of us to decide from this new perspective. In Mark 3:4 Jesus' question poses a single alternative in light of which the decision should be made. If the alternative is accepted, the required answer is clear. Mark 2:9 is somewhat similar.

It is much more common, however, for the question to appeal to an analogous situation where behavior like that of Jesus is generally accepted. We react to situations because we judge them to be like other situations that we understand and evaluate in certain ways. Our reaction can change if we discover a different likeness suggesting a different understanding of the situation and a different judgment of what is right and wrong. In the following passages from objection stories Jesus argues by analogy, asking in a question for a judgment about an analogous situation, a judgment that implies a new way of viewing the matter under debate: Mark 2:19 par.; 3:23–26 par.; Matt 12:11; 12:27 par.; 12:29; Luke 7:41–42; 11:39–40; 13:15–16; 14:5; 15:4–10. In Luke 7:41–42 and 15:4–10 we find parables with questions, suggesting that some of the parables are developed forms of these arguments by analogy. In Mark 2:17 par.; 2:21–22 par.; and 3:27 there are appeals to analogies that are not formulated as questions. The last two texts use statements with οὐδείς; and in Matthew's parallel to Mark 3:27, Mark's "no one can . . ." (οὐ δύναται οὐδείς) is transformed into "how can anyone . . . " (πῶς δύναταί τις), showing that the rhetorical questions in objection stories relate closely to implicit statements.

In some cases the argumentative question with which Jesus responds to an objection contains an appeal to Scripture (Mark 2:25–26 par.; Matt 12:5; 21:16; Luke 20:17). In the first two cases this also involves argument from analogy. The phrase "have you never read," often used to introduce these appeals to Scripture, contains a reproach for not knowing what should have been known. The question in Luke 2:49 expresses a similar reproach, although it is not an appeal to Scripture.

In addition to rhetorical questions and analogies, we often find general statements of principle in the responses in objection stories. Thus the story moves from a specific occasion to a disclosure of the basic principle by which actions and attitudes on such occasions should be governed, combining the vividness of a particular encounter with a general disclosure of God's will or the meaning of Jesus' mission. These general statements are often formulated antithetically, emphasizing the contrast between what is being said and another point of view (these are similar to some correction responses) or emphasizing two contrasting possibilities.[18] Mark 2:17 par.; 2:27; 7:15 par.; Luke 7:47; and 16:15 are examples. General statements that are not antithetical are found in Mark 2:10 par.; Luke 11:41; and 19:10.

In an objection story tension arises at an earlier point than in a correction story. In corrections it is the corrective response of Jesus that makes clear that something is amiss. This may come as a surprise. In objection stories, however, conflict is initiated by the objector. The peculiar behavior of Jesus and his disciples has been noted in the public domain and has provoked a reaction. Thus correction stories initiate tension, while objection stories are fitted to reflect the tension that already exists because of conflicts between the Jesus movement and its environment. Bultmann's assertion that the controversy dialogues are related to the "apologetic and polemic" of the early church fits many of these stories well.[19] Indeed, a few passages involve sharp counterattacks against the objecting group, suggesting hard lines of division. These are passages in which the response is long and composite, contrasting with the brief and pointed response typical of the pronouncement story (see Mark 7:1–15 par.; Matt 12:22–37; Luke 11:37–52).

However, in most cases Jesus speaks to the issue, rather than attacking the objector, and appeals for agreement in spite of the wide gulf separating the parties to the conversation. In question, analogy, and forceful statement of principle, Jesus presents his perspective, and both the power of the words and their story setting help them to take root in the memory and imagination of the reader, where they may provoke new thought. Although Jesus replies to outsiders in many of these stories, his words are also relevant to his followers. As with other groups, the special concerns and values of the Jesus movement are subject to erosion. The words of Jesus in objection stories often disclose the fundamental concerns behind peculiar practices and seek to reawaken commitment to these fundamentals.

An objection is a challenge to Jesus and his authority. Such situations carry risk for Jesus and those who honor him. The objection stories and the testing inquiries highlight the ability of Jesus to meet such challenges. The powerful wisdom and authority of Jesus stand out as they are put to the test. Thus these stories are also indirect praise of Jesus.

---

18. Compare my discussion of the antithetical aphorism in Tannehill, *Sword*, 88–101.

19. Bultmann, *History*, 40–41.

Quest Stories

Although a few possible examples of quest stories outside the synoptic Gospels have been found,[20] they appear to be rare, while this is an important group of pronouncement stories in the synoptic Gospels. Some of these stories concern people who seek for and receive healing for themselves or others. We might suppose that the synoptic quest story developed through a combination of the healing miracle story with the pronouncement story. However, this does not explain a majority of the cases. Only four of the nine stories in the synoptic Gospels concern persons in quest of healing. Furthermore, the inclusion of healing does not necessarily lead to a quest story, for there is a significant group of objection stories that report a healing. Evidently some early Christian storytellers were interested in the figure of the quester, who becomes prominent in these stories.

Quests are usually longer and more elaborate than most pronouncement stories. They can incorporate features of the other types. In them Jesus may correct and commend, or answer an objection and commend. However, these features are parts of the story of a quest, and it is this quest that provides the central tension of the story and orders the other features as a meaningful development. A quest story discloses the need of a quester and comes to an end by announcing success or failure in meeting that need. This concern with the outcome of the story for the person who encounters Jesus is unusual, for most pronouncement stories end with the pronouncement of the sage, with no indication of how those addressed are affected by this. At most there is indication of a general crowd reaction. But the quest story focuses on the quester. It is his or her need and success or failure that shape the story and are meant to gain our interest.

The pronouncement of Jesus relates to this need and has a key role in the success or failure of the quester. Jesus remains the figure of authority in the story, and he must certify the success of a quest. The pronouncement announcing the successful quest usually implies the commendation of the quester. Thus, there is a relation between the successful quest (all but one of the synoptic quest stories are successful) and the commendation story, though they differ because the quest emphasizes that a person comes to Jesus with a need and finds the solution to that need. Quests can develop further the tendency in commendation stories to present persons other than Jesus as models to be imitated. Most striking, however, is the

---

20. See John E. Alsup, "Type, Place, and Function of the Pronouncement Story in Plutarch's *Moralia*," *Semeia* 20 (1981) 25; Poulos, "Form and Function," 56–57. See also Diogenes Laertius, *Lives* VI.96–97 and Philostratus, *Life of Apollonius of Tyana* I.9.

strong tendency to present someone with a religious or social liability as a successful quester. Religious inferiors or outcasts receive Jesus' affirmation. The outcome conflicts with the usual expectations of such people. These stories are working against resistance and are seeking to change attitudes, for they present questers with disqualifying characteristics who, in the end, are not disqualified. The negative characteristics of the questers make success doubtful and add to the interest of the stories. These and other blocking factors are often highlighted within the story by being expressed as objections to the quest. The interpreter should pay close attention to such blocking factors, for they often disclose the issue on which the storyteller wants to change attitudes.

Mark 10:17–22 par. Matt, Luke (the rich man) is the only unsuccessful quest story in the synoptic Gospels. Several features of Mark's text encourage a positive reaction to the rich man and sympathy for his quest, resulting in a sense of tragedy when the conflict between riches and the demands of discipleship proves to be too great. Mark 10:28–31 par. Matt, Luke provides an alternative ending to the story of the rich man, for the disciples are pictured as responding positively to the demand made of the rich man.[21] Mark 12:28–34 (the first commandment) appears to be a quest, although the parallel versions are testing inquiries. Following Jesus' statement of the two love commandments, the scribe makes an unusually long statement (12:32–33). He praises Jesus' answer and emphasizes its importance, which might lead us to compare this story with some inverted commendation stories in which the sage or hero is praised, rather than praising another.[22] However, the scribe introduces something new when he applies Jesus' teaching to the issue of temple sacrifices. The final verse not only commends this as a correct insight but makes a declaration about the religious state of the scribe: "You are not far from the kingdom of God." Although the personal stake of the scribe in the question that he brings to Jesus is not brought out until the end of the story, this ending appears to move the story beyond commendation to quest.

In Matt 8:5–13 par. Luke, the centurion also makes a rather long statement, is commended, and receives what he seeks. If Matt 8:7 is a question indicating an initial objection by Jesus,[23] Matthew's version of this story is quite similar to the story of the gentile woman discussed be-

---

21. See Tannehill, *Sword*, 147–52.

22. See Vernon K. Robbins' discussion of laudations in "Classifying Pronouncement Stories in Plutarch's *Parallel Lives*," *Semeia* 20 (1981) 44–45.

23. See Bultmann, *History*, 39.

low. Luke 17:12–19 (the Samaritan leper) moves like other quest stories from an initial indication of a need to an announcement that the need has been fulfilled.[24] In this case this is accompanied by a strong contrast between one leper who shows gratitude and nine lepers who do not. The positive behavior of the one leper is demonstrated before the disclosure of a factor that would be negative for some hearers of this story: the leper is a Samaritan. In vv. 17–18 Jesus criticizes the nine, thereby highlighting the appropriateness of the Samaritan's behavior and making it difficult to deny that Jesus' inclusion of the Samaritan in his saving work is also appropriate.

There is a group of quest stories in which an objection must be overcome for the quest to be successful. If this is the major conflict in the story and if the climax both answers the objection and discloses the outcome of a quest, we may speak of a hybrid objection-quest. This applies to Mark 2:1–12 par. Matt, Luke (the paralytic). It also applies to Mark 7:24–30 par. Matt (the gentile woman). In the latter story Jesus expresses the objection himself and must change his mind. Jesus' final words have a double function: they adopt the woman's reply to the objection as Jesus' own position and announce the success of the quest.

In Luke 7:36–50 (the sinful woman in the Pharisee's house) Jesus and the Pharisee take contrasting attitudes to the woman, with the Pharisee objecting to Jesus' behavior and Jesus answering the objection. The woman also represents an attitude toward Jesus contrasting with the Pharisee's attitude, as is emphasized in vv. 44–46. Similar contrasting relationships are found in the Mary and Martha story (an objection-commendation), but Luke 7:36–50 is longer and the story is developed as a quest. The woman is introduced as a sinner and at the end Jesus emphasizes to her that her sins are forgiven. Although vv. 48 and 50 may seem like an appendix, they indicate that the storyteller understands the story as a quest, which ends appropriately when Jesus certifies to the woman that she has received what she needs.

In Luke 19:1–10 the story ends both with the announcement to Zacchaeus of the success of his quest and with Jesus' response to the crowd's objection, as is somewhat awkwardly indicated by the shift in the party addressed in v. 9. Finally, in Luke 23:39–43 (the requests of the crucified criminals) the quester is at center stage, as in other quest stories.

24. In the context of this story, "Your faith has saved you" refers to a salvation that includes but goes beyond healing. The strong contrast with the nine in vv. 17–18 suggests that this statement applies to the Samaritan leper in a way that it does not apply to the other nine healed lepers.

His quest is expressed late in the scene (v. 42), but it is to this quest that Jesus responds in his final pronouncement. In responding positively Jesus is also expressing approval of the penitent criminal's response to the first criminal's objection (v. 39), bringing to a resolution both the objection and the quest sequences. Since the objection presupposes the preceding crucifixion narrative, this is not a fully independent story.

Since quest stories incorporate some of the movements of the other types, they may share some of the same functions. However, quests are unique in the prominent role given to the quester. We are presented with the quester's need, and the story continues until we discover whether the quester succeeds or fails in finding the solution to that need. These features help us to experience events from the quester's perspective, and there may be other aspects of the story that encourage hope and sympathy for the quester.[25] In this way readers are encouraged to recognize their own quests in these stories or to become sympathetic to those in need. Tension arises for readers when the need of the quester encourages sympathy and the positive response of Jesus calls for a similar response from the reader, yet an aspect of the quester offends against prejudices. It is striking how many of these stories involve persons who arouse such prejudices: gentiles (Mark 7:24–30; Matt 8:5–13), a sinful woman (Luke 7:36–50) and a sinful cripple (Mark 2:1–12), a Samaritan (Luke 17:12–19), a tax collector (Luke 19:1–10), and a criminal (Luke 23:39–43). These stories function both to invite the outcasts and to create openness for them within the religious community.

The large number of these stories in Luke is noteworthy. Counting stories shared with other Gospels, Luke contains seven of the nine synoptic quest stories. Four of these are unique to Luke.

Inquiry Stories

There is an important group of testing inquiries in the synoptic Gospels. Apart from these, however, the inquiry stories in the synoptic Gospels are not a large and well-developed group. The dramatic tension that characterizes other types is reduced. In some stories the connection between the question or request and the response is not clear, and some stories, although they are marked as separate scenes through the introduction of a new character and sometimes a new setting, are dependent on previous

---

25. Such encouragement is especially clear in the story where the quester fails. Mark 10:17, 19–21 emphasize the rich man's reverential attitude, religious commitment, and Jesus' positive response.

material, providing clarification of it. Thus we find the following dependent inquiry scenes in which Jesus responds with additional explanation:

- Mark 4:10–20 par. Matt, Luke—interpretation of parable of the sower
- Mark 7:17–23 par. Matt—interpretation of defilement saying
- Mark 9:28–29 par. Matt—explanation of disciples' inability to cast out a demon
- Mark 10:10–12—explanation of divorce teaching
- Matt 13:36–43—interpretation of the parable of the weeds
- Luke 12:41–48—interpretation of parable of the watchful servants

In Mark 11:20–25 the withering of the fig tree provokes an exclamation from Peter that seems to function as an inquiry into how this could happen, since Jesus seems to be replying to such a question. This is Matthew's understanding of the scene, for in Matt 21:20 the exclamation becomes a question. Apart from the testing inquiries, the rest of the inquiry scenes are Lukan:

- Luke 3:10–14—John's instructions to social groups
- Luke 11:1–4—the Lord's prayer
- Luke 13:22–30—enter through the narrow gate
- Luke 17:5–6—faith

In the last three scenes the words of Jesus have a parallel in another Gospel, but Luke's pronouncement story setting is unique.

In the inquiry scenes listed above the focus of attention is on the teaching in the responses, and the function of the stories is to convey this teaching. The questions or requests that introduce the responses add little, except that they link the dependent inquiry scenes to preceding material, indicate the general topic of the teaching that follows, and sometimes suggest a particular application of the teaching. Luke 11:1, for instance, suggests that the Lord's prayer is an appropriate answer to a request for a basic pattern of prayer for Jesus' disciples.

Unlike the other inquiries, the testing inquiries comprise a group of fairly long,, dramatically developed stories that are fully capable of independent existence. In a testing inquiry the question or request usually comes from a hostile or skeptical party. It is designed to put the responder to the test. The responder is placed in a critical situation. There is a sense of risk, for the reputation, influence, and perhaps the safety of the responder are at stake. In the synoptic Gospels this situation may be indicated simply by a participial phrase ("testing him"), indicating the inquirer's intention. However, a testing situation also arises when the question or request concerns the status and authority of Jesus. Jesus may respond to a testing question or request by correcting it. Such stories belong with the corrections. On the other hand, if the question or request is accepted and answered, we have a testing inquiry. Although the responder is also placed in a critical situation when faced with an objection from a hostile party, the testing inquiry differs from the objection story in that the provoking element is not an objection to something already said or done.

The following stories are testing inquiries:

- Mark 10:2–9 par. Matt—divorce
- Mark 11:27–33 par. Matt, Luke—Jesus' authority
- Mark 12:13–17 par. Matt, Luke—taxes to Caesar
- Matt 11:2–6 par. Luke—John's question to Jesus
- Matt 12:38–42—first request for a sign
- Matt 16:1–4—second request for a sign
- Matt 22:34–40—the great commandment
- Luke 10:25–37—loving one's neighbor[26]

Of the stories in this list, Mark 10:2–9 is a hybrid, for vv. 5–9 both answer the initial question and correct the Mosaic permission.[27] Matthew 12:38–42 and 16:1–4 are also hybrids, combining testing inquiry with correction (as I previously explained in the section on correction stories). In addition, Mark 8:27–30 par. Luke (Peter's confession) is an inverted testing inquiry, i.e., a testing inquiry in which the person featured in the writing (Jesus) does not respond to the test but poses the testing question.[28] Mark 12:35–37 par. Matt, Luke (David's son) may also be an inverted testing inquiry. If Jesus is denying that the Christ is David's son, the story is a correction; if not, Jesus is posing a testing question. The

---

26. It is possible that Matt 12:9–14 should also be included. See the discussion of this passage and other Sabbath healing stories in the section on objection stories.

27. In Matthew's version, however, Jesus' answer to the testing inquiry is followed by two objections.

28. Matthew transforms this into a commendation story by the addition of Matt 16:17–19.

question concerns the views of a group generally presented as hostile,[29] and they will lose influence if they have no explanation. In this case, no answer is given.

The special interest of the author in the requests for a sign gives Matthew's Gospel a slight edge in the number of testing inquiries.

The repeated use of preliminary counter-questions in synoptic testing inquiries is noteworthy. These questions differ from the rhetorical questions that frequently appear in objection stories, and sometimes elsewhere. In objection stories the question is the response or an important part of it; in it Jesus is disclosing his view of the matter. In the testing inquiries Jesus' question is preliminary; it is designed to elicit an answer that will contribute to Jesus' final answer. Therefore, the inquirer's answer (or non-answer) to Jesus' question is recorded as part of the story. We find such questions in Mark 10:3; 11:29–30 par.; 12:16 par.; Luke 10:26, 36. Note also these preliminary questions in the inverted stories: Matt 22:42, Mark 8:27 par.[30] Through these questions Jesus seizes the initiative in the testing situation. Furthermore, in this way a crucial factor can be brought into the open, where it can be assessed (Mark 10:3), and the inquirers can be made to participate in answering their own questions (Mark 12:16 par.; Luke 10:26, 36), which will make the final answers more difficult to reject.

There is a significant increase in the dramatic tension in testing inquiries, compared to ordinary inquiry stories, because we are presented with a situation of risk. This tension is often developed through lengthening the story and including several exchanges of dialogue. In these stories there is interest not only in the answer to the inquiry but also in the outcome for the answerer. The responder as a person has something to gain or lose. This can emphasize the response, for an impressive response is all the more impressive when made in a situation of risk. But the testing inquiries also say something about Jesus: his claim to wisdom and authority can pass the test even of difficult questions from hostile questioners. Furthermore, in a number of cases a Christological interest appears in the issues raised, for the questions concern Jesus' authority and status (Mark 8:27–30 par.; Mark 11:27–33 par.; Matt 11:2–6 par.; Matt 12:38–42; 16:1–4; see also Mark 12:35–37 par.).

---

29. However, in Luke the source of the opinion is unclear.

30. The function of the question in Mark 8:27 par. is somewhat different. It elicits a preliminary answer that contrasts with the final one.

Description Stories

Description stories are either very rare or completely lacking in the synoptic Gospels.[31] The only possibility that I have noted is Luke 14:15–24, in which the parable of the great banquet is presented as a response to the statement "Blessed is the one who will eat bread in the Kingdom of God." The parable neither corrects nor commends this statement but reveals a concealed incongruity, for an unexpected group receives this blessing. This is somewhat like the descriptions, but I do not regard it as a clear and convincing example.

Conclusion

We have a rich group of pronouncement stories in the synoptic Gospels, especially in Mark and Luke, particularly when we consider that the Gospels are connected narratives composed of material of various genres, not just pronouncement story collections. Furthermore, the dramatic possibilities of the pronouncement story are developed. Relevant aspects of the situation are brought out, and persons other than Jesus frequently speak in direct discourse, sometimes more than once. The narrative setting does more than provide a location for a sage's word of wisdom. It helps to present Jesus' words in their significance for those who encounter Jesus, with their challenge to the surrounding world, and in situations that are critical for Jesus himself.

The typology employed in this essay helps us to do justice to the fact that a pronouncement story is a story with narrative tension and movement, not just a saying with a narrative setting that can be ignored. It helps us to determine the specific ways in which tension appears in these stories. When we consider the particular issues presented in these patterns of tension in individual stories, we can see these stories as narrations of value conflicts, investigate the relation of the story to value conflicts in the historical situation of the early church, and draw conclusions about the way that these stories were meant to influence the value orientation of their hearers and readers.

---

31. On description stories see Tannehill, "The Pronouncement Story and Its Types" (included in the present volume, 32–33).

4

Types *and* Functions *of* Apophthegms *in the* Synoptic Gospels

The reader will note that the following essay covers much of the same territory as the essays on "The Pronouncement Story and Its Types" and "Varieties of Synoptic Pronouncement Stories." The following essay, however, contains more discussion of individual pericopes and more comment on the relation of my work to the form criticism of Rudolf Bultmann and Martin Dibelius. The shift from the term "pronouncement story" to "apophthegm" does not imply a change of perspective. Since this essay first appeared in a German publication, I use the term that is most common in German scholarship.

Introduction

AN APOPHTHEGM IS A brief narrative[1] in which the climactic (and usually final) element is an utterance,[2] often expressed in a succinct and striking way, by which someone responds to something said or observed on a particular occasion.[3] In an apophthegm there is a close relation between set-

---

1. In non-Christian authors of the Roman world there are many one sentence apophthegms, with the setting of the utterance given in a participial clause and the utterance in the main clause. Most synoptic apophthegms are not that brief. However, apophthegms comparable in length to those in the synoptic Gospels are also found in non-Christian authors.

2. Ancient scholars recognized that there were other possibilities. See Heinrich Lausberg, *Handbuch der literarischen Rhetorik: Eine Grundlegung der Literaturwissenschaft*, 2d ed. (Munich: Hueber, 1973) 537–39. Lausberg reports classifications of *chriae* (a form closely related to apophthegms) indicating that an expressive action might take the place of the utterance, or the response might consist of both utterance and action. The latter, "mixed" type occurs in the Gospels, as we shall see.

3. In other writings I use the term pronouncement story to refer to the same literary genre. See especially Tannehill, "Introduction: The Pronouncement Story and Its Types" and "Varieties of Synoptic Pronouncement Stories," *Semeia* 20 (1981) 1–13, 101–19.

ting and utterance: the setting provides the stimulus for the utterance and the utterance is a response to this stimulus. The interaction between setting and utterance often contributes to the forcefulness of the utterance. While several exchanges of dialogue may occur in some apophthegms, these should lead forward to the climactic pronouncement. This pronouncement (sometimes accompanied by action) will be the dominant element in the story. In a well-formed apophthegm it will not be one of a group of sayings of more or less equal importance, nor will it be one point among many in an extended dialogue. The pronouncement may point back to some earlier element in the story, correcting, commending, or defending someone or something, but in doing so it will express a final and authoritative comment on the scene. One who relates an apophthegm intends the climactic utterance to be impressive. It is often spoken by a person of authority. The final position of the utterance contributes to the impression that it makes, as does the brevity of the rest of the story, for other interests are not allowed to compete with the dominant utterance. The utterance is often presented in striking and forceful language. Thus an apophthegm is not a neutral record of a discussion between equal parties. A particular pronouncement is presented in such a way as to make the dominant impression. I will designate the speaker of this pronouncement as the primary character of the apophthegm. In the synoptic Gospels this is usually Jesus. However, the primary character in an apophthegm need not be the most important character in the surrounding narrative. This emphasis on a particular pronouncement indicates an intention to influence the mind, will, and imagination of the hearer or reader through the pronouncement that has been given climactic position in the narrative.

The apophthegm has some elasticity. While some are very concise, others are longer, with several exchanges of dialogue and some descriptive

---

The term apophthegm is in common use by many New Testament scholars because of the influential work of Rudolf Bultmann. See Bultmann, *Die Geschichte der synoptischen Tradition*, 4th ed. (Göttingen: Vandenhoeck & Ruprecht, 1958) 8–73; *The History of the Synoptic Tradition*, rev. ed., trans. John Marsh (New York: Harper & Row, 1976) 11–69. Greek authors of the Roman period may use *apophthegma* (ἀπόφθεγμα) or *chreia* (χρεία) to refer to such stories. There seems to be some variation in what is meant by *apophthegma*. Diogenes Laertius includes sayings attributed to a specific person but without narrative setting among the *apophthegmata*. See, e.g., *Lives and Opinions of Eminent Philosophers*, trans. R. D. Hicks, LCL (Cambridge: Harvard University Press, 1950) 4:47–48. This usage of Diogenes Laertius is discussed and contrasted with that of Plutarch by Richard A. Spencer, "A Study of the Form and Function of the Biographical Apophthegms in the Synoptic Tradition in Light of Their Hellenistic Background" (Ph.D. diss., Emory University, 1976) 264–79.

detail. This need not distort the essential characteristics of an apophthegm so long as the utterance remains dominant. An unusually long story may be an indication that additional interests are threatening the dominance of an utterance within its narrative setting. Or the additional material may simply increase the suspense and make the impact of the climactic utterance all the stronger. The latter is the case in Mark 12:13–17, which is longer than many apophthegms and yet is rightly recognized as a fine example.[4]

An apophthegm is a complete narrative scene that is meaningful in itself, and the climactic utterance is significant apart from events which may have been caused by it. The relative independence of the apophthegm is usually indicated by a shift in some characters or by a shift in time and place, marking the scene as an occasion separate from other occasions. Nevertheless, an apophthegm may have a function within a larger plot if the writing of which it is a part is itself a narrative. This possibility must be kept in mind in studying the apophthegms in the Gospels.

The purpose of the following typology is different than the purpose of Bultmann's discussion of synoptic apophthegms or Dibelius's discussion of paradigms.[5] Both Bultmann and Dibelius were primarily interested in the history of the pre-Gospel tradition. I am interested in the apophthegm as an act of communication between a speaker and a listener, or a writer and a reader. This communication takes place through a story about another time and place, but this story, carefully shaped to make an impression on the reader, can have influence on the present. The interaction in the story between the setting and the response of the primary character may relate in various ways to the intended influence of the story upon the reader. If so, this should be illuminated by the following typology, which focuses on this interaction of setting and response. In the following discussion I will survey scenes in the synoptic Gospels that appear to be apophthegms, whether they were part of the early oral tradition or were composed later when the Gospels reached their final form.

It is unfortunate that the work of Bultmann and Dibelius, so stimulating to debate over the general character and history of the synoptic tradition, was less effective in stimulating new studies of the literary types of synoptic material and their possible functions. Work remains to be done

---

4. Bultmann, *History,* 26; Vincent Taylor, *The Formation of the Gospel Tradition: Eight Lectures* (London: Macmillan, 1933) 64.

5. See Martin Dibelius, *Die Formgeschichte des Evangeliums,* 4th ed. (Tübingen: Mohr, 1961) 34–66; *From Tradition to Gospel,* trans. Bertram Lee Woolf (New York: Scribner, 1934) 37–69.

in defining the types and subtypes, and in understanding their usefulness as communication. Dibelius's paradigms, although showing considerable similarity to Bultmann's apophthegms, include short miracle stories that are not apophthegms. Dibelius attempted no system of sub-types for the paradigms. Bultmann did divide the apophthegms into three classes, the controversy dialogues, the scholastic dialogues, and the biographical apophthegms. However, the last of these is a catchall for apophthegms that did not fit the other two classes, and Bultmann overlooked significant similarities and differences among texts when he was content to divide them in this way. Different typologies of the same material are possible, bringing out different features of the texts. The typology that I will propose will disclose important relationships overlooked by Bultmann and Dibelius and will allow us to further clarify the functions for which the various types of apophthegms are fitted. I will comment on the differences between my typology and the views of Bultmann and Dibelius as I discuss the different types.

There are two necessary parts to an apophthegm, the response of the primary character and the occasion stimulating that response. The latter may or may not include dialogue addressed to the primary character. The response may simply be stimulated by something observed. These two parts can be discerned even in stories that are somewhat longer than the simplest apophthegms, involving several exchanges of dialogue. The response begins when the primary character takes charge of the situation and begins to move toward the utterance that will be the climax of the story. For example, in the apophthegm about paying taxes to Caesar, the response begins in Mark 12:15, when Jesus asks for the *denarius,* and the climactic utterance is found in 12:17.

These two main parts of the apophthegm are correlative. The function of the one must correlate with the function of the other or the story will be malformed and confusing. We must look at both parts of the story in their interrelation in order to understand the function of either. I am proposing a typology based on a careful examination of the interrelation of these two main parts. This approach has the advantage of focusing on a characteristic that is essential to the apophthegm as such. Furthermore, a typology based on the varying relation between stimulating occasion and response to this occasion gives attention to the apophthegm as a whole rather than to isolated parts. Such a typology will point out significant similarities in the composition of stories belonging to the same type. It will focus attention on an element central to the story as a story, for the tension that arises between the stimulus and the response gives the story its movement and interest. The interaction of stimulus and response in an apophthegm often reflects the interaction of a person or group with the environment. Something of the social and historical setting shines through. Particularly important are the value conflicts that emerge when there is sharp conflict between the position assumed or stated in the stimulus and the position proclaimed in the response. Study of the apophthegms in light of the following typology will call attention to the principal interaction in the text, which may reflect and wish to influence an interaction of groups and values in the world in which the apophthegm was created.

Study of the relation between stimulating occasion and response in synoptic apophthegms leads to the recognition of five types, which I list in the order in which they will be discussed: 1) correction stories (or simply "corrections"), 2) commendation stories ("commendations"), 3) quest stories ("quests"), 4) objection stories ("objections"), 5) inquiry stories ("inquiries").[6] Each of these will be defined in the appropriate section below. However, it is helpful to note immediately that, while the names appear to relate to one part of the apophthegm, either the stimulus or the response, they actually characterize the apophthegm as a whole, since the parts are correlative. Thus in corrections and commendations it is the response that corrects or commends, but such a response implies that in the stimulating setting someone, by word or action, has taken a position that can be corrected or commended. On the other hand, quests, objections, and inquiries have names that refer most directly to the stimulus part of the story, but in each case the response must be appropriate to the type of stimulus if we are to have a meaningful story.

I will indicate below that some apophthegms combine several of the types. I will call these stories "hybrids." Such combinations do not necessarily indicate later corruption of the stories, for the possibility of such combinations is inherent in the types themselves. The combination of certain types of apophthegm with a miracle story is also an important hybrid in the synoptic Gospels.

The apophthegm is a rhetorical form. It is shaped so as to influence the hearer or reader and was studied in the ancient world by those who

---

6. At least one more type, description stories, must be recognized if we consider apophthegms outside the synoptic Gospels. In a description story the climactic response does not answer an inquiry, as in inquiry stories, nor does it positively or negatively evaluate a person or situation, as in corrections and commendations. It simply describes some remarkable aspect of the situation that provides the stimulus for the comment. The descriptive response often highlights some incongruity in the situation, resulting in humor, or it may bring out the tragic quality of a situation.

wished to develop their powers of writing and speaking.[7] It can also be an art form, not only delighting us with fine craftsmanship but also deepening our perception. This is the case with those apophthegms that present a vivid challenge to comfortable and customary views of what is real and important, using carefully formed narrative and speech to open eyes for a new vision. Such apophthegms speak to the imagination, provoking thought that involves the will and the emotions as well as the mind, opening new possibilities for living.[8] To be sure, not all of the texts discussed below have such power. Many of them have humbler tasks. Furthermore, it will not be possible in this article to look carefully at those apophthegms that do have imaginative power or to examine the reasons for this. The interaction between stimulating setting and response may be one contributing factor, but the literary qualities of the climactic utterance may be equally important, and the significance of each feature can only be appreciated when an apophthegm is studied as a unique whole. Here we are concerned only with a typology of the synoptic apophthegms. This will alert us to some common features of these texts that, in some cases, contribute to their imaginative power.

After some decades, New Testament scholars are again asking about the relationship between the Gospels and Greco-Roman biographies.[9] The fact that apophthegms have an important place both in the synoptic Gospels and in some of the lives of Plutarch and Diogenes Laertius should be significant for this discussion. The following typology should permit more exact comparison of different writings through considering the frequency of particular types of apophthegms in them and the functions of these apophthegms. Consideration of the relation between stimulus and

---

7. See H. I. Marrou, *A History of Education in Antiquity*, trans. George Lamb (New York: Sheed & Ward, 1956) 174–75. Marrou describes the exercises with the *chreia* that were part of the rhetorical-literary education of antiquity.

8. The importance of forceful and imaginative language in the synoptic Gospels and the relation of such language to the language of literary art are discussed by Tannehill, *The Sword of His Mouth* (1975; reprinted, Eugene, Ore.: Wipf & Stock, 2003) 11–37. This book includes discussion of a few of the synoptic apophthegms, with special attention to the literary qualities of the climactic utterance and the relation of this utterance to its narrative setting, resulting in texts with imaginative force; see 152–85.

9. See Dieter Georgi, "The Records of Jesus in the Light of Ancient Accounts of Revered Men," in *Society of Biblical Literature, Proceedings* 2 (Missoula, Mont.: Scholars, 1972) 527–42; Charles H. Talbert, *What Is a Gospel? The Genre of the Canonical Gospels* (Philadelphia: Fortress, 1977). Note also the republication of this earlier (1915) writing: Clyde Weber Votaw, *The Gospels and Contemporary Biographies in the Greco-Roman World*, Facet 27 (Philadelphia: Fortress, 1970).

response, each of which may represent a value stance, will also help us to understand how certain values characteristic of the primary characters in the apophthegms, and perhaps of the author of the writing, are being recommended to the reader, while contrary values are being attacked. This will help to clarify the value systems competing in the Roman world, value systems that were expressed by presenting the impressive wisdom of their outstanding representatives in apophthegms.

Correction Stories

Correction stories are apophthegms in which the response corrects the views or conduct of the person or group occasioning the response. The stimulus for the corrective response may simply be something observed. It may also be a statement, request, or question from a secondary character. In the case of requests or questions, the primary character does not respond by granting the request or answering the question but by correcting an assumption on which the request or question was based. The secondary character is regarded as having taken a position concerning what is good, true, or expedient, a position subject to correction by the primary character. Thus in the correction story there is always tension between the primary character and another person. This tension is not expressed until the corrective response. Initially the position corrected may seem acceptable or inoffensive. It may represent what is commonly said or done. But the primary character does not find it acceptable, resulting in tension between the characters of the story. A similar tension is present in objection stories, but it is apparent earlier in the story. In the objection story tension is expressed before the climactic response, for the stimulus is an objection against the primary character. In corrections, however, the stimulus is not an objection against the primary character. Tension between characters is often apparent also in testing inquiries. However, in a testing inquiry the stimulus consists of a question or request for information, and this question or request is not criticized and corrected but is accepted and answered.

Most of the synoptic apophthegms of this type were placed by Bultmann in the vague category of "biographical apophthegms" or under the heading "the Master is questioned (by disciples or others)" without distinguishing between responses that accept and answer a question and responses that correct the assumptions on which a question is based. One of these apophthegms, Mark 12:18–27 par., was regarded as a controversy dialogue by Bultmann.[10] Dibelius discussed only a selection of synoptic texts. Of the stories that I regard as corrections, or as hybrids combining correction with another type, Dibelius classified Mark 3:31–35; 10:13–16, 35–45; 11:15–17; 12:18–27; 14:3–9; and Luke 9:51–56 as paradigms. On the other hand, Dibelius regarded Matt 4:1–11 par. as myth.[11]

This type of apophthegm is very common in the literature of the Roman world.[12] An example of a correction story from Diogenes Laertius:

γνωρίμου ποτὲ πρὸς αὐτὸν ἀποδυρομένου ὡς εἴη τὰ ὑπομνήματα ἀπολωλεκώς, ἔδει γάρ, ἔφη, ἐν τῇ ψυχῇ αὐτὰ καὶ μὴ ἐν τοῖς χαρτίοις καταγράφειν.

When a friend complained to him that he had lost his notes, "You should have inscribed them," said he [Antisthenes], "on your mind instead of on paper."[13]

We will begin with some of the simpler examples of correction stories in the synoptic Gospels. In Matt 18:21–22 Peter asks Jesus how often he should forgive and then proposes seven times as a possible limit. In making this tentative proposal, Peter has taken a position to which Jesus can respond. Jesus does so by correcting Peter, first negating Peter's proposal and then substituting a demand that goes far beyond what Peter imagined. Both the dramatic encounter and the forcefulness of Jesus' words give imaginative power to this attack on the common assumption of a reasonable limit to forgiveness. Other brief and simple corrections include the following pericopes: the blessing of Jesus' mother (Luke 11:27–28), the strange exorcist (Mark 9:38–40 par.), the great temple buildings (Mark 13:1–2 par.),[14] and the mission of Jesus to other cities (Luke 4:42–43).[15]

---

10. *Synoptic Tradition*, 26, 49.

11. *Formgeschichte*, 40, 274–75; *Tradition to Gospel*, 43, 274–75.

12 It is the most common type of apophthegm in Diogenes Laertius' *Lives and Opinions of Eminent Philosophers*, Lucian's *Demonax*, Philostratus' *Life of Apollonius of Tyana*, and (pseudo?)-Plutarch's *Sayings of Kings and Commanders*, among other works.

13. *Lives of Eminent Philosophers*, trans. R. D. Hicks, LCL (Cambridge: Harvard University Press, 1958) 6:5. See Paula Nassen Poulos, "Form and Function of the Pronouncement Story in Diogenes Laertius' *Lives*," *Semeia* 20 (1981) 59 [53–63].

14. Matthew's version (Matt 24:1–2) is less clearly a correction because the strong praise for the temple buildings expressed in Mark is not expressed by the disciples in Matthew.

15. The Markan parallel (Mark 1:35–38) is also a correction if "All are seeking you" means that the people of Capernaum, including Simon, want Jesus to remain with them.

In Matt 8:19–22 there are two brief correction stories concerning following Jesus. In each case a proposal is made and Jesus corrects the assumptions about discipleship that lie behind the proposal. The series is expanded by the addition of a third apophthegm in Luke 9:57–62.[16] The proposals by would-be disciples in this series of apophthegms appear to be laudable or very reasonable. The correction of these proposals with words of imaginative force is a shocking attack on widely held assumptions.[17]

In some correction stories the response of Jesus is longer. Examples are the pericope on places at table (Luke 14:7–11) and the reply to the weeping women (Luke 23:27–31). In both cases Jesus responds to something observed, rather than to someone who addresses him. In Luke the Baptist's statement about the one mightier than him has become a correction story through the addition of an initial description of the crowd's attitude toward John (Luke 3:15–17). Mark 9:33–37, the discussion about greatness, is unusual in several respects. It begins with a question of Jesus to the disciples. However, this question uncovers the behavior of the disciples that Jesus wishes to correct. The corrective response of Jesus contains both a saying about being first and a dramatic action (the embrace of a child), accompanied by a statement showing that this act is intended to be an example for the disciples. The parallel versions are simpler. In Matt 18:1–4 the reference to the initial dispute among the disciples disappears, weakening the corrective force of Jesus' words, and Jesus' response introduces a long discourse. A second correction story that combines a verbal response with response through action is the so-called cleansing of the temple (Mark 11:15–17 par.).[18] The narrative begins with the corrective action of Jesus. The stimulus for Jesus' action becomes apparent through description of the activities of the persons against whom Jesus acts. The utterance follows the action, justifying and interpreting it. Both action and utterance together constitute the corrective response. In Luke's ver-

---

16. The second in Luke's series is introduced with Jesus' command "Follow me," and the man may seem to be objecting to this command, resulting in an objection story. However, there is no indication that the man knows that discipleship requires ignoring such basic family duties as the burial of one's father. The man is not objecting to a known position of Jesus. He intends to follow Jesus, but family duty appears more pressing at the moment. The story remains a correction, in spite of the slight elaboration of the beginning of the scene.

17. On the literary composition and imaginative force of Luke 9:57–62, see Tannehill, *Sword*, 157–65.

18. This type of *chreia* was recognized by ancient scholars. See Lausberg, *Handbuch*, 539.

sion (Luke 19:45–46) the narrative description is reduced, placing greater emphasis on the utterance.

An apophthegm (as defined above) must contain some narrative description that provides a setting for the primary character's utterance. However, there are cases in which the cause of the corrective response is only made clear within the response itself. In Luke 13:1–5, Jesus' statement about the slain Galileans and the fallen tower, the narrative setting simply indicates that some people bring information about the slain Galileans to Jesus. We are not told that they express an opinion about the meaning of this event. In his comment Jesus expresses (in the form of a question) an opinion that his dialogue partners may hold, and it is this opinion that is corrected. The essential elements of the correction story are still present, even though the position to be corrected, usually expressed by a secondary character, is not made clear until Jesus speaks. The pericope about the kingdom "among you" (Luke 17:20–21) is similar. Jesus' response begins with a double denial. In presenting Jesus making this denial to the persons being addressed, the story suggests that these persons hold the rejected opinions. The assumption that there are some observable signs of the kingdom's coming does seem to stand behind their question. But this is only made clear as Jesus speaks, both disclosing the assumption and correcting it. Luke 19:41–44, Jesus weeping over Jerusalem, is similar. Jesus responds to the scene observed by describing the city's blindness to the things that lead to peace, the punishment that will result, and his own despairing desire to correct this.[19]

Matt 17:24–27, on paying the temple tax, is also a correction story. The collector of the tax, in his initial question, is not simply asking for information about Jesus' practice. He is making a point. He is pointing out that Jesus does, in fact, pay the temple tax,[20] and Peter concedes that this is true. Jesus, in his conversation with Peter, responds to the point that Peter and the collector of the temple tax have agreed upon. He corrects not the fact of payment but the implication that might be drawn from that fact, that Jesus and his disciples are required to pay (and, perhaps,

---

19. Luke 14:12–14, Jesus' comment to his host on who should be invited to his parties, may also be a correction story. To be sure, there is no clear statement that the host has invited his friends and relatives, rather than the poor and crippled. But we can probably assume that this is what he has done, or is likely to do, since it is customary practice. Jesus' response includes a negation followed by "but," a structure common in corrective responses.

20. The question with the Greek negative οὐ expects an affirmative answer and can be used as a way of arguing.

also fulfill the other responsibilities of Jews). Here, as in the texts in the preceding paragraph, the position being corrected is not clear until Jesus speaks. Only when the false implication is corrected by asserting the essential freedom of Jesus and his disciples is a reason for paying recognized: "that we might not offend them."

Mark 10:35–45 par., the request of James and John, is an unusually elaborate correction story, with a number of exchanges of dialogue. The story remains a correction story, for the response of Jesus in 10:42–45 is clearly intended to correct both the request of James and John and the reaction of the other disciples (10:41), and this correction is the climactic element in the story. The previous dialogue, in which Jesus tests the resolve of James and John yet denies their request, is preliminary to the final correction. The parallel in Luke (Luke 22:24–27) is much simpler, describing briefly the disciples' dispute and presenting Jesus' corrective response.

In the section on inquiries we will note that the synoptic Gospels contain an important group of testing inquiries, in which a question or request is addressed to Jesus by a hostile or skeptical party in order to test him. This motif of testing heightens the tension in a story, for Jesus seems to be placed in a difficult situation. There is also a small group of testing corrections. They differ from the testing inquiries in that Jesus does not answer the question or accept the request but responds by correcting the assumptions on which they were based.

Mark 8:11–12, the refusal of a sign, is a testing correction. However, the stories of request for a sign in Matt 12:38–42 and 16:1–4, although they contain a strong corrective element, provide a positive response to the request by pointing to the sign of Jonah. These two scenes are hybrid stories, combining correction with testing inquiry. In addition to Mark 8:11–12, we find testing corrections in Matt 4:1–11 par., the temptation, and Mark 12:18–27 par., the question about the resurrection. The temptation story belongs among the apophthegms, for it fits the definition at the beginning of this article and the interaction between the devil and Jesus clearly belongs to the corrective type. Here we find a tripling of the stimulus and response. There are three exchanges between the devil and Jesus, each consisting of a proposal and a corrective response. At the same time, the story emphasizes that this is a test of Jesus. In Mark 12:18–27 par. the correction takes place on two levels, and the story contains a double stimulus and response. The question of the Sadducees in Mark 12:23 receives a response in 12:25, which corrects the assumption on which the question was based. However, the story begins by indicating the position of the Sadducees with regard to the resurrection (12:18). This position is corrected in 12:26–27. Although we are not explicitly told that Jesus is being tested, this is implied by the situation. The Sadducees ask a trick question which is designed to embarrass Jesus. The question is based on a premise that the questioners do not accept. Thus it does not arise from their search for truth but from their hostility to Jesus and hope of undermining his authority.

There are also hybrid apophthegms that combine correction with another type of relation between stimulus and response. These stories will be discussed later, after introduction of the other types in these hybrids. I will simply list the texts here. The following texts combine correction and commendation, and are discussed in the section on commendations: Mark 3:31–35 par.; 10:13–16 par.; and 14:3–9 par. The following texts, discussed in the section on inquiries, combine correction and testing inquiry: Matt 12:38–42; 16:1–4; and Mark 10:2–9.

There are some additional stories in the synoptic Gospels that probably should be included among the correction stories. However, they contain some unusual features, making judgment more difficult. In some cases the stimulus is vague or is vaguely related to the response, so that the story lacks a sense of dramatic conflict on a sharply focused issue. The parable of the pounds in Luke 19:11–27 is introduced with a reference to the false opinion that the kingdom was to appear immediately.[21] It is evidently intended by the Evangelist to correct this opinion. However, the parable also contains other themes, so that setting and response do not fit especially well. The introduction to the parable of the Pharisee and tax collector (Luke 18:9–14) indicates that it was told "to some who trusted in themselves that they were righteous and despised others." This does not go beyond what can be drawn from the story itself. This general statement weakens the sense of dramatic concreteness, of witnessing a particular personal confrontation, which is characteristic of many synoptic apophthegms. Matthew 11:20–24, the woes on the Galilean towns, begins with a similar general indication of the group being addressed. Luke 12:13–21, the scene which includes the parable of the rich fool, has the common features of a synoptic apophthegm, but only Jesus' refusal in 12:14 is addressed directly to the person who makes the initial pro-

---

21. Note that a parable may be part of an apophthegm, serving as the primary character's response. This is common in Luke. The setting of the Pharisee and tax collector and of the rich fool will be discussed immediately. The parables in Luke 15 are presented as Jesus' response to an objection, and the parable of the good Samaritan is a response to a testing inquiry (Luke 10:25–37).

posal. The following words are addressed to a larger group. Nevertheless, they constitute a correction of the attitude toward money represented by the request in 12:13. Luke 9:52–56, the inhospitable Samaritans, clearly involves a correction of James and John by Jesus. However, the best attested reading does not include quotation of Jesus' words of rebuke. Since these words would be the climax of a correction story, it is unusual for an author to be content with the general statement that Jesus rebuked them. The fact that many manuscripts supply the words of Jesus at this point shows an awareness that such words are appropriate at this point in this type of story. Finally, Luke 13:31–33, the warning about Herod, may be a correction story, although the primary point in Jesus' response is obscure.[22]

The apophthegm is not a neutral mode of expression. The story is shaped so that the words of one person make the dominant impression. Other opinions are not given equal importance. In the correction story other opinions are expressed in order to be corrected by the words forming the climax of the story, words that are often phrased in a memorable and forceful way. Although the responses in some apophthegms contain brief reasons for the judgments that are made, the apophthegm as a genre does not permit much reasoned discussion and careful argument within the story. It is too brief, too one-sided in presentation of options, too concerned with the rhetorical impact of words. But an apophthegm can provoke imaginative thought from the reader. Through the imaginative force of a good apophthegm a possibility may become sufficiently arresting and challenging to entice readers to reconsider old assumptions. This is important, for generally our thinking runs in well-worn ruts. We assume that the familiar is the true and find nothing new to explore. Challenging words presented with imaginative force in a dramatic scene can rescue us from these well-worn ruts.

This applies to correction stories, as well as to other types of apophthegms. The correction story is especially useful when it is important to emphasize the difference between the view of the primary character and another perspective. An objection story is a natural choice when a conflict between views is already perceived. But there are cases where such a conflict is not perceived or is not taken with sufficient seriousness. Here the correction story can be helpful. It can make the one view stand out against the other, showing that a choice must be made, a choice that may

---

22. Mark 12:35–37 par., David's son, is a correction story if Jesus' questions imply that the Christ cannot be son of David. See the remarks on this text in the section on "Inquiry Stories."

involve abandoning past securities. In most cases this disturbing choice is forced upon the supposed followers of Jesus or anonymous persons from the crowd, while those who wish to oppose Jesus appear in other types of apophthegms.[23]

In many apophthegms there is tension between what is being recommended and another view, often a view that is widely accepted.[24] In the correction (and objection) stories this tension is dramatized. The poles are represented by persons in the dramatic scene. Some of the correction stories seem to be designed to catch the reader between these poles. Readers, whether of the first century or the present, can recognize similarities between the attitudes being corrected and their own attitudes but may also be attracted or shaken by Jesus' challenge. Then the tension in the story is reproduced in the reader, who must struggle to reorder the memories, meanings, and goals that structure life. This requires struggle, for many of these correction stories challenge old securities, including the security provided by family and home, deep desires, including the desire for status, and the assumption that we can place "reasonable" limits on the demands that others make on us. One of the values of this typology is that it discloses this important group of correction stories within the synoptic apophthegms and shows the importance of the challenge that they present.

The correction stories mentioned above vary greatly in the degree to which they develop the potentiality of such stories to challenge prevailing assumptions with imaginative force. Some, such as Matt 8:21–22 par., are outstanding examples of such power; some are not. It is not merely the presence of conflict that gives such power to some stories. The importance for human existence of the issue addressed and the literary power of the climactic response must also be considered, as well as the interaction of the response with its setting.[25]

The prominence of correction stories in material unique to Luke is noteworthy.

---

23. The testing corrections and hybrid correction-testing inquiries are exceptions, for in most of them Jesus responds to Pharisees, scribes, or Sadducees.

24. On the value of tension in the language of the Gospels see Tannehill, *Sword*, 51–56.

25. Tannehill, *Sword*, 39–200, discusses features of synoptic sayings that contribute to their literary power, suggesting the features that may be important in the study of the sayings found within apophthegms.

Commendation Stories

Commendations are the complement of corrections. The latter involve a corrective response to a position taken by the secondary character; the former contain an affirmative response. In other words, the primary character of the story, the person whose words are climactic and authoritative, commends or praises something said, done, or represented by a secondary character in the story. This approving response is more than a simple statement such as "I approve" or "Yes, I agree," for such weak statements would tend to undermine the dominant role of the primary character. The response often discloses a previously hidden value or importance in the position being commended. There is often an element of surprise to the commendation in light of common standards of judgment. Something commonly despised or ignored is being praised. Thus tension with another perspective can be present here also. In the pure commendation story this other perspective remains a tacit aspect of the story. It is not represented by a character in the story or expressed by the narrator of the story. We often find hybrid stories, however, that combine correction and commendation or objection and commendation. Such stories usually have three characters, one of them presenting a negative judgment contrasting with Jesus' positive judgment or a negative action contrasting with the action being commended. In these stories the negative possibility is expressed clearly and contributes to the dramatic tension of the story.

In commendations the person commended is often presented as an example to be imitated. The climactic utterance points back to something represented or demonstrated by the secondary character and discloses its value and importance so that others may imitate this model.

Later I will indicate that commendation is frequently important in another type of story, the quests. These stories begin by presenting a person in search of something important to human fulfillment and then relate how, in encounter with Jesus, this person either succeeds or fails in attaining the goal. Success is indicated by Jesus' commendation. Such stories will not be discussed in this section.

Commendations are less frequent than corrections in both the synoptic Gospels and in the non-Christian literature of the Roman world. An example of a commendation from (pseudo?)-Plutarch:

> πένητος δὲ ἀνθρώπου μῆλον ὑπερφυὲς μεγέθει προσενέγκαντος αὐτῷ δεξάμενος ἡδέως, νὴ τὸν Μίθραν, εἶπεν, οὗτός μοι δοκεῖ καὶ πόλιν ἂν ἐκ μικρᾶς μεγάλην πιστευθεὶς ἀπεργάσασθαι.

> A poor man brought to him an apple of extraordinary size which he accepted with pleasure, and at the same time he [Artaxerxes Mnemon] remarked, "By Mithras I swear it seems to me that this man would make a big city out of a small one if it were entrusted to his charge."[26]

Of the texts to be discussed in this section, which include commendations and the hybrid correction-commendations and objection-commendations, Bultmann listed Mark 3:31–35; 10:13–16; 12:41–44; 14:3–9; and Luke 10:38–42 among his biographical apophthegms. He discussed Matt 16:13–19 under the heading of "historical story and legend."[27] In the other texts discussed here, Bultmann considered the narrative setting to be secondary and classified only the sayings that they contain. Dibelius regarded Mark 3:31–35; 10:13–16; and 14:3–9 as paradigms and classified Matt 16:13–19 and (with some hesitation) Luke 10:38–42 as legends.[28] Dibelius believed that an interest in the piety of secondary characters indicated that a story was a legend.[29] We will see that secondary characters are important in both commendations and quests, in commendations as positive models, in quests as persons who arouse sympathy because of their goals and who may also be positive models in attaining them. More than pious curiosity is at work here, for the positive presentation of these characters contributes to the impact of these stories upon the reader.

The words praising Peter in Matt 16:17–19, not found in the parallel accounts, turn the confession of Peter (Matt 16:13–20) into a commendation story. In this case the commended statement of Peter is elicited by Jesus' inquiry. The commendation is lengthy and contains a good deal of new information, rather than simply proclaiming and justifying a particular judgment about what has happened. For this reason Jesus' words about Peter (at least vv. 18–19) are less tightly tied to their setting than is common in apophthegms. Furthermore, the statement by Jesus about the scribe and his treasure (Matt 13:51–52) seems to be intended by the Gospel writer as a commendation of the disciples' understanding. These verses refer back to the preceding parables, so are not a fully independent

---

26. *Sayings of Kings and Commanders,* trans. F. C. Babbitt, LCL (Cambridge: Harvard University Press, 1968) 174A. Compare Plutarch, *Life of Artaxerxes,* LCL (Cambridge: Harvard University Press, 1954) 4:4. For a commendation with more elaborate narration see Plutarch, *Life of Alexander,* LCL (Cambridge: Harvard University Press, 1958) 14:1–3.

27. Bultmann, *History,* 29–37, 257–59.

28. Dibelius, *Formgeschichte,* 40, 112, 115–16; *Tradition to Gospel,* 43, 115, 118–20.

29. *Formgeschichte,* 111–12; *Tradition to Gospel,* 114–15.

scene. Jesus' response to the return of the seventy (two) in Luke 10:17–20 is also a commendation scene. To be sure, v. 20 corrects, but even this subordinate note of correction serves to emphasize the greatness of the privileges granted to Jesus' followers.

The best examples of synoptic commendation stories are hybrid in type, combining correction and commendation or objection and commendation. Both of these combinations dramatize a contrast, either between Jesus' response to someone and the response of another character or between two secondary characters, with Jesus commending the one at the expense of the other. There are three persons or parties in these stories, and Jesus takes the side of one party against the other. The contrast in these stories helps readers to recognize that the view being recommended is a challenge to other ways of thinking or acting, which the readers may share. In affirming, the story also negates, which increases its power to move the reader toward clear decision. The presentation of Jesus' word as part of a dramatic conflict increases its power to attack the rejected perspective with imaginative force.[30]

A hybrid story need not be long and elaborate. Mark 10:13–16 par., the blessing of the children, combines correction (of the disciples) and commendation (of the children) in a brief story. There are three important characters (individuals or groups), and Jesus responds to both of the other characters. While correcting the disciples, he also commends the children for what they represent. They are models for others to follow; they represent those who are able to receive the kingdom. This function of a character as a positive model is characteristic of commendations.[31] The same combination of correction and commendation is found in the story of the anointing woman at Bethany (Mark 14:3–9 par.). As in the blessing of the children, Jesus and another character make contrasting judgments about a third party, in this case the woman. The story recommends Jesus' judgment by placing his words in climactic position in an apophthegm. The climactic utterance of Jesus in Mark 3:31–35 par. also involves both correction and commendation. "Those around" Jesus are commended by being designated his mother and brothers, and the previous use of these family titles to refer to Jesus' natural family is corrected. Although, in

---

30. Tannehill, *Sword*, 152–57. On the dramatic quality of synoptic anecdotes see Amos N. Wilder, *Early Christian Rhetoric: The Language of the Gospel* (1964; reprinted, Cambridge: Harvard University Press, 1971) 51–54.

31. The role of the child in Mark 9:33–37 is different, for 9:37 speaks not of being like a child but of receiving a child. Thus it is Jesus' embrace of the child that is exemplary. This is part of his correction of the disciples, rather than being a commendation of the child.

contrast to the two stories just discussed, the corrected statement (that of the messengers) is not intended as a negative statement about a third group (those around Jesus), the messengers represent both Jesus' natural family and the common assumption that the bonds and responsibilities of the natural family, signified by the titles "mother" and "brothers," are primary. Jesus attacks this assumption by giving these words, first used in the story in their literal sense, a metaphorical twist. At the beginning the narrator of the story as well as the messengers in the story use the key terms "mother" and "brothers" in their normal, literal sense, so there is a sharp shift in perspective as the story moves from the initial narration to the climactic statement of Jesus.[32] The story of the widow's offering (Mark 12:41–44) is similar. Jesus' commendation of the widow involves a comparison with the gifts of the rich. The statement that the widow "put in more than all" conflicts with another way of judging the value of offerings, which is based upon the economic value of the gifts. The latter perspective controls the introductory narration, for we are told that the rich were putting in much, while the widow put in only two *lepta*. Jesus' commendation of the widow also corrects this perspective. This is a correction not so much of the rich contributors as of the ordinary way of judging, assumed at first in the narration, which values the gifts of the rich highly.[33]

A story very similar to the blessing of the children and the anointing woman can be produced by combining objection and commendation instead of correction and commendation. Then the negative judgment by a secondary character is directed not merely at a third party but also at Jesus, as an objection to his behavior, because he has allowed something to happen. This is the case with the story of Martha and Mary (Luke 10:38–42), in which Jesus' response both commends Mary and responds to Martha's objection. In Luke 19:37–40 the entry into Jerusalem is expanded into an objection-commendation scene by the addition of an objection by Pharisees to the behavior of the disciples and Jesus' response. Jesus, by emphasizing the necessity of the disciples' joyful praise, not only replies to the objection but also commends the disciples. In Matt 21:14–16 a similar scene is placed in the temple.

The function of commendation stories is to recommend to the reader certain persons or what they represent. The latter is much more com-

32. On Mark 3:31–35 see further Tannehill, *Sword,* 165–71. Luke's version of this story (Luke 8:19–21) lacks some of the dramatic emphasis found in Mark.

33. Luke's version (Luke 21:1–4) omits the statement that the rich were putting in much and so removes the tension between the narration and Jesus' statement.

mon in the synoptic stories, since the stories seldom focus on persons who are important as unique, historical individuals.[34] In this way the values important to a religious perspective are being presented with imaginative appeal. It is not Jesus alone who represents positive values within synoptic apophthegms. He is the figure of central authority and so guides the reader by what he is and what he values. But some of these values can be demonstrated best by secondary figures, people similar to those whom readers may encounter and with whom readers may identify. These values are in competition with the values of the surrounding world. They are presented in stories that challenge and attack these competing values. This competition is reflected in the commendation of persons who, by other standards, seem unimportant: children and a poor widow. It also appears in the strong tendency to form hybrid stories, combining correction and commendation or objection and commendation in order to contrast the new values strongly and dramatically with the values that control common life.

Quest Stories

In a quest story someone approaches the primary character in quest of something very important to the well-being of the quester. The story captures the interest of the reader by focusing attention on whether the quester will obtain what he or she is seeking. The story begins by introducing the quester and the quest; it ends by indicating the success or failure of the quest. An important question or request directed to Jesus may begin the action. Jesus may raise an objection or correct the quester, but the story does not end at that point, and within the context of the story as a whole the question or request will be recognized as valid and important. In some cases there is no verbal question or request, but an action indicative of the quest is narrated. In the quest story Jesus remains the primary character, the figure of authority whose response will be decisive, but the quester is also very important. The central tension in the story, and the focus of the reader's interest, concerns the success or failure of the quest, and the story encourages the reader's sympathy with the quester. The quest is one with which the reader can sympathize, and there may be other features to the story that present the quester in a favorable light, even when he or she fails. Suspense is often heightened by the presence of an obstacle to the desired goal. An objection is raised by a third party or by Jesus himself, or Jesus poses a difficult condition. This helps both to

---

34. Matthew 16:13–20 is an exception. Perhaps also Mark 14:3–9.

maintain interest in the quest and to clarify the specific issue with which the story is dealing, the issue that is crucial for the outcome. If the quest is indeed central to the story, its success or failure will be indicated at the end. While many apophthegms end with Jesus' word without indicating how the secondary character responded to that word, leaving unclear the final relationship between Jesus and the secondary character, the quest does come to a clear resolution. If the quest succeeds, Jesus' final words are a commendation of the quester. This highlights the importance of the quester and what he or she represents. The majority of quests do, in fact, contain a prominent statement of commendation, but they are distinct from commendation stories in that they begin by presenting a person with a quest, and this quest remains the controlling interest throughout, while the various parts of the story serve to advance or hinder movement toward the goal. Because of the features noted above, quests tend to be longer and more elaborate than most apophthegms.

Preliminary investigation of the vast number of apophthegms in the literature of the Roman world suggests that the quest is rare outside the synoptic Gospels. However, the following story may qualify as a brief quest in which the quester fails:

> ἤθελέ τις παρ' αὐτῷ φιλοσοφεῖν. ὁ δέ οἱ σαπέρδην δοὺς ἐκέλευσεν ἀκολουθεῖν. ὡς δ' ὑπ' αἰδοῦς ῥίψας ἀπῆλθε, μετὰ χρόνον ὑπαντήσας αὐτῷ καὶ γελάσας λέγει, τὴν σὴν καὶ ἐμὴν φιλίαν σαπέρδης διέλυσε.

> Someone wanted to study philosophy with him, and he [Diogenes], giving him a Nile perch, commanded the fellow to follow him. When for shame the man threw it away and departed, he met him some time later and, laughing, said, "A Nile perch dissolved the friendship between you and me."[35]

The stories to be discussed as quests appear in all three of Bultmann's categories of apophthegms: controversy dialogue, scholastic dialogue, and biographical apophthegm. The following stories are included in the controversy dialogues: Luke 7:36–50; Mark 7:24–30; and Matt 8:5–13.[36] Mark 12:28–34 and 10:17–22 are designated scholastic dialogues, and Luke 17:12–19 and 19:1–10 are biographical apophthegms.[37] Dibelius

---

35. My translation; for the text, see Diogenes Laertius, *Lives of Eminent Philosophers*, 6:36.

36. Bultmann, *History*, 20, 21, 38–39. Bultmann noted that in the last two cases Jesus is overcome in debate, an unusual feature.

37. Ibid., 21–23, 33–34, 54.

included two quests (Mark 2:1ff. and 10:17ff.) among his paradigms and three (Luke 7:36–50; 17:12–19; 19:1–10) among the legends, noting the importance given to the sinful woman and to Zacchaeus in two of the last three stories.[38]

Mark 10:17–22 par. is the only quest story in which the quest is a failure. Nevertheless, it gives to the quester a prominent role and presents him as a figure with whom the reader can sympathize. The story begins to unfold when the man asks, "What shall I do to inherit eternal life?" The rest of the story concerns his discovery of what this requires of him and his decision that he cannot fulfill this requirement. The quest for eternal life is one that the original readers of this story would probably share. Furthermore, the religious earnestness of this man is emphasized. He has kept all the commandments listed by Jesus (Mark 10:19–20), and Jesus' affirmative response is made clear by the statement that Jesus "loved him" (Mark 10:21; only in Mark). The reader is expected to share Jesus' affirmative response. This may be the reason why the crucial, but possibly prejudicial, fact that he is rich is disclosed only at the end of the story. The importance of the quest and the positive presentation of the quester make his final failure poignant. Success can come only by fulfilling a difficult condition. Faced with this, the man turns away. Since the condition has not been met, the scene comes to an end without the statement of commendation found in other quests, leaving Mark 10:21 as the climactic statement of Jesus.[39]

Mark 10:28–31 par. provides an alternative ending to the rich man's story. The disciples and the rich man represent contrasting responses to the challenge of Jesus in Mark 10:21. The disciples have left their possessions and have followed Jesus (Mark 10:28 par.).[40] They will receive what the rich man sought, eternal life (Mark 10:30 par.; see Mark 10:17 par.). Thus, the rich man's quest is presupposed, and Peter, in behalf of the disciples, makes that quest his own (Mark 10:28 par.). Therefore, we are still dealing with a quest story. In all three Gospels Jesus in reply affirms that this quest will be successful. However, Mark alone speaks of a reward "in this time" that will consist of "houses and brothers and sisters and moth-

38. Dibelius, *Formgeschichte*, 40, 111, 115, 117–18; *Tradition to Gospel*, 43, 114, 118, 120–21.

39. Mark 10:23, 25 could fit into the scene as a final statement by Jesus about the rich man. Matthew and Mark, however, present these words as part of a new (though related) scene with new characters. In Luke 18:24–25 the break between scenes disappears.

40. The emphatic ἡμεῖς shows that a contrast between the disciples and the rich man is intended.

ers and children and fields," a reward that will come "with persecutions." While the context leads the reader to expect a promise of eternal life, this strange reward is unexpected. It has a humorous undertone that debunks the feeling that much has been sacrificed and so a glorious reward is due.[41] This surprising, critical note is missing in the accounts of Matthew and Luke, where we find the straightforward statements of commendation typical of the successful quest.[42]

Mark 12:28–34, the story of the great commandment, is a quest, although the parallel accounts in Matthew and Luke, which correspond only with the first half of Mark's story, present this scene as a testing inquiry. In Mark the statement of Jesus concerning the love commandments is followed by an unusually lengthy statement by the secondary character, in which the scribe approves Jesus' views and draws out their implications through a comparison with sacrifice. The interaction ends with Jesus' commendation of the scribe, making him an example of religious insight. Indeed, Jesus indicates that the scribe is "not far from the kingdom of God," the object of religious quest emphasized in the synoptic Gospels. This ending focuses attention on the personal religious state of the scribe. The interaction begins when the scribe poses a question important for a religious quest in the context of Judaism. It stops when Jesus affirms that the scribe has the insight necessary for a successful quest. Even at the beginning the scribe's favorable attitude toward Jesus is indicated (v. 28), distinguishing this scribe from others and helping the Christian reader to sympathize with him.

Mark 2:1–12 par., the healing of the paralytic, is often regarded as a healing story that has been expanded by the later insertion of a controversy about Jesus' authority to forgive sins.[43] While this may have happened, it cannot be said that this is a poorly formed story because Jesus responds to two concerns, the need of a paralytic and the objection of the scribes. We will see that the two stories to be discussed next, Luke 7:36–50 and 19:1–10, show the same combination of response to the quest of someone in need and to an objection by a third party. In these stories the objection serves as a complicating element in the quest. It is an obstacle that must be overcome and so heightens the tension in the story. Indeed, in these three

---

41. On Mark 10:28–30, see Tannehill, *Sword*, 147–52.

42. To be sure, Matt 19:30 par. does add a note of caution.

43. Bultmann believed that Mark 2:5b–10 was "a secondary interpolation." See *History*, 14–16. Vincent Taylor believed that this section was part of an independent pronouncement story, with the original beginning and ending cut away when the combination was made. See Taylor, *Formation*, 66–68.

stories and in Mark 7:24–30, Luke 23:39–43, and perhaps Matt 8:5–13 objections assume such importance that it may be appropriate to speak of them as hybrid objection-quest stories. The fact that in the healing of the paralytic the answer to the objection is reserved until the climax of the story is an indication of the importance of the objection sequence. On the other hand, the details concerning digging through the roof and lowering the paralytic on his mat (missing in Matthew) heighten narrative interest in the quest of the paralytic and his friends. They, like Zacchaeus, must overcome an obstacle in order to encounter Jesus. Their resourcefulness, the favorable response of Jesus in Mark 2:5, and the need of the paralytic encourage the reader's interest in and sympathy for their quest. The story ends with the success of the quest. However, the healing, together with the words that lead up to it and interpret it, has a double function; it fulfills the need expressed in the quest and demonstrates that the Son of Man has authority to forgive, responding to the scribes' objection. The healing is an integral part of the response to the objection, as well as answering the need of the paralytic. Thus it is appropriate that Jesus' final words address both the scribes (Mark 2:10) and the paralytic (2:11).[44]

Luke 7:36–50, the sinful woman and the Pharisee, is unusually long for a synoptic apophthegm. This is due primarily to the unusual length of Jesus' reply to the Pharisee, which contains a parable and its application. The organization of the story, however, is similar to apophthegms already discussed. This story resembles the story of Martha and Mary, which I designated a hybrid objection-commendation. Both stories contain three characters, and the two secondary characters are contrasting figures. In both an objection is raised against Jesus' behavior, as well as the behavior of the third character. In both Jesus responds to the objector, defending himself, commending the other person who has been attacked, and contrasting that person with the objector. However, the story of the sinful woman does not end with Jesus' reply to the objector. Jesus turns to the woman and speaks directly to her about her religious state in vv. 48 and 50. This focuses attention on the meaning for the woman of her encounter with Jesus. The story's interest in this indicates that it is a quest story. The object of the woman's quest is not expressed in words at the beginning of the story, but it is made clear that she is a sinner, i.e., one in need of forgiveness, and her love for Jesus is portrayed in detail. The story ends by affirming that she has found what she needs. Thus this story

---

44. Mark 2:9–12 is another example of a response that involves both word and action. See above, n.18.

differs from the story of Martha and Mary in its fuller presentation of the woman and in the interest shown in her quest. But Simon the Pharisee is equally important in this story. Much of the dialogue of Jesus is with him and responds to his objection. In this dialogue Simon and the woman are compared, keeping both figures before the reader. It is appropriate, then, to describe this story as a hybrid objection-quest.

In the story of Zacchaeus (Luke 19:1–10) the prominent role of the quester is especially noticeable. Not only is Zacchaeus named but his characteristics, his desires, and his actions are reported in some detail. In vv. 3–4 we are told of Zacchaeus's desire to see Jesus, the problem that he faces, and his unusual solution to the problem. This bit of vivid narration underscores Zacchaeus's eagerness and helps the reader to experience events from his point of view, creating sympathy for him. The statement that Zacchaeus wished to see Jesus conceals a quest, the full dimensions of which are apparent only at the end of the story. Zacchaeus's real need is indicated by what he in fact receives through Jesus (see vv. 9–10). This salvation, involving a reaffirmation of his place among God's people, is the object of his quest, whether we are to picture Zacchaeus as aware of this at the beginning of the story or not. There are two obstacles that must be overcome: the first, preliminary obstacle of Zacchaeus's difficulty in seeing Jesus, the second the objection against Jesus and Zacchaeus in v. 7. In both cases the crowd, which is the third character of this story, is the source of the problem, suggesting that isolation from the community and restoration to it ("He also is a son of Abraham") is a major issue in this story. The confusion in v. 9 as to whether Jesus is speaking to Zacchaeus or to the crowd is caused by an awkward handling of the double function of Jesus' final words: Jesus is both responding to the crowd's objection and affirming the successful completion of Zacchaeus's quest. This story not only resembles the story of the sinful woman in its theme of forgiveness for the outcast but also in its reference to an objection from a third character. The objection is expressed rather late in the story (v. 7), but both Zacchaeus's clear change of behavior (v. 8) and Jesus' final words (vv. 9–10) seem to be designed to respond to it, indicating that this story also is a hybrid objection-quest.

Mark 7:24–30 par., the Syrophoenician woman, reports a miracle and contains features typical of miracle stories. However, the story focuses attention on the dialogue between Jesus and the woman, and Bultmann was right to include it among the apophthegms.[45] The interaction be-

---

45. Bultmann, *History*, 38.

tween the two characters begins with the woman's request for help, and the story ends with the announcement, both in Jesus' words and through narrated action, that she has been granted what she sought. This is typical of the successful quest.[46] Also typical are the heightening of tension through emphasis on an obstacle to the quest and the importance given to the quester within the story. In this case the woman's importance is indicated by the fact that it is her clever word in Mark 7:28 that determines the course of events. It is unusual, but significant for the impact of the story, that it is Jesus who raises the objection that is an obstacle to the woman's quest. To overcome the objection of one who is presented throughout the Gospels as the chief figure of authority would seem to be exceedingly difficult. This makes the woman's triumph all the more striking. Since Jesus remains the figure of authority, he must correct himself and confirm the woman's triumph (7:29). Jesus' final statement indicates both that the objection has been overcome and that the quest is successful, and we may include this story with the hybrid objection–quests previously discussed. Such a story could have a significant impact on the early church's debate about the Gentiles. Confronted with such a woman and such a surprising turn of events, Christians who were first inclined to share Jesus' negative attitude would be challenged to follow Jesus in his change of mind. In Matt 15:21–28 the tension of the story is heightened by three rebukes of the woman's request before her statement that wins Jesus' favorable response.

Matt 8:5–13 is quite similar to the story of the Syrophoenician woman in that it is a successful quest story concerning a Gentile who seeks healing for someone close to him. The similarity is even closer if we understand 8:7 not as Jesus' agreement to the centurion's request but as a surprised question indicating unwillingness: "Shall *I* come and heal him?!"[47] Then here also Jesus initially rejects the request but finally commends the centurion and grants his request. The initial rejection is lacking in Luke 7:1–10, and Jesus' final statement is much shorter, for Matthew's

---

46. These features are also typical of the healing miracle, which raises questions about the boundaries between healing miracles and quests. Besides the four miracle stories discussed in this section, miracle stories in which Jesus' commendation of faith is prominent (see, e.g., Mark 5:25–34 or the much shorter parallel in Matthew) are especially close to quests.

47. This is Bultmann's view. See *History*, 38–39. This translation explains the emphatic ἐγώ. It means "I, a Jew," who cannot be expected to do such things for Gentiles. This also explains the fact that the centurion responds by conceding that he is not worthy to have Jesus come.

version adds a general statement about Gentiles and Jews in the kingdom.

Luke 23:39–43, the two crucified criminals, is not completely independent of the rest of Luke's passion story, for v. 39 is an objection to Jesus' failure to save himself and those with him. In this case the second criminal, rather than Jesus, responds to the objection against Jesus. The second criminal then makes a request of Jesus. The request of this quester is expressed late in the story (v. 42), but the situation of need is clear from the beginning of the scene, for all of the parties are hanging on crosses. Jesus speaks to the second criminal, affirming that his quest will be successful. However, this seems also to be a response to his general attitude toward Jesus, including his reply to the first criminal's objection. If that is so, we have another objection-quest story, similar to the story of the Syrophoenician woman, in which Jesus' final words both complete the quest sequence and ratify the correctness of a previous response to an objection. The clear difference in the attitude of the two criminals toward Jesus encourages readers to view the second criminal positively.

Luke 17:12–19, the Samaritan leper, is another Lukan quest story. It begins with the announcement of a need and, as in Luke 7:50 and 19:9, ends with Jesus certifying that the quester's need for salvation has been met. The healing takes place early in the story, and the story focuses on what happens afterwards, coming to a climax with Jesus' words. No objection against Jesus is expressed. Nevertheless, this story is like Luke 7:36–50 in that a positive response to Jesus is graphically depicted and is contrasted with the attitude of another party. The story appeals to those who find Samaritans offensive to rethink their prejudice in the light of this individual. We are not even told that he is a Samaritan until his gratitude has made a positive impression. Then Jesus underscores the importance of this gratitude by criticizing the nine lepers who fail to show it and declares that the Samaritan shares in the salvation that Jesus brings.

Quests share some of the functions of other types of apophthegms. Those quests that incorporate objections function in part like objection stories, defending with imaginative force certain distinctive perspectives in conflict with other views. Quest stories also clarify the demands of discipleship (Mark 10:17–22 par.) and Jesus' understanding of the law (Mark 12:28–34 par.). However, the distinctive function of quests appears in connection with the important role of the quester in these stories. His or her movement from seeking to finding determines the limits of these stories, and the tension of this movement encourages the reader to become involved in the quester's concerns. Furthermore, the quester is presented in a favorable light and does or says things that give evidence of the sincerity and importance of the quest. All of this encourages the reader to experience the events of the story from the quester's perspective. The reader may recognize his or her own quest portrayed in the story, or the reader may become more sympathetic to those in positions of special need and more open to sharing Jesus' ministry to such people. In this way attitudes can change.

It is noteworthy that many of the stories depict a religious outcast as a successful quester. The quest stories present us with Gentiles (the Syrophoenician woman, the centurion), a Samaritan leper, a sinful paralytic, a sinful woman, a tax collector, a condemned criminal. By showing Jesus responding favorably to such people, assumptions about who may share in God's salvation are being attacked.

Objection Stories

In objection stories an objection is raised against the words or actions of the primary character or his close associates, and a response is given by the primary character to this objection. The objection story has three parts: 1) the cause of the objection, which is often depicted at the beginning of the story, 2) the objection, which is often expressed as a question asking why something is being done, and 3) the response to the objection. While the cause of the objection is often an event narrated prior to the objection, it is sometimes absorbed into the objection. Then we encounter the cause only as the objectors refer to it. Furthermore, objectors occasionally anticipate that the primary character will act in a way of which they disapprove. This will develop into an objection story if the anticipation is correct. The story may end with the primary character both completing the anticipated action and defending his action in response to the objection (see Mark 3:1–6). The response often corrects an assumption basic to the objection, which makes this type similar to correction stories. However, there is a significant difference between the two types. In the correction story tension arises when Jesus declares his disagreement with a position assumed, through word or act, by someone else. It is Jesus' response that makes the conflict clear. In objection stories the position of Jesus or his disciples is the beginning of the development, conflict appears in the objection, not just in the response, and Jesus must correct an attitude critical of himself. Because of this, the tension in the story focuses on Jesus. He is being challenged, and the reader will want to know whether he can meet the challenge. An objection situation can be a crisis for Jesus and those who honor him. In this respect objection stories are similar to testing inquiries. A testing inquiry is also a crisis for Jesus, but the crisis arises not through an objection to something already said or done but through a question posed by a hostile or skeptical person. In a testing inquiry the question is an open question, asking Jesus to declare his position where that position is not yet clear. In an objection the objector may also raise a question, but this is really a request for justification of a position already taken by Jesus. The question will ask why Jesus thinks or acts as he does, rather than what Jesus thinks.

This type of story is fairly common in the literature of the Roman world. I give a brief example:

> ὀνειδιζόμενός ποτε ὅτι πονηρῷ ἀνθρώπῳ ἐλεημοσύνην ἔδωκεν, οὐ τὸν τρόπον, εἶπεν, ἀλλὰ τὸν ἄνθρωπον ἠλέησα.
>
> Being once reproached for giving alms to a bad man, he [Aristotle] rejoined, "It was the man and not his character that I pitied."[48]

Objection stories are closely related to Bultmann's controversy dialogues. The following texts, listed by Bultmann as controversy dialogues, are discussed in this section: Mark 2:15–17 par., 18–22 par., 23–28 par.; 3:1–6 par., 22–30 par.; 7:1–15 par.; Luke 13:10–17; 14:1–6. Bultmann included two stories (Mark 2:1–12 par.; Luke 7:36–50) that I have already discussed as objection-quests. He also included Mark 11:27–33 par., which appears to me to be a testing inquiry.[49] He omitted a number of stories that I will include, partly because he was not concerned with all the stories in the Gospels but primarily with the pre-Gospel tradition and partly, perhaps, because he did not include scenes with objections from people who are not consistent opponents of Jesus. In the first part of his discussion of apophthegms, Bultmann correctly distinguished stories beginning with an action that causes an objection from stories beginning with a question from opponents concerning Jesus' position, which is not known.[50] Later, however, the three texts of the latter type listed by Bultmann (Mark 12:13–17 par.; 12:18–27 par.; 10:2–12 par.) are included in his general discussion of controversy dialogues.[51] Of the texts

---

48. Diogenes Laertius, *Lives of Eminent Philosophers*, trans. R. D. Hicks, LCL (Cambridge: Harvard University Press, 1950) 5:17. See Nassen Poulos, "Form and Function," 57.

49. Bultmann, *History*, 12–21.

50. Ibid., 12–21, 26–27.

51. Ibid., 48–49.

discussed in this section, Dibelius included Mark 2:15ff., 18ff.; 3:1ff.; 6:1ff.; and Luke 14:1ff. among his paradigms.[52]

In both Mark 2:15–17 par., the meal with the tax collectors and sinners, and Mark 2:23–28 par., plucking grain on the Sabbath, the objectionable action is narrated before the objection is made. While the objection in Mark 2:24 is expressed through a question of why the disciples are acting as they are, the parallel in Matt 12:2 has an accusing statement. The function of this element in the story remains the same. The question about fasting, Mark 2:18–22 par., does not begin by narrating the objectionable act. The prior behavior being criticized is described within the objection itself. This is also true of Mark 3:22–30, the Beelzebub controversy. In Matthew's and Luke's versions, however, this scene is introduced by an exorcism, which becomes the specific cause of the accusation (Matt 12:22–24, Luke 11:14–15). In this story an objection setting is used to introduce a fairly extensive discourse by Jesus. We will note further examples of this below. The objection stories, especially, show a tendency to expand the response of Jesus by combining sayings or adding arguments to a saying that could stand alone. Mark 3:22–26 would be a better example of an apophthegm, for the addition of vv. 27–30 somewhat reduces the climactic effect of vv. 24–26. Matthew 12:22–37 carries considerably further this tendency to construct an extensive discourse.

Mark 6:1–6, the rejection at Nazareth, which was regarded by Bultmann as a biographical apophthegm,[53] appears to me to be an objection story. Here also Jesus' activity causes a negative reaction, and Jesus responds to these negative views. Jesus' wisdom and mighty acts, when viewed in light of his origin, are the cause of the negative reaction. The reference to Jesus' ordinary origin as part of their own community (Mark 6:3) constitutes an objection, and the negative implications of the remarks are underscored by stating that the people took offense at him. The saying of Jesus in Mark 6:4 is a relevant response. It not only describes how Jesus and other prophets are treated but subjects this treatment to criticism. The saying points to rejection at home as the strange exception to the honor that a prophet rightly receives. The strangeness of this exception casts doubt upon its justice.

The Sabbath healings are objection stories that also show the characteristics of miracles, but they vary somewhat in their composition. The composition of Luke 13:10–17 is the simplest. Here the healing on the Sabbath is completed first. This causes an objection, which leads to Jesus'

---

52. Dibelius, *Formgeschichte*, 40; *Tradition to Gospel*, 43.
53. Bultmann, *History*, 31–32.

response. In Mark 3:1–6 par., however, the healing is Jesus' final action in the story. Nevertheless, Jesus, in his words and actions in 3:4–5, is responding to his opponents. In 3:2 the position of the opponents is made clear: They anticipate that Jesus may heal on the Sabbath and take a strong negative attitude. They not only object; they intend to use this case as basis for a legal accusation. Here we have an anticipatory objection, an objection against a possible or contemplated action.[54] Since Jesus does act as anticipated, the character relationships typical of the objection story are preserved. The opponents are objecting to the way that Jesus does, in fact, act within the story, and Jesus' words and acts in 3:4–5 are a response to that objection.[55] The response consists of both word and action. In 3:4 Jesus poses a question, a question that interprets the situation by indicating that one must choose between doing good and doing evil. Following the silence of his opponents, Jesus answers his own question as to what is right by his act of healing. Thus the healing here has multiple functions within the story. Anticipated, it is the cause of the objection and, performed, it is part of Jesus' response to that objection. It is also a response to the crippled man's need, as in other healing miracles. In Matt 12:9–14, which differs in a number of ways from Mark's version, Jesus' words are more independent of the healing and respond to an explicit question of whether it is lawful to heal on the Sabbath. This suggests that the author of Matthew may have conceived the story as a testing inquiry (12:10b–12) in the framework of a healing miracle. However, the indication that Jesus is being questioned in order to be accused suggests that the questioners anticipate Jesus' position and oppose it. Their anticipation proves correct. They oppose the position that Jesus takes in the following verses. Luke 14:1–6 also contains a question about whether it is lawful to heal on the Sabbath. The fact that it is expressed by Jesus in Luke's story is incidental. It could equally well have been expressed by the Pharisees,

---

54 Compare Matt 3:13–15 and the following story from Plutarch's *Life of Alexander*, trans. B. Perrin, LCL (Cambridge: Harvard University Press, 1958) 16:2: . . . τοῦ δὲ Παρμενίωνος, ὡς ὀψὲ τῆς ὥρας οὔσης, οὐκ ἐῶντος ἀποκινδυνεύειν, εἰπὼν αἰσχύνεσθαι τὸν Ἑλλήσποντον εἰ φοβήσεται τὸν Γρανικὸν διαβεβηκὼς ἐκεῖνον, ἐμβάλλει τῷ ῥεύματι σὺν ἴλαις ἱππέων τρισκαίδεκα. ". . . when Parmenio, on the ground that it was too late in the day, objected to their risking the passage, he [Alexander] declared that the Hellespont would blush for shame, if, after having crossed that strait, he should be afraid of the Granicus, and plunged into the stream with thirteen troops of horsemen." See Vernon K. Robbins, "Pronouncement Stories in Plutarch's *Lives of Alexander* and *Julius Caesar*," in *SBLSP 1978*, 2 vols. (Missoula, Mont.: Scholars, 1978) 2:27.

55 If Jesus were to reject the anticipated action, we would have a correction story.

for it is implicit in the situation. This question does not have the same function as the question in Mark 3:4, which implies its own answer and is part of Jesus' response to his opponents. The opposition of the lawyers and Pharisees is indicated in 14:1 and 6. Unlike Mark 3:1–6 par., Jesus responds first with the healing, then with a pronouncement, making clearer that the pronouncement is a defense of the healing against those who oppose such action.

There are passages in which an objection situation provides the setting for a rather long discourse that is not limited to refuting the objection but becomes a general attack on the group objecting. Although the apophthegm appears to be stretched beyond its proper shape in these passages, I will discuss them briefly. Mark 7:1–15 par. is an example.[56] The protest of the Pharisees and scribes at the behavior of the disciples, for whom, it is assumed, Jesus is responsible, provokes a counterattack by Jesus, centering on the tradition of the elders. Only 7:15 speaks specifically to the issue of defilement in eating, the subject of the objection. Although this Markan material is rearranged in Matt 15:1–14, the basic interaction is the same, except that Matthew adds a second protest from the Pharisees (transmitted by the disciples) and a further attack by Jesus (15:12–14). Similar general attacks on the group represented by the objecting person are found in Luke 11:37–52, where Jesus addresses a series of woes first to a Pharisee who objects to Jesus' failure to wash and then to a lawyer who objects to what Jesus has been saying. More closely related to the specific objection but still quite lengthy is Jesus' response to the Pharisees and scribes in Luke 15. To their protest against his behavior with sinners, Jesus replies with three parables, one of them rather long. Some of the material mentioned in this paragraph is found in another Gospel without the introductory objection.

While many of the objections come from the Pharisees and scribes, stories of the same type arise when Jesus responds to objections from people who are not his consistent opponents. Matthew 3:13–15 presents a little objection scene in which John the Baptist is the objector. He objects not because he is hostile to Jesus but because he at first believes that the proposed baptism is beneath Jesus' dignity. Luke 2:41–51, the boy Jesus in the temple, a story that Dibelius regards as an outstanding example of a legend,[57] has, along with its legendary features, the essential features

---

56. Mark 7:15, although addressed to a broader audience, seems to be a necessary part of Jesus' response to the objection. Verses 17–23, however, are an attached inquiry scene that will be discussed below under inquiries.

57. Dibelius, *Formgeschichte*, 103–6; *Tradition to Gospel*, 106–9.

of an objection story. The introductory narrative is unusually long, but the story comes to its climax with the mother's protest against her son's behavior and Jesus' reply. If Mark 9:9–13 par. is intended to make sense as a meaningful conversation, the disciples are apparently expressing an objection by referring to an opinion of the scribes (v. 11) that seems to call in question Jesus' anticipation of resurrection in the near future (see vv. 9–10). In Mark 8:31–33, Peter's reaction to the first announcement of the passion, we find an objection sequence with a disciple as the objector. While Mark simply says that Peter "began to rebuke" Jesus, Matt 16:22 fills out the objection with a direct quotation.

The last example also belongs to a group in which the objection is provoked not by an action of Jesus or the disciples but by Jesus' teaching. When Jesus' teaching is the first step in the interaction of characters, the balance of emphasis among the parts of the scene may shift. When the scene begins with an objectionable action, the emphasis clearly lies on Jesus' response to the objection. When it begins with Jesus' teaching, the response to objection may simply reinforce the initial teaching and be subordinate to it. In Mark 8:33, Jesus' response not only crushes Peter's objection but also shows how crucial it is that the disciples accept Jesus' previous words about the passion. In Mark 10:23–27, the dialogue with the disciples on the rich entering the kingdom, the amazement and question of the disciples in vv. 24 and 26 function as objections to the statements of Jesus. The response of Jesus to the disciples clarifies the implications of what he has said but is not the climax of the dialogue. The parallel texts in Matt 19:23–26 and Luke 18:24–27 have the same basic composition but eliminate the first response of the disciples. In Luke 16:14–15 a brief objection scene is attached to Jesus' preceding teaching about possessions but remains subordinate to that teaching. In Luke Jesus' words about the wicked tenants of the vineyard provoke a protest, which is followed by a Scripture reference supporting what Jesus has already said (Luke 20:16–18). The dialogue with the disciples in Matt 19:10–12, which is attached to Jesus' teaching about divorce, allows Jesus to clarify the application of that teaching in light of the demands of the kingdom. This is an objection scene if v. 10 is meant as a protest against the severity of Jesus' teaching on divorce or against the limitation it places on married missionaries.[58] Matthew 19:3–12 appears to be a dialogue that begins as a testing inquiry and continues with two objections, one from the Pharisees and one from the disciples. Each of Jesus' three replies is roughly equal in

---

58. See Tannehill, *Sword*, 134–40.

importance, so this passage moves away from the climactic ending typical of the apophthegm.

The importance of the sequence of objection and response in synoptic apophthegms is underscored when we recall that we have already discussed several groups of texts in which objections have an important role. They include the hybrid objection-commendation (Luke 10:38–42; 19:37–40; Matt 21:14–16), discussed in the section on commendations. They also include Mark 2:1–12 par.; Luke 7:36–50; 19:1–10; 23:39–43, which are objection-quests, as well as the quest stories in which Jesus himself raises an objection (Mark 7:24–30 par. and probably Matt 8:5–13).

In objection stories Jesus, and sometimes his disciples, encounter a challenge. Their behavior and ideas are called in question and must be defended. This gives narrative interest to these stories, for the reader or hearer will want to know whether the challenge can be met and how. This also suggests that the chief function of the objection stories is to support and reinforce the distinctive perspectives of the Jesus movement in the face of challenges from conflicting views. So Bultmann was correct in relating his controversy dialogues to the "apologetic and polemic" of the early church.[59] Although there is a tendency toward the expansion of objection stories through the addition of arguments,[60] these stories rely less upon rational argument, which would require much fuller discussion, than upon words of imaginative force. Such words can provoke the hearer into questioning assumptions and priorities that seemed self-evident by giving imaginative power to a new perspective. Although shaped by the struggles of the early church, such words are not simply weapons to conquer opponents. They speak equally to the serious follower of Jesus, whose commitment is always a struggle against other commitments and desires. The words of Jesus set forth his radical call in its distinctiveness and seek renewed and deepened commitment. To be sure, there are some scenes that have become general polemics against an opposing group (Mark 7:1–15 par.; Luke 11:37–52). Here we may find polemics in the narrow sense of an attack on others who are clearly distinct from the attackers. The fact that the early church broke with Judaism and that the scribes and Pharisees appear in the Gospels so frequently as objectors or testers and so seldom in other roles also makes it easy to regard Jesus' words in objection stories as attacks on outsiders. However, the disciples of Jesus occasionally

---

59. Bultmann, *History*, 40–41.

60. Note the additions to Markan stories in Matt 9:13; 12:5–7; 12:11–12. This process of adding arguments is probably already at work in Mark. Mark 2:25–26 may be an example.

object,[61] and in many objection stories Jesus' words are sufficiently radical to challenge followers as well as critics.

Inquiry Stories

Inquiries contain a question or request for instruction as the stimulating element. The response provides the answer. The question may be expressed fully or it may simply be stated that a question was asked by someone about a particular topic. Questions may also occur in the types of apophthegms previously discussed, but the inquiry scene lacks the distinctive characteristics of the other types. The primary character does not respond to the question by correcting the assumption on which it is based, as in a correction story. Rather, the question is accepted as valid and some answer is given. The question is not an objection to something that has been said or done. The story lacks the special features of a quest. As a result, attention focuses upon the content of the teaching provided in response to the question. While the content of the teaching is important in stories of the other types as well, the other types narrate an event in which something important happens to the participants. Instruction is given, but at the same time the acts or views of a person are evaluated with words of correction or commendation. Or we learn of the success or failure of a quester in reaching a goal, or of the success or failure of someone in responding to an objection. Dramatic interaction between the characters and the dramatic tension that accompanies the risk of loss or gain are generally more prominent in the other types than in the simple inquiry. While a dramatic scene attracts our interest to the climactic saying, presenting it as a decisive utterance in a situation of high tension, the situations depicted in simple inquiries are generally not of this kind. Therefore, the setting contributes less to the saying's force, although it may clarify the topic being discussed or suggest the application of the teaching to a particular group or problem.

The decrease in dramatic tension just noted does not apply to a significant group of stories that I will call testing inquiries. In these stories Jesus is being tested as he is asked a question; he is being placed in a situation of risk by a hostile or skeptical group. These tend to be well-developed, independent stories, while many of the simple inquiry sequences are attached to and dependent on teaching or an event preced-

---

61. See Mark 8:31–33 par.; 9:9–13 par.; 10:23–27 par.; and Matt 19:10–12. The disciples appear more often in correction stories as the cause of Jesus' corrective statement than as objectors.

ing them. In the latter cases the development of the larger scene involves not just inquiry-response but teaching/event-inquiry-response, and the inquiry is a request for explanation of what precedes it. The inquiry sequence is dependent on its context in that the topic for the inquiry is drawn from the preceding material. Nevertheless, these inquiry sequences are almost always marked off as separate scenes by the introduction of a new conversation partner and usually also by a shift in location (e.g., to a house) or situation (e.g., in private).[62] Thus they are presented to the reader as separate, short encounters between persons, after the manner of apophthegms, rather than as part of the preceding teaching. The great majority of these inquiries dependent on preceding material are requests for clarification from the disciples. When we are aware of the four types previously discussed and recognize the stories belonging to them, it is surprising how little synoptic material is left for the inquiries, except for the testing inquiries and these scenes, probably late and redactional in origin, in which the disciples request additional explanation.

In the non-Christian literature of the Roman world we also find apophthegms of the inquiry type, like the following story about Pittacus:

ἐρωτηθεὶς δέ ποτε τί ἄριστον, τὸ παρὸν εὖ ποιεῖν.

Once, when asked what is the best thing, he replied, "To do well the work in hand."[63]

At first Bultmann correctly distinguishes Mark 12:13–17 par. and 10:2–12 par. from stories in which the conduct of Jesus or his disciples provokes an objection, but the distinction is later lost, for Bultmann includes these two passages in his general discussion of controversy dialogues.[64] I regard Mark 12:13–17 par. and 10:2–9 par. as testing inquiries. Bultmann also includes the following testing inquiries in his controversy

---

62. Luke 3:10–11 is an exception, for there is no indication of a shift either in conversation partner or in setting. This inquiry, however, is parallel to two more in Luke 3:12–14, which do introduce new conversation partners. A new conversation partner but not a new setting is indicated in Matt 13:10; 15:15; Luke 8:9; 12:41; and 14:15. Mark consistently indicates both sorts of shift in introducing these dependent inquiry scenes.

63. Diogenes Laertius, *Lives of Eminent Philosophers*, trans. by R. D. Hicks, LCL (Cambridge: Harvard University, 1950) 1:77. See Paula J. Nassen, "The Pronouncement Story in Diogenes Laertius' *Lives and Opinions of Eminent Philosophers*: A New Classification," in *SBLSP 1978*, 2 vols. (Missoula, Mont.: Scholars, 1978) 2:12 [11–19]. For an inquiry with a more elaborate setting see Plutarch, *Life of Caesar*, LCL (Cambridge: Harvard University Press, 1958) 63:4 (mentioned by Robbins, "Pronouncement Stories," 37).

64. Bultmann, *History*, 12–21, 26–27, 48–49.

dialogues: Mark 11:27-33; Matt 22:34-40, 41-46; Luke 10:25-37.[65] Of the testing inquiries, Dibelius includes only Mark 12:13ff. among his paradigms.[66] Of the inquiries in which there is no indication of testing, Bultmann includes only Mark 11:20-25, the comment on the withered fig tree, in his list of apophthegms,[67] and none of these texts appears in Dibelius's list of paradigms.

We will begin with scenes in which the disciples inquire about something that has happened or that has just been said by Jesus, for this is the largest group of inquiries that do not involve testing. These scenes are dependent on preceding material and provide additional instruction and clarification. For instance, a group of Jesus' followers inquire about the parables following Jesus' parable of the sower. Jesus replies both with words about "those outside" and with an allegorical interpretation of the parable (Mark 4:10-20 par.). There is a subordinate note of criticism of the disciples' lack of understanding in Mark's version. Mark 7:17-23 par., Jesus' explanation following his statement of what defiles a person, is similar. We also find scenes in which the disciples inquire and Jesus answers their inquiry following the healing of the epileptic boy (Mark 9:28-29 par.), Jesus' teaching about divorce (Mark 10:10-12), the parable of the tares (Matt 13:36-43), and the parable of the waiting servants (Luke 12:41-48).[68] In Mark 11:20-25 the cause of the inquiry is part of the inquiry scene itself. Peter sees the withered fig tree, exclaims about it, and Jesus responds with words about faith. Peter's exclamation seems to function as a request for explanation of how such a thing could happen, for Jesus responds by providing such explanation. That is the way in which the scene is understood in Matt 21:18-22, where the exclamation becomes an explicit question as to how the fig tree withered.

In two disciple inquiry scenes the disciples do not respond to previous teaching or a previous event but simply raise a question or request instruction about something important to them. In Luke the Lord's Prayer is presented as a response to a disciple's request for instruction (Luke

---

65. Ibid., 19-20, 51.

66. *Formgeschichte*, 40; *Tradition to Gospel*, 43.

67. He also discusses Mark 7:1-23 and 10:2-12, longer stories that conclude with disciple inquiry scenes. See Bultmann, *History*, 17-18, 26-27.

68. There is also a brief inquiry and reply in Luke 17:37, following Jesus' eschatological teaching, but there are no signs that this verse is meant to be an independent scene, so it cannot be accounted an apophthegm. In Mark 13:3-4 par. the disciples respond to Jesus' prophecy of the destruction of the temple with a question. Jesus' response, however, is a long discourse that exceeds the limits of an apophthegm.

11:1–4), and Jesus is also responding to a request when he speaks about faith in Luke 17:5–6.

In a few cases the inquiry comes from someone outside the circle of Jesus' followers. In Luke 3:10–14 we find three inquiries from different groups addressed to John the Baptist and caused by his preaching. In Luke 13:22–30 Jesus responds with eschatological warnings to a question about the number to be saved. Here the question is not presented as a response to what Jesus has just said.

The inquiries include some rather loosely constructed dialogue scenes. While in most apophthegms stimulus and response are carefully matched, there are inquiries in which the response strays from or goes beyond what is asked, drawing from the question a general topic for comment. In Luke 12:41–48 Peter asks for whom the preceding parable is meant, but in the answer Jesus seems less concerned with the identity of the servant than with the consequences of faithfulness and unfaithfulness. While Luke 13:24 is related to the preceding question of whether few will be saved, Jesus continues with eschatological warnings that leave the question of few or many behind. Finally, in Luke 17:5–6 Jesus responds to the apostles' request to increase their faith by emphasizing how powerful faith is. The response picks up the general topic of faith but it is not clear that it fulfills the request.

The focus of attention in the inquiry scenes above is almost entirely on the content of the teaching provided in the response. The function of these inquiry stories, then, is to convey this teaching. These stories also suggest the relevance of this teaching to the life of the church, for much of this teaching is given to the followers of Jesus in response to their questions. In some cases the introductory question or request suggests a particular application of the teaching. In Luke 11:1–4, for instance, the fact that the Lord's Prayer answers the disciple's request indicates that it is meant to be a basic pattern of prayer for Jesus' followers. In a number of cases the inquiry scene as a whole is secondary to, and an application of, teaching given in preceding material. The explanation and application of the teaching about defilement in Mark 7:17–23 par. is an example. An inquiry scene following words or acts was a useful way of emphasizing and clarifying the preceding material, thereby providing some interpretation of it and applying it to the church's life.

In contrast to other inquiries, the synoptic testing inquiries form a group of well-developed, fully independent stories with considerable dramatic interest. Like other inquiries, the testing inquiry is structured by a question or request that is accepted and answered by the primary character. In the testing inquiry, however, this question or request is designed to test the primary character. The inquirer is usually hostile or skeptical and the situation is critical for the one being tested, for failure to provide an impressive answer will at least mean loss of influence and may be dangerous in other ways. The tension in the story focuses on the primary character, who is put in a difficult situation. In this respect testing inquiries resemble objection stories. However, the tension does not arise from an objection to something already said or done. The inquirer is not reacting negatively to the primary character's position but must ask what the primary character's position is. There must be some indication that the inquiry involves a test. In the synoptic Gospels this is often stated directly in a participial phrase ("testing him"), but certain other situations may also involve testing, as when Jesus is asked about his status and authority. Jesus may respond to a testing question or request by correcting, as in the question about the resurrection (Mark 12:18–27 par.). I have included these stories with the corrections. If the testing question or request is accepted and answered, we have a testing inquiry, as in the texts discussed below.

In Mark 12:13–17 par., the question about the census tax, the danger and deceitfulness of the question put to Jesus is emphasized. The hostile intent of the secondary characters is made clear at the beginning: they wish to "catch" Jesus by something that he says. The question is preceded by an elaborate compliment, which contrasts in its verbosity with the terse dialogue that follows. The repetitive verbosity of the compliment makes it sound overdone and hollow, and these words are directly labeled as hypocrisy in Mark 12:15. Nevertheless, Jesus must "teach in truth the way of God," and so some answer is necessary. Thus the hostile questioners are able to force Jesus into a difficult situation in which he is being tested, as the first words of Jesus' response (12:15) indicate. These features of the text add to the tension of the situation and heighten the reader's interest in knowing whether Jesus will be able to escape the trap and meet the test. This interest is increased as Jesus requests the coin and asks a question about it. The point of this question is not immediately clear. The reader awaits the outcome in order to discover the coin's purpose. Thus everything points forward to the climactic command in 12:17, with its terse and forceful language. With these words Jesus meets the test, as is certified by the amazed response of the hearers. Thus the central development of the story is the movement from a dangerous question that tests

Jesus' courage and insight to disclosure of how Jesus met the test successfully.[69]

While Mark's story of the great commandments is a quest, in which the questioner is presented in a favorable light, agrees with Jesus, and is declared to be not far from the kingdom, the parallel story in Matt 22:34–40 is a testing inquiry. The features indicating favorable evaluation of the questioner are absent, and instead we are told that the questioner is "testing" Jesus. The related scene in Luke 10:25–37 is also a testing inquiry. The question asked by the lawyer would be appropriate in a quest story (see Mark 10:17 par.). The fact that the lawyer answers Jesus' counterquestion about the law correctly might suggest that he is a person of insight. But the sympathy for the quester commonly promoted in quest stories is undermined when we are told that the lawyer asked his initial question in order to test Jesus and continued the conversation in order to "justify himself." Furthermore, we are not told how the lawyer responded to Jesus' final challenge. To be sure, the sense of a crisis for Jesus is not as strong here as in Mark 12:13–17 par. and Matt 22:34–40, which are part of a series of testing questions in the temple. The fact that the dialogue develops through a preliminary counterquestion by Jesus in Luke 10:25–37 and in Mark 12:13–17 par. is noteworthy. This feature seems to be common in testing inquiries. We will find it again in Mark 10:2–9 and 11:27–33 par.[70]

The stories in which Jesus responds to a request for a sign are also testing inquiries. These stories depict a critical situation for Jesus, for these requests raise the question of whether Jesus is able to demonstrate his divine authority. In Matt 12:38–42 scribes and Pharisees test Jesus by requesting a sign.[71] Jesus' response contains a correction: a generation seeking a sign is evil, and in the judgment this generation will be condemned. Nevertheless, Jesus indicates that there is a sign, the sign of Jonah, which provides a positive answer to the testing request. In Matt 16:1–4 Jesus again responds to a request for a sign from people who are "testing" him (16:1) by pointing to the sign of Jonah. This story, like Matt 12:38–42, is

69. On Mark 12:13–17 see further Tannehill, *Sword,* 171–77.

70. Jesus frequently responds with a question in objection stories also. See Mark 2:19; 2:25–26; 3:4; 3:23; Matt 12:5; 12:11; 12:26–27; 21:16; Luke 2:49; 11:40; 13:15–16; 14:5; 15:4; 15:8; and 20:17. However, in these stories the question is argumentative and constitutes the reply or an important part of it. In the tests just mentioned the counterquestion is preliminary and elicits a response useful for Jesus' final reply.

71. The Lukan parallel (Luke 11:29–32) lacks this request, and Jesus' words are not presented as a response to a dialogue partner or to an observed event. Thus Luke's version is not an apophthegm.

a hybrid, combining correction and testing inquiry, for Jesus both corrects and answers the request. While the reference to the sign of Jonah is not developed in 16:1–4, the correction is prominent. This is true whether we follow the shorter or longer text,[72] for the words about the weather in this context serve to correct the assumption of the Pharisees and Sadducees that they are able to recognize and judge signs.

Mark 10:2–9, the question concerning divorce, also combines testing inquiry and correction. We are told that the Pharisees ask their question in order to test Jesus. Jesus responds with a counterquestion concerning the commandment of Moses. The answer states a position on divorce contrary to the one that Jesus will take. This procedure makes the contrary view available for correction. The response of Jesus in 10:5–9 is both a correction of this view and an answer to the initial testing question. In Matt 19:3–9 the elements of the story are rearranged so that the reference to the Mosaic certificate of divorce becomes an objection to the position that Jesus has already taken. Thus we have a testing inquiry combined with an objection.

Mark 11:27–33 par., the question about Jesus' authority, is also a testing inquiry. To be sure, the double question in 11:28 refers to Jesus' activity and might be understood as an objection to the things that Jesus has been doing. This question, however, seems less concerned with objecting to specific activities of Jesus than with inquiring about what lies behind them. It seems to be designed to elicit a statement from Jesus about his personal claim, leaving open the possibility that Jesus is acting with proper authority.[73] There is no explicit statement that Jesus, in being asked this question, is being tested. However, to be questioned about one's authority is a personal test, particularly when the question comes from a hostile group. The question focuses on Jesus himself and the basis of his work, not just on a particular position that he has taken. To fail to clarify and establish one's authority would ordinarily lead to the loss of influence that is always possible in a testing situation. As in some other testing inquiries, Jesus replies with a counterquestion. Here, however, an answer to Jesus' question is refused and Jesus, in turn, refuses to answer.

72. Most of Matt 16:2–3 is textually suspect.

73. Hultgren attempts to reconstruct an earlier version of the story. See Arland Hultgren, *Jesus and His Adversaries: The Form and Function of the Conflict Stories in the Synoptic Tradition* (Minneapolis: Augsburg, 1979) 68–75. His reconstructed version is considerably shorter, ending with Jesus' question in v. 30 and including only the second of the two questions in v. 28. He insists that the story was originally linked with the temple cleansing, although this link has been broken in Matthew and Mark. The reconstructed text could be an objection story, but Mark's text is a testing inquiry.

Thus the scene comes to an end without the expected answer to the testing question. While those who refuse a test run the risk of being regarded as incapable of answering, the opponents' refusal here provides justification for Jesus' refusal.

Probably we should also include the Baptist's question (Matt 11:2–6 par.) among the testing inquiries. While the question is not posed by a hostile party, it does focus on Jesus' personal claim and so raises the issue of the degree of authority and importance to be attributed to him. A question about one's status and authority establishes a testing situation. In this respect this story resembles the story just discussed (Mark 11:27–33 par.).

Jesus may appear in testing inquiries not only as the one tested but also as the tester. This is the case in the confession of Peter (Mark 8:27–30 par.). Here again the question of Jesus' position and authority is raised, but now Jesus asks the disciples. The disciples' insight is being tested. This is a critical situation for them because they must make a statement to and about their own leader. Statements to and about a superior are risky because of the power of that person's displeasure. The question to the disciples is preceded by a question about the opinions of other people, making Peter's answer stand out in contrast to these opinions.[74] Mark 12:35–37 par., the Christ and David's son, may also be a testing inquiry in which Jesus is the tester. While Jesus alone speaks in the scene, a dialogue situation is suggested, for Jesus begins by referring to the opinion of others and he ends with a question.[75] Those who hold the opinion owe an answer to the question but evidently fail to provide it. If Jesus' words imply that the Christ is not David's son, they are a correction of that opinion. If it is possible to explain how the Christ can be both David's Lord and his son, the scribes are being presented with a difficult question.[76] It has a riddle-like quality and functions as a test of their insight, a test that they fail.

Narration of a story as a testing inquiry heightens the tension in the scene, since the situation involves personal risk for the one being tested. This increases the reader's interest in the event and usually increases the reader's concern for the one tested, who in the Gospels is ordinarily a person of importance to Christian readers. This tension can emphasize the climactic response, for an impressive answer is all the more impressive in

74. This testing inquiry is the first part of a more elaborate scene that continues until Mark 9:1.

75. In Matthew's version an actual dialogue is narrated (see Matt 22:41–42), bringing out the opinion about the Christ that Jesus will discuss.

76. So in Mark, while Matthew refers to the Pharisees and Luke leaves the source of the opinion indefinite.

a testing situation where the risk is high. But these stories also emphasize that Jesus, the one who can meet such tests, is a person of insight and authority. To some extent all of the apophthegms in which Jesus' words are central not only tell us what Jesus said but present him to us as a person of insight and authority. This presentation is more impressive in a testing situation. A testing situation focuses our attention on the adequacy of Jesus in meeting the test, and the testing inquiries of the Gospels affirm his adequacy again and again. The subjects discussed in testing inquiries also show an unusually strong concern with Christological issues, including Jesus' authority (see Matt 11:2–6 par.; 12:38–42; 16:1–4; Mark 8:27–30 par.; 11:27–33 par.; 12:35–37 par.).

It is noteworthy that when we consider the two collections of Markan "controversy dialogues" investigated by Albertz,[77] we find that they differ. Mark 2:1–3:6 is composed of objection stories (2:1–12 is a hybrid objection-quest), while Mark 11:27–33, 12:13–37 is dominated by testing questions.[78]

We have a rich group of apophthegms in the synoptic Gospels, and the dramatic possibilities of the genre are well developed. The narrative setting does more than provide an incidental location for Jesus' sayings. The apophthegms present Jesus in interaction with other persons, thereby conveying a sense of the challenging power of his words. The typology developed in this essay helps us to do justice to the fact that apophthegms are stories with narrative tension and movement. The typology enables us to observe and describe common patterns of narrative tension and development, showing that some of these stories are more complex than they seem, and helping us to recognize the ways in which value conflicts are mirrored in them. The typology also helps us to recognize the ways in which these brief stories are shaped to influence the readers' or hearers' basic attitudes, perceptions, and commitments.[79]

---

77. See Martin Albertz, *Die synoptischen Streitgespräche: Ein Beitrag zur Formgeschichte des Urchristentums* (Berlin: Trowitzsch, 1921) 5–36.

78. This includes Mark 12:18–27, a testing correction. Mark 12:28–34, however, is an exception. This quest becomes a testing inquiry in Matthew.

79. I discuss this aspect of apophthegms further in "Attitudinal Shift in Synoptic Pronouncement Stories" in Richard A. Spencer, ed., *Orientation by Disorientation: Studies in Literary Criticism and Biblical Literary Criticism Presented in Honor of William A. Beardslee* (Pittsburgh: Pickwick Publications, 1980) 183–97.

5

The GOSPELS and NARRATIVE LITERATURE

While the following essay includes a section on pronouncement stories, it considerably broadens my discussion of formal types of Gospel literature to include parables, wonder stories, and promise and commission epiphanies, as well as some longer narrative sequences within the Gospels. I also provide some guidance on reading a complete Gospel as a narrative. This discussion should help readers to be aware of some of the actions and relationships that define typical Gospel narratives, which the creative storyteller can modify for his or her special purposes.

THE GOSPELS AND NARRATIVE literature can be studied on several levels, for example, the level of complete Gospels and the level of the short narrative episodes that they contain. These episodes follow recognizable patterns, and those that follow the same pattern may be classed as examples of the same literary type. This article will first examine types of short narratives in the Gospels and then will discuss the Gospels themselves as extended narratives containing these short narrative forms.

Types of Narrative in the Gospels

Certain stable patterns of short narrative are found within the Gospels and the surrounding culture. The repetition of these patterns is evidence that they were found to be effective and worthy of imitation. Within first-century Mediterranean culture, the development of literary skill consisted, in part, in the mastery of these narrative patterns. The patterns were seldom used rigidly; they could be adapted to the content of the story, and skillful storytellers could employ these patterns creatively.

Patterns of short narrative may be studied by form critics, who will ask about the function of each type within a community's life; by rhetorical critics, who will ask how each type is able to affect an audience; and by literary critics, who will ask how these short patterns enrich the larger narrative, helping to create a complex communication that deepens our experience of humanness.[1]

Short narrative types include pronouncement stories, parables, wonder stories, and promise and commission epiphanies. Before considering complete Gospels as narratives, one should also note several longer narrative sequences within the Gospels in which scenes are linked by clear plot developments. These represent narrative at an intermediate level between the short episode and a complete Gospel.

Pronouncement Stories

Within the Gospels are a number of short narratives in which Jesus responds to a person or situation, and this response is the main point of the narrative. These narratives may be called pronouncement stories. Matthew 18:21–22 provides an example:

> Then Peter came and said to him, "Lord, if another member of the church sins against me, how often should I forgive? As many as seven times?" Jesus said to him, "Not seven times, but, I tell you, seventy-seven times."

A pronouncement story is a brief narrative in which the climactic (and often final) element is a pronouncement that is presented as a particular person's response to something said or observed on a past occasion. Pronouncement stories have two main parts: the pronouncement and its setting—i.e., the response and the situation provoking that response.[2] In some cases an expressive action, making a point without speech, or a response combining speech and action may substitute for the pronouncement.

The pronouncement story is closely related to a form widely used in the Greco-Roman world, the *chreia*. An ancient educational textbook, Theon's *Progymnasmata*, defines the *chreia* as "a concise statement or action, which is attributed with aptness to some specified character or to something analogous to a character."[3] Although a *chreia* may sometimes simply indicate the person who is the source of the statement or action,

---

1. See Carl R. Holladay, "Contemporary Methods of Reading the Bible," in *NIB* 1:125–49.

2. See Tannehill, "Introduction: The Pronouncement Story and Its Types," *Semeia* 20 (1981) 1 (in present volume 19–20).

3. See Ronald F. Hock and Edward N. O'Neil, *The Chreia in Ancient Rhetoric*, vol. 1: *The Progymnasmata*, SBLTT 27 (Atlanta: Scholars, 1986) 83.

it often provides a brief setting, presenting the statement or action as a response in a particular situation. It is then equivalent to a pronouncement story. One of Theon's examples shows how concise a *chreia* can be: "Alexander the Macedonian king, on being asked by someone where he had his treasures, pointed to his friends and said: 'In these.'"[4] Most examples of pronouncement stories in the Gospels are significantly longer, yet retain the same basic structure. Furthermore, Theon required his students in their exercises to take a concise *chreia* and expand it.[5] Thus there is some flexibility in the length and amount of detail among them.

The pronouncement story is generally equivalent to Rudolf Bultmann's *apothegms* and overlaps to some extent with Martin Dibelius's *paradigms*.[6] The pronouncement story is very selective in what it presents; it is not to be confused with a full report of a dialogue. Where there are two parties in the scene, they are generally not given equal attention. The scene is rhetorically shaped so that the concluding response makes the chief impression, due to its climactic position, and often due to the forceful language used in the pronouncement. Thus the little scene serves to display the wit and wisdom of a particular person, whose pronouncement or significant action is presented for admiration and often for emulation. When these stories present persons and highlight values that represent the cultural heritage, they maintain cultural continuity. Yet pronouncement stories may also have a sharply critical edge, undermining confidence in accepted values and seeking to replace them.

The pronouncement stories in the Gospels often present two contrasting attitudes to a situation, one in the setting and the other in the response. As the brief scene unfolds, there is a sharp shift from one attitude to the other. The setting, by expressing one attitude, makes it available for challenge. The hearer or reader is invited to make the shift traced in the scene or, at least, to reaffirm a previous decision of this kind. It is easy for persons of a different time and culture to lose a sense of the challenge in many of these pronouncements, since we may not have an investment in or attraction to the position being challenged. Yet the reason for emphasizing the climactic pronouncement and contrasting it with an initial

---

4. Ibid., 91–93.
5. Ibid., 101–3.
6. See Rudolf Bultmann, *The History of the Synoptic Tradition*, rev. ed., trans. John Marsh (New York: Harper & Row, 1976) 11–69; and Martin Dibelius, *From Tradition to Gospel*, trans. Bertram Lee Woolf (New York: Scribner, 1934) 37–69.

attitude is best understood when we recognize that a significant shift in attitudes and values is being advocated.[7]

Pronouncements featured in these stories seem designed to be provocative and memorable rather than to present reasoned arguments for a position. Nevertheless, a response may include a rationale (a brief supporting reason, attached with "for" or "because"). Furthermore, there are some scenes, especially controversy scenes, in which arguments are developed. Burton Mack has studied an ancient school exercise called the "elaboration" of the *chreia* (a prescribed way of developing arguments in defense of a *chreia*), and he and Vernon Robbins have found traces of similar argumentative patterns within some Gospel pronouncement stories.[8]

Pronouncement stories are numerous in the synoptic Gospels, and they contribute much to the impression of Jesus and his message that we receive there. In spite of their brevity, many of these scenes have a dramatic quality, as Jesus interacts with other parties. The dramatic setting helps to make the climactic saying of Jesus impressive and forceful.

The nature of the dramatic interaction can be clarified by dividing pronouncement stories into subtypes. Below I present a typology of pronouncement stories based on the relation between their two essential parts, the setting and the response. Viewed from this perspective, there seem to be five subtypes of Gospel pronouncement stories.[9]

Correction Stories

In the dialogue between Peter and Jesus quoted above, Peter proposes that he might forgive up to seven times and Jesus corrects him by saying, "Not seven times, but . . . seventy-seven times" (Matt 18:21–22). In correction stories, the response corrects the views or conduct of another party. The response may be prompted by something observed, or it may be caused by a statement, request, or question. In the case of requests or questions, the response does not grant the request or answer the question but corrects

---

7. See Tannehill, "Attitudinal Shift in Synoptic Pronouncement Stories," in *Orientation by Disorientation*, ed. Richard A. Spencer, PittsTMS 26 (Pittsburgh: Pickwick, 1980) 183–97.

8. See Burton L. Mack and Vernon K. Robbins, *Patterns of Persuasion in the Gospels*, FF (Sonoma: Polebridge, 1989).

9 For further discussion and examples, see Tannehill, "Introduction: The Pronouncement Story and Its Types" and "Varieties of Synoptic Pronouncement Stories," *Semeia* 20 (1981) 1–13, 101–19; idem, "Types and Functions of Apophthegms in the Synoptic Gospels," in *Aufstieg und Niedergang der Römischen Welt*, II.25.2, ed. Wolfgang Haase (Berlin: de Gruyter, 1984) 1792–829. (These three articles are included in the present volume.)

an assumption on which the request or question was based, turning the encounter in a new direction. By word or action the person encountering Jesus has taken a position, and Jesus responds with a correction. Among the other correction stories in the synoptic Gospels are Matt 8:19–20 par. (the homeless Son of Man); 8:21–22 par. (let the dead bury the dead); Mark 9:33–37 par. (who is greatest?); 9:38–40 par. (the strange exorcist); 10:35–45 par. (request of James and John); 13:1–2 par. (the great temple buildings); Luke 9:61–62 (plowing and looking back); 11:27–28 (blessing of Jesus' mother); 14:7–11 (places at table); and 17:20–21 (God's reign among you).

There is always tension in a correction story. This tension does not appear until the corrective response, for the person who encounters Jesus is neither criticizing nor testing him, and the attitude expressed in the setting may seem quite acceptable. The corrective response introduces tension and opens up distance. The response challenges commonly accepted thought and invites change. These stories are useful where crucial decisions are being ignored and where there is a tendency to reduce the vision of Jesus to the ordinary.

Discussion of Gospel pronouncement stories has been strongly influenced by controversy dialogues (called "objection stories" below), in which Jesus responds to critics. The correction stories, however, are equally important, and they are addressed not primarily to critics but to Jesus' followers and other persons attracted to him.

Commendation Stories

Commendations are similar to corrections, except that Jesus responds by commending what he has seen or heard. Pure commendation stories are rare in the synoptic Gospels, but in Matthew, Peter's confession has been turned into a commendation story, for the emphasis now falls on Jesus' laudatory response to him (Matt 16:13–20).

As in the correction stories, there is often an element of tension in commendation stories. There may be a surprise in the commendation, for Jesus may praise someone or something commonly ignored or despised. The tension with another standard of judgment may be dramatized in the story by introducing a third character (who may be an individual or a group) whose words or actions express a contrasting view. The result is a "hybrid" story in which the response will probably have a double function: to commend one party and correct another, or to commend one party and respond to the objection of another. This feature of the stories expresses tension with other views in the social context. Thus there is an indication that these stories, too, attempt to cause or reinforce a shift of attitude on the part of hearers or readers. An example of a hybrid story is Mark 10:13–16—Jesus' blessing of the children—in which Jesus both corrects the disciples and commends the children by associating the reign of God with them. In this case Jesus' affirmation of the children is expressed both in words and in action. Other examples of hybrid correction-commendation stories are Mark 3:31–35 par. (Jesus' true family); 12:41–44 par. (the poor widow); and 14:3–9 par. (the woman who anoints Jesus). Hybrid objection-commendation stories are found in Matt 21:14–16 (the children's praise) and Luke 10:38–42 (Mary and Martha).

Many Gospel pronouncement stories indirectly praise Jesus, since they present his responses for admiration. Commendation stories show, however, that Jesus is not the only representative of positive values. The neglected and despised people praised by Jesus also represent positive values. Thus these people function as models for the hearer or reader.

Objection Stories

In a number of stories, Jesus must answer an objection. These stories frequently have three parts, moving from description of an action to an objection to that action, and then to the response. The first element, however, may appear only in the objection itself. In Mark 2:15–17 the three elements appear in sequence: the meal with tax collectors and sinners is described, the scribes object, and Jesus responds with sayings that first draw an analogy with a physician and then disclose the fundamental principle that guides his ministry.

The objection is often expressed as a demand for justification, using a question beginning with "Why?" In these stories, which are often called "controversy dialogues," tension is introduced not by Jesus (as in correction stories) but by the party expressing the objection. Here the tension focuses on Jesus, for he is being challenged. (This is true even if the disciples are addressed, for the teacher is responsible for his disciples.) The response may consist of a rhetorical question, an analogy, or a fundamental statement of principle.

Although disciples may sometimes object, as in Mark 8:31–33, many of the objections come from the scribes and Pharisees. The formation and transmission of these stories doubtless reflect the need of the early church to defend the distinctive practices and perspectives of the Jesus movement within its historical context. The apologetic needs of the church are probably reflected in a tendency to expand Jesus' response into a series of arguments. This does not mean that these stories function only to support the early church against outside critics. Followers of Jesus would seldom be as clear and deeply committed to a position as Jesus is in these stories. They continue to be a challenge to Jesus' followers to clarify and deepen their commitment.

Some additional objection stories in the synoptic Gospels are Mark 2:18–22 par. (question about fasting); 2:23–28 par. (plucking grain on the sabbath); 3:20–30 par. (the Beelzebul controversy); 7:1–15 par. (eating with defiled hands); and Luke 2:41–51 (the boy Jesus in the temple).

There is an overlap of objection stories with wonder stories (discussed below) in the sabbath healing stories. The objection-response sequence is primary when the story ends with Jesus' response to the objection, as in Luke 13:10–17 and 14:1–6. It may still be very important when the scene ends with the healing, as in the story of the man with a withered hand (Mark 3:1–6 par.), where the healing is part of Jesus' response to the implied objection of the opponents.

Quest Stories

These stories tend to be longer and more complex than most pronouncement stories and may include features of the other types. Jesus responds to an issue raised in the scene, but now this response is part of a story in which someone is in quest of something important for human well-being. This quest is sufficiently important that we are told its outcome. In other words, the scene does not end simply with Jesus' impressive response, as in many pronouncement stories. There is some resolution, positive or negative, to the other person's quest. As a result, the person coming to Jesus receives more attention in the narrative than in many pronouncement stories. In a sense it is this person's story, for the scene is shaped by his or her desire, expressed at the beginning, and ends when this desire succeeds or fails. Since we are asked to look at events in the light of this person's need and desire, sympathy for him or her is encouraged, although the social standing of the person may hinder this.

An obstacle, sometimes expressed as an objection or a difficult condition, may surface within the scene, and Jesus' response will be crucial at this point. The objections that may occur in quest stories make them similar to the objection stories just discussed, but here the objection functions as an obstacle within a quest. Several of these stories involve healing or exorcism and are similar to other wonder stories. If we simply group them with wonder stories, however, we will ignore their structural similarity with quest stories that lack healing or exorcism. An interesting example of a quest story that includes both an objection and an exorcism is the story of the Syrophoenician woman (Mark 7:24–30), who seeks the exorcism of an unclean spirit from her daughter. The exorcism itself is reported very briefly, however. The main emphasis is on the dialogue between the woman and Jesus. The story is unusual in that Jesus himself objects to the woman's quest and even more unusual because the woman is able to change the mind of Jesus, who normally is viewed as the final authority. The woman's daring rejoinder enables the quest to move to a successful conclusion. The prominent role she plays and the way in which the quest shapes the whole story show that this is something more than an objection story. It is a quest story.

The social status of the questers is a significant factor in quest stories. The one quester who fails is from high social rank (Mark 10:17–22 par.), while successful questers—like the Syrophoenician woman, the centurion (Matt 8:5–13 par.), the sinful woman in the Pharisee's house (Luke 7:36–50), the Samaritan leper (Luke 17:12–19), Zacchaeus (Luke 19:1–10), and the crucified criminal (Luke 23:39–43)—are aliens and outcasts. Thus these stories reverse social judgments and undermine prejudices; they both invite the outcasts and help to create openness for them in the community.

Inquiry Stories

These scenes move from a question or request for instruction to the answer. Questions may also be found in other types of pronouncement stories, but the inquiry story lacks the distinctive characteristics of the other types. The responder does not correct an assumption behind the question, as in a correction story, nor does the question express an objection, as in an objection story. There is a straightforward movement from question to answer, which means that attention tends to focus almost entirely on the content of the answer. Examples are Luke 11:1–4 (the Lord's Prayer); 13:22–30 (enter through the narrow door); and 17:5–6 (increase our faith). There is generally less dramatic tension in these scenes than in other pronouncement stories.

There is dramatic tension, however, in one subgroup, the testing inquiries, for in these scenes Jesus is being tested by a hostile or skeptical party. The tension focuses on Jesus, who is put in a difficult situation. Failure to give an impressive answer would result in loss of influence and might be dangerous in other ways. On the other hand, an impressive answer is all the more impressive in a situation of risk. Matthew 22:34–40 (the greatest commandment); Mark 11:27–33 par. (by what authority?); and 12:13–17 par. (paying taxes to Caesar) are examples of testing inquiries.

Parables

Parables are figurative language. They are imaginative narratives composed in order to illuminate a subject that lies beyond the literal subject matter of the story. Scholars commonly distinguish three subtypes: the similitude, the parable proper, and the example story.[10] We may speak of the first two as metaphorical narratives, for they refer indirectly to a sphere of meaning that is normally distinct from the literal content of the story, suggesting a connection between the two. The similitude (e.g., the mustard seed, Mark 4:30–32) is brief and focuses on an event that happens repeatedly, such as the growth of seed. Even so, it has the basic components of a narrative: events happening to one or more participants in a setting. The parable proper (e.g., the prodigal son, Luke 15:11–32) is a more fully developed story that narrates a unique and sometimes surprising sequence of events. It may have several scenes and tends to have a larger number of characters. The example story (e.g., the rich fool, Luke 12:16–21) is different in that the second level of meaning does not pertain to another sphere (as in metaphor) but to the sphere of meaning of which the story itself is a part. The example story still works as a trope; it suggests much more than its literal meaning. But the trope is not metaphor but synecdoche, in which the story is a part standing for a larger whole that must be imagined.

Metaphors often have bundles of associations and, therefore, are capable of complex development. Just as a poem may draw repeatedly from the image field suggested by a root metaphor, so also a parable may develop the image field of a metaphor through narrative. Thus linking a mustard seed metaphorically to the reign of God may lead to a narrative development from sowing to growth of the seed to the mature bush, all in some way suggestive of God's reign. In a similitude the brief narrative recalls what everyone would expect in the situation. The new element arises from the metaphorical transfer of meaning to a different sphere. In the parable proper the course of the narrative is not predictable at the beginning; indeed, some surprising things happen. Yet these stories make

---

10. In the Gospels the term for "parable" (παραβολή) is used more broadly, being applied even to short aphorisms. My discussion is confined to narratives.

use of stereotypical associations, which bring with them an initial set of expectations and identifications. Thus first-century hearers would expect that a king (Matt 18:23), a father (Luke 15:11), or a landowner (Matt 20:1) might represent God. This sort of identification need not be an allegorical misreading of the parable. Stereotypical associations establish a set of expectations that the parable can use. Hearers, having made the initial identifications, discover that the parable is using traditional associations to produce unexpected results. The parable can set the traditional associations in motion, in part by reinserting them into the human sphere from which they were drawn and using fresh human experience to reimagine how God as father or owner might act.

The parables inhabit a different narrative level from that of other stories being discussed in this essay. The narrator is Jesus, a participant in the events of the larger narrative. Thus we are dealing with embedded narrative, an act of narration that occurs within the narrative world being constructed by the Gospel narrator. Techniques of narrative analysis are useful at both levels.

Narrative analysis is especially helpful in interpreting parables that are more complex. It is useful to ask whether the parable builds up to a climax at which a decisive event or crucial decision takes place. Then the prior narrative will prepare for this climax, and anything that follows will clarify its results. If the parable story can be understood according to this or some other pattern, it can be apprehended as a whole, and the function of each part within the whole becomes clear. This approach guards against the tendency to isolate an element of the story in order to derive some special meaning from it. Interpretation must concentrate on the climax of the story, to which the rest of the story contributes, if it is to do justice to the parable as a whole. Thus an interpretation of the parable of the vineyard workers (Matt 20:1–16) as primarily a call to missionary work in God's vineyard would be inadequate because it ignores the climax of the parable, which focuses on the unusual way in which the wages were paid.

The parable of the vineyard workers also exemplifies a common narrative technique: the narration of a series of events in parallel form, with a difference that will prove to be significant. The parallelism makes the difference stand out so that its significance can be considered. In the case of the vineyard workers, we have parallel accounts of hiring workers. Those hired at midday fade out of the story at the time of payment so that the story can concentrate on those showing the greatest difference, the workers hired at the beginning of the day and those hired one hour before the end. The parables avoid unnecessary descriptive detail. This encourages the comparison of persons who are essentially alike except for one characteristic, which is thereby isolated for consideration.

Through construction of such contrasts, the narrator controls the issues that are brought to the hearer's attention. In a story of a man with two sons, we may guess at the beginning that the two sons will differ in some way that will be important to the story. Such is the case in the parable of the prodigal son (Luke 15:11–32), but this parable also presents two contrasting responses to the younger brother's homecoming. Here the contrast is between the father and the older brother, who remain in conflict at the end of the story. The development of two major contrasts adds to the complexity of this parable.

There are other ways in which the narrator guides the hearer's focus of attention. For instance, a moment of crucial decision may be emphasized by reporting a person's deliberation as internal speech (see Luke 16:3–4 in the parable of the dishonest steward). Here the progress of the narrative has slowed in order to give detailed attention to this moment. In other cases expansion of direct discourse between two parties may highlight a central issue. In the parable of the talents the expanded dialogue between the third servant and the master is where the main issue is clarified and resolved (see Matt 25:24–30).

The parables are attractive and interesting as stories, which serves their goal of persuasion. Some parables explicitly ask for a verdict from the hearer, as in the ones that begin "Which one of you . . . ?" (e.g., the lost sheep, Luke 15:4–7). In other cases Jesus is depicted as rendering a verdict himself (e.g., the parable of the Pharisee and the tax collector; see Luke 18:14). Some parables are open-ended because there is an unresolved conflict at the end (e.g., the prodigal son, Luke 15:11–32). Nevertheless, the story makes clear where the narrator's sympathies lie. The parables may be even-handed in allowing conflicting perspectives expression within the story. This does not mean, however, that these views are given equal value. The workers who labor all day in the sun express their objection strongly, but the owner of the vineyard has the last word (Matt 20:11–15).

Although in the Gospel of John parables are not characteristic of Jesus' teaching, as they are in the synoptic Gospels, John does contain some related forms. We find, for instance, the short simile of the grain of wheat that dies but is fruitful (John 12:24). In John 10:1–5, Jesus speaks figuratively of the shepherd, the sheepfold, and sheep. This is called a *paroimia* (παροιμία), a "figure of speech" (10:6). It describes customary activities, like the synoptic similes, yet a greater variety of details appears. The figurative language is then interpreted, and Jesus specifically identifies himself with the gate of the sheepfold and the shepherd (10:7–18). This section of John is rather similar to the parable of the sower (Mark 4:3–8, 14–20) in its movement from figurative language to allegorical interpretation.

Wonder Stories

Although these scenes are usually called miracle stories, the term *miracle* is best avoided because it means to many an act of God that violates the laws of nature. Nature itself was understood differently by those who told the Gospel wonder stories, for it was widely assumed at that time that the physical world was open to the operation of divine and demonic powers. Nevertheless, there was a strong sense, then as now, of the difference between the usual and the wonderful. The indications of amazement at the end of many of these stories attest to that difference. The wonder stories tell of occasions when God's power surprises people whose expectations are limited to normal human experience. In the Gospels the wonder is almost always a gracious act of help from God, although wonders of punishment are also possible (see Mark 11:12–14, 20–21; Acts 5:1–11). Thus the wonder stories attest to the belief that, unusual as it may be, God's grace is available even for bodily needs and dangers.

In the synoptic Gospels these wonders are sometimes called *dynameis* (δυνάμεις), literally "powers"—i.e., manifestations of divine power or "mighty acts" (cf. Matt 11:20–23; Mark 6:2, 5). The Fourth Gospel prefers to speak of Jesus' "signs" (*sēmeia*, σημεῖα; see John 2:11 and 12:37).

In the early Gospel tradition, Jesus' wonders were an integral part of the outburst of hope for overcoming evil associated with the coming of God's reign. Jesus' healing ministry is summarized in words that recall scriptural prophecies of salvation (Matt 11:5 par.; compare Isa 35:5–6; 61:1), and the continuation of that ministry through the disciples is associated with the approach of God's reign (Luke 10:9). Jesus' exorcisms, especially, reveal the conquest of evil power through the appearance of God's reign (Matt 12:28–29 par.).

Most Gospel wonder stories can be divided into six types (although some of the stories have affinities with more than one type).[11] Discussion

---

11. This typology is my adaptation of Gerd Theissen, *The Miracle Stories of the Early Christian Tradition*, trans. Francis McDonagh (Philadelphia: Fortress, 1983) 85–112.

of these six types will help us to recognize common patterns and themes, although the point of emphasis will vary among stories of the same type.

Exorcism Stories

In this type of wonder story, Jesus encounters a person possessed by a demon and forces the demon to leave, enabling the person to return to a normal life. The demon is evil, but the possessed person is not, for the demon is an alien force that can be expelled. When the exorcism takes place, the story focuses on the interaction between Jesus and the demon (or unclean spirit). It is the demon who speaks with Jesus; the possessed person is so controlled by the demon as to be incapable of independent thought or action. Jesus addresses the demon directly and powerfully, forcing it to submit and depart.

The exorcism in the Capernaum synagogue (Mark 1:21–28 par.) presents such an encounter in brief form. The exorcism of the Gerasene demoniac (Mark 5:1–20 par.) and of the possessed boy (Mark 9:14–29 par.) are more complex examples of this type. In the former, Jesus' interaction with the demons goes through several steps. There is also considerable interest in depicting the original condition of the possessed man and the change that takes place in him. In the latter story, the father of the boy assumes a major role, especially in the Markan version. The father requests help, and his faith is important; both features draw this story close to healing stories, which will be discussed next. However, the workings of the evil spirit and Jesus' command for it to depart are also vividly depicted. Perhaps we should speak of the story of the possessed boy as a mixed form. It is distinctly different from the story of the Syrophoenician woman (Mark 7:24–30 par.), where, even though the woman's daughter is possessed by an unclean spirit, no attention is given to Jesus' confrontation with the spirit. Therefore, the Syrophoenician woman's story should not be included among the exorcisms.

Healing Stories

In this type of wonder story, Jesus responds to the bodily need of another person, and the principal interaction is between Jesus as healer and the person in need (in some cases also the representative of this person, such as a mother or father). Normally the healing story presents an encounter with Jesus, together with indications of the type of illness or disability a person suffers (sometimes with emphasis on its severity), then reports the healing itself. This is often followed by an action demonstrating that the healing has taken place or a response of amazement or praise from witnesses. Frequently the action begins when persons address Jesus with a request for healing, either for themselves (blind Bartimaeus, Mark 10:46–52 par.) or for another (Jairus's daughter, Mark 5:21–24, 35–43 par.). In some episodes, however, Jesus takes the initiative. This is the case in two of the four Johannine healing stories (John 5:2–9; 9:1–7). Also in the raising of the widow's son (Luke 7:11–17) there is no request for Jesus' help; rather, Jesus' action is due to his compassion (7:13). The healing stories are the largest group of wonder stories in the Gospels.

In the story of the hemorrhaging woman (Mark 5:25–34), the cure takes place relatively early in the scene (v. 29). This is a sign that a physical cure is not the sole concern. The story continues for five more verses as Jesus searches for the woman and the woman reveals herself with fear and trembling. How will Jesus respond to an unclean woman who has violated purity laws by touching him? The healing (which responds to her social isolation as well as to her physical need) is not complete unless she is free of social condemnation for violating religious taboos.

Jesus does not condemn her but commends her for her faith (Mark 5:34). Faith is an important theme in the healing stories. Sometimes Jesus asks for faith from those who come for healing (Matt 9:28–29; Mark 5:36 par.; John 4:48–50). Most striking are the cases in which Jesus commends someone's faith. These people become models of the faith that others should show in similar situations. Such people persist in reaching out to Jesus for help when blocked by the crowd or separated by a social barrier (e.g., the hemorrhaging woman; blind Bartimaeus, who is at first rebuked by the crowd, Mark 10:46–52 par.). The same kinds of people demonstrate faith in quest stories involving healing (e.g., the centurion, Matt 8:5–13 par.; the Canaanite woman, Matt 15:21–28; the Samaritan leper, Luke 17:12–19). These stories, however, differ from healing wonders in that the questing persons raise problems other than their physical afflictions that Jesus must resolve with an authoritative pronouncement. Faith is presented in these healing and quest stories as resolute action that, in spite of society and its taboos, reaches out to Jesus as the source of help. It is the opposite of resigned acceptance of suffering.[12]

Healing stories, as well as other types of wonders, may take on symbolic meaning. This is especially characteristic of the Gospel of John (note that John 9 begins with the healing of a blind man and ends with climac-

---

12. A point emphasized by Antoinette Clark Wire, "The Structure of the Gospel Miracle Stories and Their Tellers," *Semeia* 11 (1978) 106–8 [83–113].

tic statements about spiritual sight and blindness), but it is also true of some scenes in the other Gospels. For instance, it is significant that healings of a deaf man and a blind man surround Jesus' harsh words about the disciples' deafness and blindness in Mark (see 7:31–37; 8:18, 22–26).

Provision Stories

Some wonder stories can be called provision stories because Jesus provides food or drink for a crowd in a surprising way. In the Gospels we find not only stories of Jesus feeding crowds in the wilderness (Mark 6:34–44 par.; 8:1–10 par.), but also stories of Jesus providing wine for a wedding (John 2:1–11) and great catches of fish (Luke 5:4–7; John 21:1–14). The great catches of fish in Luke and John are elements within commissioning stories focusing on Simon Peter. The provision stories tend to attract symbolic significance. Thus the feeding stories recall the feeding of Israel with manna in the wilderness and suggest the formation of a new people under God's care. When the great catch of fish in Luke 5:4–7 is followed by Jesus' call to share his work of "catching people," the catch of fish becomes a symbolic promise of success in the future mission. The imagery of wedding and abundant wine in John 2:1–11 suggests the new time of fulfillment that is replacing the old order.

There are three provision stories in John (2:1–11; 6:1–15; 21:1–14) but only four healing stories and no exorcisms.

Controversy Wonders

Stories of this type are actually a mixed form, for they follow the pattern of pronouncement stories involving controversy (called "objection stories" above) as well as wonder stories. The emphasis may not fall on the wonder. In two sabbath healing stories special to Luke (the bent woman, 13:10–17; the man with dropsy, 14:1–6), Jesus' principal pronouncement follows the healing, taking climactic position. In the case of the bent woman, the cure takes place early in the scene and is the cause of the controversy, a subordinate position. I would classify these two stories as objection stories, not wonder stories. Even in the stories of the paralyzed man (Mark 2:1–12 par.) and the man with the withered hand (Mark 3:1–6 par.), which do end with a healing, Jesus' interaction with his critics is very important, and the point being scored has more to do with Jesus' authority and insight into God's will than with his power to heal. In these two stories the wonder is significant not only for the person healed and as a disclosure of the power of the healer but also because it speaks to the issue of controversy. The healing is itself part of Jesus' answer to his opponents.

Classification of literary types is not an end in itself. It is a means of calling attention to various patterns in stories so that we can understand each story better. When a story does not fit easily into a single category, it is useful to compare it to several types, for this may show that several important developments are taking place at the same time.

The story of the paralyzed man is a case in point. It has features of healing stories, quest stories, and objection stories. The ending is typical of a healing story, but this story is more complex than most healings. The striking action of digging through the roof shows a determination that makes the paralyzed man's party stand out as remarkable people, giving them the importance typical of quest stories, and the controversy over forgiveness functions like the obstacle that appears in other quest stories. But the controversy with the scribes is also like objection stories, and the proclamation that "the Son of Man has authority on earth to forgive sins" (Mark 2:10 NRSV) is clearly a central feature of this scene. Thus this scene is both the story of a successful quest, which involves healing, and a revelation of Jesus' authority within a controversy wonder. The tension of desire in the quest and the tension of challenge in the objection are resolved at the same point, for Jesus' answer to the objection requires both words and healing action (2:9–12). Classification of the story is less important than recognizing both of these developments.

In John 5 and 9 also, Jesus' healings are connected with controversy, but John develops the controversies not within the healing scene but through lengthy dialogue and monologue following it.

Rescue Wonders

These relate how someone in danger (especially from a storm at sea or imprisonment) is rescued through altering natural forces or physical objects, such as the wind, chains, or prison doors (see Acts 12:1–11). Probably the stilling of the storm in Mark 4:35–41 par. belongs in this category, although Jesus addresses the sea as if he were exorcising a demon, and the concluding question ("Who then is this?") suggests that the scene is also an epiphany. Rescue wonders encourage the belief that God's power can intervene in situations of danger.

Epiphany Wonders

These are stories in which the wonder primarily demonstrates Jesus' divine power and authority. This can be an aspect of the other wonder stories, but I will reserve this term for stories in which epiphany is the primary concern, for exorcism, healing, provision, controversy, and rescue are absent or secondary. The transfiguration story is a clear example (Mark 9:2–8 par.). We should probably also include Jesus' walking on the water, for the rescue of the disciples from the wind is secondary to the revelation concerning Jesus, at least in Mark 6:45–52 and John 6:16–21.

We should not assume that each type of wonder story has a single function. Even brief stories are often more complex than that, and their functions may shift with social setting. Perhaps we may say, however, that the wonder stories were told to elicit the praise of God and wonder at Jesus' power often depicted at their end. Through presenting Jesus as the mediator of God's saving power, these stories could both call new people to trust Jesus as healer and rescuer and reinforce such faith within the church. In particular, these stories encourage belief that God's saving power extends to those who are suffering physically and those who are socially excluded because of demonic possession and uncleanness. These stories call people out of resigned acceptance of their physical and social limits by providing examples of liberation from evil powers and models of daring faith—a faith that goes beyond expected behavior in order to reach out to the power that saves.

Promise and Commission Epiphanies

In addition to the wonder stories of Jesus' earthly ministry, there are stories that report the surprising appearance of God or a messenger of God (in the Gospels, an angel or the risen Christ) who brings a message containing a promise or a commission (or both). The promise and commission will refer to events beyond the scene itself. The best examples in the Gospels are the annunciation scenes in the birth narratives and some of the resurrection appearances.

Benjamin Hubbard has called attention to a series of "commissioning stories" in the Hebrew Bible and the New Testament.[13] In discussing some of the same stories, I have chosen a longer title in order (a) to limit

---

13. Benjamin J. Hubbard, *The Matthean Redaction of a Primitive Apostolic Commissioning: An Exegesis of Matthew 28:16–20*, SBLDS 19 (Missoula: Scholars, 1974); idem, "Commissioning Stories in Luke–Acts: A Study of Their Antecedents, Form and Content," *Semeia* 8 (1977) 103–26.

consideration to stories that report an epiphany and (b) to call attention to the fact that the message may contain a promise as well as authorization and instruction to do something (a commission). Thus in the Lord's appearance to Isaac in Gen 26:23–25 (a brief example of the form) the message consists entirely of reassurance and promise. The message for the future concerns what God will do rather than commanding Isaac to do something. In some cases the message announces the future birth of a child. Raymond Brown has called attention to the precedents in the Hebrew Bible for the Gospel annunciations of birth.[14] These scenes are a subtype of the promise and commission epiphanies.

Hubbard has analyzed the commissioning stories into seven components: the *introduction,* which sets the scene; the *confrontation* (God or God's messenger appears); the *reaction,* in which the person addressed responds, often expressing fear or unworthiness; the *commission* (the core of the message, which, as I explained above, may emphasize the divine promise as much as or more than the human task); the *protest* (the person addressed may claim that the promise or commission is impossible); the *reassurance,* which may occur after the reaction of fear, the commission, or the protest; and the *conclusion,* which rounds off the scene.[15] Not all components are found in every example. The appearance of God's messenger and the message delivered are the essential elements.

The annunciations of birth in Luke 1:5–38 are examples of the full form. Following the introductions, we are told of the confrontation with the angel (vv. 11, 28), Zechariah's and Mary's disturbed reactions (vv. 12, 29), the angel's reassurance ("Do not be afraid," vv. 13, 30), the promise and commissioning (vv. 13–17, 31–33), and the protest (vv. 18, 34), followed by reassurance (or reinforcement) through additional signs of divine power (vv. 19–20, 35–37). The annunciation in Matt 1:18–25 lacks a reaction and protest from Joseph, but the situation and content of the message closely resemble other examples of the birth announcement subtype.[16]

Many of the Gospel resurrection scenes follow a similar format. In Mark's depiction of the empty tomb (16:1–8), the story moves from introduction (vv. 1–4) to confrontation with the messenger (v. 5); reaction ("They were alarmed," v. 5); reassurance ("Do not be alarmed," v. 6); mes-

---

14. Raymond S. Brown, *The Birth of the Messiah* (Garden City, N.Y.: Doubleday, 1979) 156–59.

15. Hubbard, "Commissioning Stories," 104–5.

16. See Brown, *Birth,* 156.

sage, including commission and promise (vv. 6–7); and conclusion (v. 8). Matthew's version of this scene is followed by an encounter with Jesus in which the sequence of confrontation, reaction, reassurance, commission, and promise is quickly repeated (Matt 28:9–10). The final scene in Matthew (28:16–20) concentrates on Jesus' speech, but the following elements are still clear: introduction, confrontation ("When they saw him," v. 17), reaction (v. 17), reassurance (v. 18),[17] commission, and promise (vv. 19–20).

Not only Matthew but also Luke and John contain appearances of the risen Jesus to groups of disciples, and these scenes follow the same basic pattern. In Luke 24:33–49 the reassurance following the disciples' fear is greatly expanded, so that we have these divisions: confrontation (v. 36), reaction of fear (v. 37), reassurance (vv. 38–43), commission and promise (vv. 46–49). In John 20:19–23 the confrontation is described at the end of v. 19. The repeated "Peace be with you" probably functions as reassurance, not just greeting, and Jesus' showing of his hands and side has a similar function. The reaction of the disciples is joyous, not fearful, in this scene. The scene ends with the commission (vv. 21b–23).[18]

These stories present the holy God and the risen Christ as the source of the promise and mission that guide the church. They also seek to suggest the awesomeness of human encounters with this transcendent source. Borrowing the Hebrew Bible's pattern of epiphany scenes serves to support this sense of awe. The focus of the scenes is on the message of promise and commission that is delivered.

Longer Narrative Sequences

Despite the episodic quality of much of the Gospel material, there are portions of the Gospels in which we find clear plot developments through a series of interrelated scenes. These narratives are significantly longer than the small units we have discussed to this point and represent an intermediate level between the short episode and a complete Gospel narrative. As examples I will briefly discuss the Markan passion narrative, the Lukan birth narrative, and the Samaritan narrative in John.

---

17. Also in Luke 1:19 the speaker emphasizes his authority in order to reassure someone who is doubtful.

18. Neyrey understands John 20:24–29 as the protest and reassurance that commonly follow a commission. These are presented, however, as a separate scene. See Jerome H. Neyrey, *The Resurrection Stories*, ZSNT (Wilmington, Del.: Glazier, 1988) 27, 76–78.

Although some parts of Mark 14–15 might be told as separate stories, the significance of each scene is enhanced by its place within the larger narrative, and there are a number of indications of careful literary construction binding the sections of these chapters together.

There are at least two complementary approaches to the literary study of the Markan passion narrative (Mark 14–15). First, one may seek to understand this story as a representative of a story genre with a relatively fixed plot and set of characters. Thus one can discuss the Markan passion narrative as a variation on Jewish stories of the persecuted righteous one or of the wise person who is the object of a conspiracy but is vindicated.[19] This approach may help us to sense some of the echoes of familiar stories of the endangered Joseph, Esther, Daniel, etc., that first-century readers might have heard in the passion account and also help us to understand some of the significant points of difference from the common pattern. Second, one may study the literary composition of the Markan narrative itself, seeking to understand its plot lines, characterization, and rhetoric. I will briefly discuss the Markan passion narrative from the second perspective.

The Gospel of Mark, like other narratives, can be studied in the light of its overall plot. Such study would show that the passion narrative is the climax of Mark because each of three important plot lines is brought to a dramatic point of decision, as three continuing participants interact with one another.[20] I am referring to the plot lines centering on (1) Jesus, who has received a commission from God and must fulfill that commission; (2) the disciples, who have received a commission from Jesus and should fulfill that commission; and (3) Jesus' opponents, who want to destroy him. From one perspective, the passion story is a narrative of how Jesus' opponents succeed in carrying out their desire to shame and kill him. From another perspective, it is a narrative of Jesus fulfilling his commission from God, which since 8:31 is known to include rejection and death. From a third perspective, it is a narrative of the disciples who have been called to follow Jesus, which means taking up their own crosses and losing their lives (8:34–35), but who instead desert Jesus in order to save their lives. Each of these plot lines is prepared in Mark 1–13, and

---

19. See George W. E. Nickelsburg, "The Genre and Function of the Markan Passion Narrative," *HTR* 73 (1980) 153–84, for comparisons of Mark's passion narrative to Jewish literature; see also Burton L. Mack, *A Myth of Innocence: Mark and Christian Origins* (Philadelphia: Fortress, 1988) 249–69.

20. See Tannehill, "The Gospel of Mark as Narrative Christology," *Semeia* 16 (1979) 60–62, 76–77 (in the present volume 163–65, 177).

each is carefully developed in the passion story, resulting in significant characterization of all three parties.

The narrative's rhetorical shape begins to appear when we note the techniques used to highlight certain events so that they will make a strong impression on readers. Jesus predicts his betrayal by Judas (Mark 14:18–21), the flight of the disciples (14:27), and Peter's denial (14:30), thus calling readers' attention to these events before they happen. This is part of a strong emphasis on the disciples' failure in the passion story. The narrative also reinforces Jesus' experience of rejection by repeated mocking scenes (14:65; 15:16–20, 29–32), placed after each of the main events following Jesus' arrest (the Sanhedrin trial, the Pilate trial, and the crucifixion). These mocking scenes are also important because they contain ironic testimony to Jesus' true status. The narrative also contrasts Jesus' bold confession, which leads to his death, and Peter's denial by inserting Jesus' interrogation by the Sanhedrin into the story of Peter's denial (14:53–72).

Furthermore, dramatic moments are used for significant disclosures about Jesus. The Sanhedrin trial builds to a climax with the high priest's direct question about Jesus as Messiah. In this setting of official interrogation, Jesus publicly reveals the messianic secret, even though it costs him his life (Mark 14:61–62). At an equally dramatic moment, Jesus, approaching death, cries out, "My God, why have you forsaken me?" (15:34). This cry epitomizes the meaning of the passion events for Jesus. He has been rejected by the leaders of Israel and deserted by his own disciples. Rejection by humans raises sharply the question of divine abandonment, since with his death Jesus' mission comes to nothing. This cry, of course, also seeks an answer from God, which comes not as rescue from death but as resurrection.

The Lukan birth narrative (Luke 1:5–2:40) also shows signs of careful literary construction. We find, for instance, balanced scenes and motifs used in connection with John the Baptist, on the one hand, and Jesus, on the other. (Note especially the parallels between the two annunciation scenes in 1:5–25 and 26–38.) The angelic announcements in these scenes share connecting themes with the prophetic hymns that follow (1:46–55, 68–79; 2:29–32; see also 2:10–14). These announcements and hymns gradually disclose the Lukan understanding of the purpose of God to be realized through John and Jesus, providing a basis for interpreting the rest of the Gospel narrative. Full understanding comes only through considering these revelatory scenes together. They come to a climax with the presentation of Jesus in the Temple, where Simeon's oracle (2:29–32) announces God's salvation in its full scope (encompassing both Israel and the Gentiles), and where his warning to Mary (2:34–35) provides the first indication of the resistance that Jesus must face.

The Lukan birth narrative, especially through the angelic announcements and prophetic hymns, interprets the future work of John and Jesus in the context of the divine purpose, providing a preview of the later narrative and a basis for understanding its importance. Other peoples will share in the salvation, but the birth narrative emphasizes the fulfillment of promises of salvation for Israel. Because of this emphasis, the rest of the narrative is not a simple story of success, for the expectations aroused at the beginning are not fully realized. Much of Israel, in fact, rejects salvation through Jesus, creating tension between the hopes and expectations aroused at the beginning and the actual course of the narrative. This twist in the plot has a tragic effect.[21]

The Samaritan narrative in John 4:1–42 is a unified dramatic dialogue in which persons other than Jesus have important roles and in which each section contributes to a significant development, leading to a conclusion. Thus it is useful to analyze the statements of participants as actions within a plot and as disclosures of character. Setting is also important, for the location in Samaria is appropriate to the dialogue, and Jacob's well provides the initial topic (water) for the conversation.

To be sure, this narrative, like other sections of John, contains some shifts that, at first, are puzzling. Part of the time Jesus is talking with the Samaritan woman; part of the time with his disciples. The conversation begins with the subject of water (4:7–15), then shifts to the woman's husbands (4:16–18), to worship (4:20–24), to food (4:31–34), and to the harvest (4:35–38). Yet each part contributes to the forward movement of the narrative. To some extent the woman and the disciples balance each other as Jesus' conversation partners. While one occupies the foreground, the other is in the background. Nevertheless, we are made aware of the absent party's activity. The woman struggles to understand the water that Jesus offers; the disciples struggle to understand the food that Jesus is eating. All are led through a revelatory process that begins with ironic misunderstanding. The woman comes to recognize who Jesus is, and Jesus teaches the disciples about his mission and their place within it. This teaching includes helping the disciples to understand and accept Jesus'

---

21. See Tannehill, *The Narrative Unity of Luke–Acts: A Literary Interpretation*, vol. 1: *The Gospel according to Luke*, FF (Philadelphia: Fortress, 1986) 15–44; and idem, "Israel in Luke–Acts: A Tragic Story," in Tannehill, *The Shape of Luke's Story: Essays on Luke–Acts* (Eugene, Ore.: Cascade, 2005)105–24 (orig. pub. 1985).

mission among the Samaritans, for the brief discourse about the harvest (4:35–38) is a commentary on Jesus' encounter with the Samaritan woman and the people of her town.

On the one hand, the narrative portrays a revelatory process in which Jesus carries out the mission to which he refers in 4:34 and discloses to the disciples their role in it. On the other hand, the narrative portrays the Samaritan's coming to faith, with each stage of dialogue and movement making its contribution. The Samaritan woman not only comes to faith (her progress indicated by her reactions to Jesus) but also becomes Jesus' witness, the founding missionary for her community. Through the indirect language of symbolism and irony, and through the text's narrative form, we are invited to participate in a "revelatory dynamic." It is the text as narrative that presents revelation as dynamic process. Thus the narrative form of the text is not an accidental feature that can be ignored.[22]

Even when the Samaritans come to Jesus, the narrative of this process is not quite ended. The narrative quickly draws a distinction between secondhand faith, based on the woman's testimony, and firsthand faith, based on encounter with Jesus himself. Then the narrative sequence closes with a confession of faith suitable to the missionary breakthrough that it presents.

The Gospels as Narratives

Form criticism is accustomed to study a small unit of tradition apart from its Gospel context, and the liturgical reading of the Gospels also conditions us to focus on isolated units within the Gospels. Yet these small narrative units are found within a larger narrative frame, consisting of the Gospel itself. Compared to modern narrative, the synoptic Gospels seem very episodic, consisting, in part, of short scenes placed in a sequence with few connecting threads of plot. Nevertheless, attentive reading of a Gospel as a unitary narrative can help us to understand the functions of the parts within the whole.

In studying the Gospels as wholes, it is also appropriate to ask whether they belong to a larger literary genre. Much of the material within the Gospels conforms to generic types. Is this true also of the Gospels themselves? Until recently it was the conviction of many scholars that the Gospels are a unique kind of literature. In part this was due to the belief that they, as "popular" writings, could not be compared with contem-

---

22. See Gail R. O'Day, *Revelation in the Fourth Gospel: Narrative Mode and Theological Claim* (Philadelphia: Fortress, 1986) 89–96; see also 49–89.

porary Greco-Roman literature. This belief has been waning, and now a number of scholars argue that the Gospels belong within the genre of ancient biography.[23]

The Gospels share with ancient biography some general similarities of content, form, and function. In content, they focus on the life of one person, especially that person's public career. In form, they fit, to various degrees, the pattern of ancient biographies that frame a person's public career with narratives of origin and youth, at the beginning, and death, at the end. In between, biographical presentation could be chronological, but not necessarily so. The subject's words and deeds were used to illustrate character, and various short genres, such as the pronouncement story, were incorporated into the biography for this purpose. In function, many ancient biographies were concerned with praising their subject as an exemplar of the virtues to be honored and emulated in the community. The Gospels have a similar function for the Christian community, while serving other functions as well.

The genre of the Gospels continues to be a subject of debate. Adela Yarbro Collins, for instance, denies that Mark is a biography. Although it may be concerned with the identity of Jesus and presents him as a model, these are not its main purposes. Basically, it records events that changed the world—eschatological events. Thus she classifies it as apocalyptic history.[24]

Luke, too, might be regarded as history, for it is part of a two-volume work that includes Acts. This could make some difference in our understanding of Luke, for biography presents a person's deeds and words as illustrations of character, while history is interested in a person's achievements in so far as they had consequences for society. Yet "during the late Hellenistic period history and biography moved closer together with the increasing emphasis on character in historiography. Biography and history became more and more difficult to distinguish."[25] The fact that one genre can be embedded in another might also suggest that Luke can be regarded as a biography even if Acts, and Luke–Acts as a whole, is placed in another category.

---

23. See, e.g., David E. Aune, *The New Testament in Its Literary Environment*, LEC (Philadelphia: Westminster, 1987) 17–67. The following paragraph is based on Aune's work.

24. Adela Yarbro Collins, *The Beginning of the Gospel: Probings of Mark in Context* (1992; reprinted, Eugene, Ore.: Wipf & Stock, 2001) 1–38.

25. Aune, *The New Testament*, 30.

Narrative criticism of the Gospels frequently distinguishes between a Gospel as story (the basic events and characters that provide the content of a narrative) and as discourse (the particular perspective from which this story is told and the rhetorical means of expressing that perspective). As Seymour Chatman writes, "The story is the *what* in a narrative . . . discourse the *how*."[26] This distinction calls attention to a narrative's discourse. We are encouraged to recognize that a narrative is always being told from some perspective and that particular techniques are being used to shape it to that perspective. In other words, the distinction encourages us to consider a narrative's rhetoric.

Studying how a story is told calls attention to the voice telling the story, the voice of the narrator. The Gospel narrators seldom speak in the first person, choosing to efface themselves in order to focus attention on their story. Yet the narrator of a Gospel is the voice through which a particular set of interests, norms, and values is presented.

The interpretive role of the narrator is most obvious when the narrator provides explanations in narrative "asides" and gives "inside views" of the characters. The narrator assumes the privilege of interpreting the inner working of human hearts and making judgments about them, as when the narrator of Mark, following the disciples' encounter with Jesus walking on the sea, states that the disciples' "hearts were hardened" (6:52). An interpretive perspective shapes the narrative in many other ways. Someone has decided which character is most important, deserving to be put in the center of the narrative. Furthermore, certain characters are presented as trustworthy and insightful. They are "reliable characters" in the sense that they become spokespersons for the perspective that is being expressed by the writing as a whole. In the Gospels, of course, Jesus is not only given central importance but also functions as the most reliable character. The underlying perspective of the narrative need not be fully and directly expressed by the narrator because it can be conveyed through Jesus' words and actions. Jesus can provide commentary on the narrative, including norms for judging persons and events, through his parables, for instance.[27]

26. Seymour Chatman, *Story and Discourse: Narrative Structure in Fiction and Film* (Ithaca, N.Y.: Cornell University Press, 1978) 19.

27. See Mary Ann Tolbert, *Sowing the Gospel: Mark's World in Literary-Historical Perspective* (Minneapolis: Fortress, 1989) 148–59, 233–39. Tolbert has studied the implications of the parable of the sower (Mark 4:3–9, 14–20) and the parable of the wicked tenants (Mark 12:1–12) when understood as commentary on Mark's narrative as a whole.

The small narrative units discussed above are placed in a sequence in the Gospels. As a result, one scene influences our understanding of another. One factor in this process is the "primacy effect," which suggests that material placed early in the narrative takes on special importance.[28] We need to orient ourselves at the beginning of a narrative. The perspective established there will continue to influence our understanding of characters until we are told something that indicates a change in them or requires us to change our opinion of them. This observation should help us to recognize the importance of the promise and commission epiphanies (annunciation scenes) in the birth narratives of Matthew and Luke. They serve to connect Jesus to the purpose of God, provide initial statements of that purpose, and disclose the commission from God that Jesus must fulfill. The narrative that follows is to be interpreted in the light of these initial disclosures. We are guided in interpreting Jesus' ministry not only by the birth narratives in Matthew and Luke but also by such key scenes as Jesus' announcement in the Nazareth synagogue (Luke 4:16–19). We should expect complications to develop, for the beginning of a narrative will not disclose everything. In the Gospels, Jesus encounters hardened hearts and deaf ears, not only in other religious leaders but also in his own disciples. Such conflict adds suspense to the narrative and raises the question of how Jesus' commission can still be fulfilled. The conflict leads to a crisis in the passion story. In this and other ways individual units of tradition become part of a developing plot that moves through conflict to a crisis and its results.

Thus the order of events in a Gospel is important. A Gospel's narrative rhetoric, however, also appears in variations of frequency and duration.[29] Repetition (an increase in frequency) and extended duration (a slowing of narration to give greater attention to a scene) indicate emphasis. When an event is emphasized in these ways, we must seek to understand how it is being understood and why it is important. Some types of repetition provide stability to the story by contributing, for instance, to characterization. If a person does something once, we may take note but reserve conclusions about the person. If the person does it twice or more, we conclude that it is characteristic of this person. Thus we are told twice that the disciples have failed to understand about the loaves (Mark

28. On the primacy effect, see Menakhem Perry, "Literary Dynamics: How the Order of a Text Creates Its Meanings," *Poetics Today* 1 (1979) 53–58 [35–61; 311–61].

29. Gérard Genette discusses narrative time in terms of order, duration, and frequency. See his *Narrative Discourse: An Essay in Method*, trans. Jane E. Lewin (Ithaca, N.Y.: Cornell University Press, 1980) 33–160.

6:52; 8:17–21) in boat scenes following the two feedings of multitudes. This repetition suggests that the problem is not minor and temporary but arises from the basic character of the disciples.

The narrator may repeat the same type of event, as in the example above, or may repeatedly refer to a single event. We may be told about an event in advance (a preview), told about it as it happens, and then be reminded of it later (a review). In Luke, Jesus begins to announce his coming rejection and death in 9:22. The repeated previews lead up to the passion story itself. Then the messengers at the tomb and the risen Jesus remind his followers of his words and their fulfillment because they have not been properly understood (24:6–7, 25–27, 44–46). The emphasis on this theme through repetition not only indicates its importance but also prods the reader to consider why Jesus' death was "necessary" (24:26) and how it fulfills Scripture (24:27, 44–46).

Although they have not been discussed in this article, it should be noted that the sayings of Jesus—and the extensive discourses that may be composed of these sayings—are part of the narrative. To speak is a narrative action, and what Jesus says may be studied for what it reveals about him, what norms it establishes in judging the behavior of others, and the intended and actual effect of his speech on later events in the narrative.

Studying the Gospels as narratives (a literary approach) does not conflict with an interest in their historical and social settings. A narrative not only creates a narrative world, but it also depends on and comments on a preexisting social world. Our understanding of how a text functioned within a past social context can make an important difference in our view of that text's significance.

Scholars attempt to reconstruct the social contexts of the Gospel tradition, thereby providing additional contexts for the sayings and stories beyond the literary context of a Gospel. As a result, important issues may emerge. If, as Burton Mack has argued, some of the pronouncement stories arose from the disappointing experience of a group of Jesus' followers who had sought to bring synagogues to faith in Jesus, an early function of these stories may have been to justify the Christian side of a bitter conflict, reinforcing a negative stereotype of scribes and Pharisees in the process.[30] We should note the hypothetical character of such historical reconstructions and the fact that the Gospel traditions passed through several stages of use, during which their functions may have changed. Even at a particular time and place, a tradition may have had multiple

---

30. Mack, *Myth*, 192–207.

functions. Nevertheless, such historical reconstructions are valuable, not because they specify, once for all, the significance the material must have, but because they suggest ways in which the material might have been employed and help us consider whether it should be used in the same way today.

Telling the stories of Jesus did and will have a function within a social context, producing results that are good or evil. Retelling and interpreting these stories is an act for which we must take ethical and religious responsibility, with as much awareness of the consequences as possible. The Gospels reveal their original social contexts only in a general way. Through intense labor and some guesswork, scholars attempt to be more specific, with results that force us to think in new ways. Nevertheless, the fact that the Gospels themselves do not specify these social settings may, if we choose, be viewed as a gift. Thereby the Gospels free themselves, and the stories they contain, to function in various ways in different historical and social contexts. This is not to say that any narrative unit will fit any situation; rather, many texts have more possibilities of social significance than are commonly recognized. Furthermore, it is right to remember that in reading the Gospel narratives we are reading about another time and place. While we may affirm the continuing relevance of these words, a story about the past does not decide for us how it is relevant to the present. That involves ethical and religious decisions for which we must take responsibility.

6

"You Shall Be Complete"— If Your Love Includes All
Matthew 5:48

The following brief textual note is an attempt to explain a verse that is puzzling, especially in its usual translation "Be perfect" (NRSV, NIV). Close attention to the verses immediately preceding helps us to understand the particular point of these words.

IN HIS REVIEW OF scholarship on Matthew's Sermon on the Mount, Warren Carter selects Matt 5:48 as one of two "difficult verses" that require special comment, and he begins his brief discussion by saying, "The command in 5:48 to be 'perfect' has long troubled interpreters."[1] I believe that this troublesome verse can be better understood if we recognize that it is an appropriate conclusion to the teaching about love of enemies in Matt 5:43–48.

Previous commentators, of course, have noted the connection of Matt 5:48 to the material that precedes it. Some emphasize that this verse is a fitting conclusion to the section that begins in 5:17 or 5:20, which consists primarily of the six so-called antitheses.[2] This is a defensible reading of 5:48 in context, for in 5:20 we read that the righteousness of Jesus' disciples must exceed the righteousness of the scribes and Pharisees, and each of the antitheses presents instruction that exceeds the commands in the Mosaic law. Thus this instruction can be understood to have a completeness, a perfection, lacking in past teaching.

---

1. Warren Carter, *What Are They Saying About Matthew's Sermon on the Mount?* (Mahwah, N.J.: Paulist, 1994) 95.

2. For instance, in his recent commentary Carter says, "This verse sums up all six examples. The greater righteousness (5:20) which embodies God's empire imitates God in '*wholeness*'" (see *Matthew and the Margins: A Sociopolitical and Religious Reading* [Maryknoll, N.Y.: Orbis, 2000] 157; italics in original). Carter, like other commentators, interprets "perfect" in terms of wholeness of commitment.

Other commentators may agree with this reading, but they also note that 5:48 is an integral part of 5:43-48, the last of the six sections of antitheses. I accept this view and will argue that its connection with 5:43-47 gives to v. 48 a special nuance that should not be missed. Although the view presented below is not entirely new, I think a careful statement of the reasons for it and implications of it will be useful.[3]

We should note, first of all, that only the connection with the immediately preceding verses helps to explain the second half of 5:48, the comparison with the heavenly Father's completeness or perfection. Taken by itself, v. 48 contains the startling idea that the earthly creature can share the divine Creator's perfection, a perfection that could include divine power and wisdom. Furthermore, Jacques Dupont notes that it is highly unusual, in the Bible and Jewish tradition, to describe God as "perfect."[4] This term is not used as a general divine attribute. This observation suggests that there may be a special reason in this context for the use of this unusual description of God. We find this special reason in vv. 45-47. In v. 45 love of enemies is described as the way to become "sons of your Father in the heavens," for it imitates the heavenly Father, whose benevolence includes the evil and the good, the righteous and the unrighteous. The imitation of God advocated in v. 45 prepares for the imitation of God advocated in v. 48. The connection between vv. 45 and 48 indicates that the completeness or perfection that the heavenly Father and the disciples can share is the completeness of a love that excludes no one, even someone who is evil.

The train of thought in 5:43-48 supports this view. The first verse of this section reminds the reader that the command to love in Lev 19:18 can be, and, as human behavior attests, usually is understood to be limited in scope. It applies to the neighbor, the one "close" (πλησίον) to oneself, and not to others, especially not to the enemy. But v. 44 removes

---

3. Although I developed my interpretation independently, I note the following brief statements of a similar view. W. D. Davies and Dale C. Allison Jr., *A Critical and Exegetical Commentary on the Gospel according to Saint Matthew*, ICC (Edinburgh: T. & T. Clark, 1988) 1:562-63: "The immediate context of 5.48 is the most important key to its understanding. The tradition demanded love of neighbor, but Jesus demands love of enemy, which means, in effect, love of all. . . . And in this lies perfection: love of unrestrained compass lacks for nothing. . . . It is perfect." Donald A. Hagner, *Matthew 1-13*, WBC 33A (Dallas: Word, 1993) 135: "This verse [v. 48] confirms the argument of v. 45 and properly forms the conclusion of the pericope. The disciples . . . are to be 'perfect' . . . —that is, they are to be like their Father in loving their enemies."

4. Jacques Dupont, "'Soyez Parfaits' (Mt., V, 48) 'Soyez Miséricordieux' (Lc., VI, 36)," in *Sacra Pagina*, ed. J. Coppens et al., BETL 12-13 (Paris: Gabalda, 1959) 152.

all limits to the love commandment by including even the enemy. This instruction is supported in v. 45 by insisting that God's loving action extends to all, both the evil and the good, and those who want to be "sons" of God should act as God does. Further support is provided by vv. 46–47, which revert to the contrary case of love limited by reciprocity—loving "those who love you" or "your brothers only." There is nothing "extraordinary" (περισσόν) about that. It is an inadequate standard for those who are children of the heavenly Father, from whom much more is expected. Against the limitation on the love commandment expressed in v. 43 and assumed by the behavior described in vv. 46–47, v. 48 calls for completeness: "You, therefore, shall be complete [by showing complete love, inclusive of all] as your heavenly Father is complete [as shown by God's complete love, demonstrated in nature, as v. 45 notes]."

"You" (ὑμεῖς) in v. 48 is emphatic, since Greek nominative pronouns are not used except for emphasis. It emphasizes the contrast between Jesus' disciples and those described in vv. 46–47. This feature ties v. 48 directly to the preceding verses and justifies reading οὖν as inferential: "therefore."[5] These details establish the connection with the preceding argument and support the view that the completeness required of disciples in v. 48 consists primarily of the complete love that includes even enemies.

The word that I have translated "complete" (τέλειος and its plural form) is usually translated "perfect." Both are appropriate translations.[6] However, when τέλειος contrasts with a significant lack or limitation and indicates a state in which that lack or limitation is overcome, the translation "complete" is preferable. This is the case in Matt 5:43–48, as indicated above. It is also the case in the only other use of the word in Matthew. In 19:20–21 the rich young man asks, "What do I still lack?" and Jesus replies, "If you want to be complete (τέλειος) . . ." (i.e., overcome this critical lack). This connotation of the word is also apparent in James 1:4.[7] Furthermore, Ulrich Luz notes that there is a "quantitative

---

5. "The particle οὖν ("therefore") serves as both a transitional and an inferential conjunction, denoting that the sentence to follow is a consequence of the preceding argument." Hans Dieter Betz, *The Sermon on the Mount*, Hermeneia (Minneapolis: Fortress, 1995) 320–21.

6. Walter Bauer, *A Greek-English Lexicon of the New Testament and Other Early Christian Literature*, revised by Frederick W. Danker, 3d ed. (Chicago: University of Chicago Press, 2000), s.v. 1.b: "perfect, complete."

7. Noted by E. Yarnold, "Τέλειος in St. Matthew's Gospel," in *SE* 4 (1968) 271 [269–73]. Yarnold adds, "The word τέλειος literally means 'complete.' Usually the context makes it clear in what the completeness consists."

element in the Matthean conception of righteousness," as indicated by the references in 5:20 and 5:47 to what "exceeds" or is "more," and he surmises that this applies also to 5:48.[8] The translation "complete" helps to express the contrast with love that is incomplete in quantity because it excludes some.

I would like to add two suggestions: First, it may be important to place Matt 5:48 within the large historical context of the ancient world, where completeness or perfection can express the supreme goal of a religious and/or moral quest. We find hints of this when we consider that our verse may contain intertextual echoes of Lev 19:2 ("You shall be holy, for I the LORD your God am holy") combined with Deut 18:13, which in the LXX reads, "You shall be complete/perfect (τέλειος) before the Lord your God." One would also need to consider the importance of perfection in Qumran[9] and in Greek thought.[10] Against this broad background, Matt 5:48 gives one answer to the quest for perfection. It does not simply state that completeness or perfection is required. It reveals what kind of perfection is appropriate to the life of the disciple. This perfection consists (not exclusively, perhaps, but preeminently) in the complete love that includes even the enemy.

Second, it may be worth noting that the verb ἔσεσθε in Matt 5:48 is ambiguous. It is true that a future indicative verb can express a command, as the LXX version of the Decalogue demonstrates (Exod 20:3–17), and I do not deny that Matt 5:48 expresses a requirement for disciples. However, it can also be read as a promise, or as hovering between command and promise.[11] The translation "You shall be complete" (in contrast

---

8. Ulrich Luz, *Matthew 1–7: A Commentary*, trans. William C. Linss, CC (Minneapolis: Augsburg, 1989) 346.

9. See Gerhard Delling, "τέλος κτλ.," in *TDNT* 8:73; Béda Rigaux, "Révélation des Mystères et Perfection à Qumrân et dans le Nouveau Testament," *NTS* 4 (1958) 237–62; Paul J. du Plessis, *TELEIOS: The Idea of Perfection in the New Testament* (Kampen: Kok, 1959) 104–15.

10. See the section on "The Concept of the Perfect Man in Philosophy" in Gerhard Delling, *TDNT* 8:69–72. See also du Plessis, *TELEIOS*, 74–94.

11. See Betz, *Sermon on the Mount*, 321, who comments, "It is not clear from the outset whether ἔσεσθε is merely an imperative . . . , or a prediction or an eschatological promise. . . . Grammatically as well as contextually, one could justify each of the options. . . . My suggestion is that the ambiguity is intended precisely to combine the various aspects, none of which can be isolated without losing grasp of the theology of the SM as a whole." John Wesley interprets Matt 5:48 as a promise in his *Explanatory Notes upon the New Testament* (London: Methodist Publishing House, n.d.), ad loc.

to the NRSV "Be perfect" and the RSV "You, therefore, must be perfect") is an attempt to preserve this significant ambiguity.

As I understand it, the final verse of the antitheses in the Sermon on the Mount is still a challenging and troubling verse. It is not troubling because it is a vague and general demand for perfection, with implications difficult to comprehend. It is challenging and troubling because it is a focused demand, and we can understand where we fall short. It attacks our tendency to limit our love to those near to us—our family, friends, and nation—while neglecting others and destroying our enemies through state executions and war. There is still reason to describe Matt 5:48 as a "difficult" verse.

PART II

The Gospel *of* Mark

7

The Disciples *in* Mark:
The Function of a Narrative Role

The Mark Seminar of the Society of Biblical Literature was the setting of exciting discussions in the early 1970s, as the first stages of what came to be called "narrative criticism" unfolded. An early version of this essay was presented to the Mark Seminar. Here I concentrate on one story line within the Markan narrative—the Markan story of the disciples—and trace their story from the beginning to the end of Mark, after laying the foundation for a new approach.

This essay, I believe, both demonstrates the value of the method, new at the time, and illuminates Mark's message. If we do not approach Mark as a continuous narrative, with a beginning and an ending, between which significant developments take place, we are reduced to saying that the disciples are sometimes presented favorably and sometimes not. But if we think in terms of narrative plot, and the implied evaluation of characters as the plot develops, we see that the Markan presentation of the disciples is not at all fuzzy or muddled. Rather, in the course of events a significant change takes place, and particular narrative techniques are used to emphasize this change.

This essay has been translated into German. See "Die Jünger im Markusevangelium—die Funktion einer Erzählfigur" in Der Erzähler des Evangeliums, ed. Ferdinand Hahn (Stuttgart: Katholisches Bibelwerk, 1985) 37–66.

The Study of Narrative Composition

Norman Perrin has argued that, since "the evangelists are genuinely authors," it is necessary to develop a "general literary criticism" of the synoptic Gospels and Acts that will borrow perspectives from non-biblical literary studies.[1] This general literary criticism must include, according

---

1. Norman Perrin, "The Evangelist as Author," in idem, *Parable and Gospel*, ed. K. C. Hanson, FCBS (Minneapolis: Fortress, 2003) 55–56 [51–63]; orig. pub. 1972.

to Perrin, "a concern for the composition and structure" of these writings and "a concern for protagonists and plot."[2] The following study is an attempt to respond to Perrin's challenge. It will show that close attention to the composition of the Markan narrative can guide us to a better understanding of the disciples' role in Mark. It will discuss the function of the disciples in the implicit dialogue between author and reader. It will also point to some resources in non-biblical literary studies that may help us to understand these matters.

Redaction criticism has not fully recognized the importance of studying the composition of each Gospel. Primary attention is often given to the study of additions and changes made by an evangelist in using source material. In the study of Mark this easily leads to dubious speculations, since the source material can only be inferred indirectly. Furthermore, additions and changes to source material do not in themselves reveal the concerns and emphases of the author. The question of what is emphasized in a writing is logically separate from the question of the origin of material within it. An addition or change by an author may reflect only a passing concern of minor importance. The composition of the writing as a whole must indicate to us that a greater concern is involved. On the other hand, an author may quote material without change but shape his or her writing to show that this material is centrally important and has a significance both greater and different than it may have had in previous tradition. The study of modification of the tradition can provide suggestions of possible concerns of the author. We can only specify the nature and importance of these concerns by studying the composition of the writing and the function of the modified material within it.[3]

This point has not been completely ignored in previous redaction critical work. For instance, the possible thematic relations between the modification of tradition in a text and other material in the Gospel have been considered. The outline of a Gospel has also been a subject of frequent study. This usually results in a topical outline with neat divisions. Such an outline may be appropriate to a well-constructed essay, but it is not necessarily appropriate to a narrative. There are special aspects of *narrative* composition that biblical scholars will continue to ignore if there is not greater awareness of how stories are told and how they communicate.

2. Ibid., 61–62.

3. Quentin Quesnell seems to be making a similar point when he distinguishes material that is "redactional by nature" from what is redaction "in fact"; see *The Mind of Mark: Interpretation and Method through the Exegesis of Mark 6:52*, AB 38 (Rome: Pontifical Biblical Institute Press, 1969) 51–52.

The Disciples in Mark 137

In the following discussion I will suggest some ways in which we can begin to do justice to the fact that Mark is a narrative.

Fortunately, a wide range of resources outside of biblical studies can help us develop a better understanding of narrative composition and communication. Among these are discussions of the novel. Some readers may be disturbed by my appeal to discussions of fiction, especially the novel, in the interpretation of Mark. It is proper to be cautious at this point. Certainly not all features of the modern novel can be found in Mark or in other ancient narratives.[4] Nor would I want to call Mark "fiction." However, there are qualities that all narratives share and further qualities that various narratives may share, even when some make use of historical fact, if the author has a strong, creative role.[5] Because of the importance of the novel in modern literature, qualities of narrative are often discussed in terms of the novel. With proper caution the biblical scholar can learn from this discussion.

We sometimes forget that a story represents a narrator's choices. Because we are familiar with certain stories and story types, the story seems obvious and necessary. However, just as the writing of history involves interpretation, so does telling a story. This is true both of stories that have a factual foundation and those that do not. Even when it reports actual events, a story represents a narrator's choices, for few events of our world are important enough to be remembered in story, and the narrator must choose how to tell the story. This choice will reflect the narrator's selective emphasis and values, and the story's composition helps to communicate the narrator's emphasis and evaluation to the reader. There are more ways of telling a story than we usually realize. Narrators choose the way that fits their purposes or limit their purposes to the narrative forms at their disposal. Conscious or unconscious choices by a narrator shape a narrative, leading us to view characters and events in a particular light.

---

4. Robert Scholes and Robert Kellogg give considerable attention to narrative prior to the novel in their book *The Nature of Narrative* (New York: Oxford University Press, 1966). There has been a strong interest in clarifying, through the construction of abstract "grammars" of narrative, the structures and relationships basic to all narrative. In this discussion examples simpler than the novel are often chosen. See, e.g., Vladimir Propp, *Morphology of the Folktale*, 2d ed. (Austin: University of Texas Press, 1968); Claude Bremond, *Logique du récit* (Paris: Seuil, 1973); and Tzvetan Todorov, *Poetik der Prosa* (Frankfurt: Athenaeum, 1972 [translation of *Poétique de la prose*]).

5. Theodore J. Weeden refers to Livy's indirect methods of interpreting historical characters, influencing the reader's attitudes; see *Mark: Traditions in Conflict* (Philadelphia: Fortress, 1971) 15–16. Weeden believes that Livy's approach is similar both to Greek drama and to Mark.

Narrative Rhetoric in Mark

One helpful approach to Mark is the study of narrative roles.[6] I will confine myself to the role of the disciples in Mark, although study of other narrative figures and groups would probably be fruitful.[7] While recent scholarship has recognized that there are remarkable features to the treatment of the disciples in Mark, there has been little agreement on the significance of the author's handling of this group. We will see whether consideration of the role of the disciples in the Markan narrative can bring greater clarity.

The author of Mark narrates a single, unified story. While the story's unity results primarily from the persistence of a single central figure, Jesus, a group of companions, or "disciples," appears early in the Gospel and plays a continuing role. To be sure, in different scenes the focus of attention may expand to a large group of "those around" Jesus (Mark 3:34; 4:10) or contract to the twelve or an individual among the twelve, but there are some common characteristics that define the group, despite its varying size.[8] It consists of those who have responded positively to Jesus and his message and are bound to Jesus in a continuing bond. While those healed by Jesus may or may not have a continuing relationship with him, the "disciples," those who "follow" Jesus, do have such a continuing

---

6. Claude Bremond, *Logique du récit*, presents a comprehensive and systematic study of narrative roles. It would have been possible to utilize Bremond's categories in the following discussion. However, these categories, which are quite abstract, would have made it more difficult for me to make my points clearly and concisely.

7. The roles of Jesus, as he interacts with others in the Gospel story, are, of course, especially important. It may be possible to gain new insight into the Christology of Mark by concentrating not on the titles applied to Jesus but on the narrative functions that Jesus performs within the Markan story. This will require a comprehensive view of narrative role interaction in Mark. Many characters in the Gospels appear only in a single scene. Still, study of the relationships and situations of these characters, together with possible developments within the scene, may be rewarding. Furthermore, different persons, whether members of a designated group or not, may have similar roles in similar narratives, for example, the miracle stories. Study of the similarities and variations in these roles may be worthwhile.

8. Robert P. Meye, in *Jesus and the Twelve: Discipleship and Revelation in Mark's Gospel* (Grand Rapids: Eerdmans, 1968), argues that "the evangelist Mark equates discipleship and Twelveship throughout his narrative" (228). However, there is evidence to the contrary. It is made clear in 4:10 that the following discourse, with its private explanation of the parable of the sower, is addressed not only to the twelve but to a larger group. In 4:33-34 the author generalizes the pattern of the preceding narrative (public teaching in parables followed by private explanation) and notes that the private explanation is given to Jesus' "disciples."

relationship. Because there is continuity of persons and characteristics, we can also observe developments. When in reading a story we encounter the same person or group more than once, it is right to ask if the relationship between the scenes enriches our understanding of the characters. Certain scenes reinforce what we already know about a character or group, other scenes reveal new characteristics, still others indicate significant shifts and developments. The meaning of each scene is enriched if we can understand it in relationship to all the other scenes. In the story each scene then becomes part of a significant development that moves toward an end. Below we will try to discover whether the scenes in which the disciples have important roles fit together into a unity with significant development. The author will enable us to follow this development, not by describing developing states of mind from the inside, but by narrating significant words and actions that indicate a shifting relation to Jesus.

In reading a text we are continually seeking to establish connections among the parts of what we read. Possible connections are multiple and some authors may seek to hold open many of these possibilities so as to engage the active imagination of the reader.[9] Our imaginations are more active in reading stories than we realize. The brief scenes in the synoptic Gospels are like pen and ink sketches in which an artist, with only a few strokes, has suggested some forms, relying on the viewers to fill in the rest with their imaginations. Reduction of shapes to a few lines is also a means of emphasis, and the selective emphasis of the artist may help us to see the subject in a new way. This is also true of the succinct narrative scenes in the synoptic Gospels. In our study of Mark we must pay special attention to the way that narrative composition indicates emphasis and suggests negative or positive evaluation of the actions of the disciples. Here we are dealing with what we might call narrative rhetoric.[10] This narrative rheto-

---

9. Wolfgang Iser speaks of the "potential multiplicity of connections" in a literary text. Readers must work out connections for themselves. Because the text requires the reader to be creatively active in this way, the reader becomes involved in events, and they seem real even when they are "far from his own reality." "The literary text activates our own faculties, enabling us to recreate the world it presents. The product of this creative activity is what we might call the virtual dimension of the text, which endows it with its reality. This virtual dimension is not the text itself, nor is it the imagination of the reader: it is the coming together of text and imagination"; see *The Implied Reader* (Baltimore: Johns Hopkins University Press, 1974) 278–79.

10. Wayne C. Booth, in his book *The Rhetoric of Fiction* (Chicago: University of Chicago Press, 1961), argues that "the rhetorical dimension in literature is inescapable" (105). Among other things, this involves "the ordering of intensities" in a literary work (60) and the use of "reliable commentary" (169), in which a narrator or other person in

ric reveals the standpoint of the author, or, more cautiously, the "implied author," that is the author insofar as he or she is immanent in the work.[11] The rhetoric of a story also reflects, by anticipation, a dialogue between author and reader. Writing a story, although it may involve persons and events quite distinct from the world of the author and reader, is, nevertheless, communication between author and reader.[12] At various points the author's reasons for narrating this story for a group of readers may become especially apparent. Furthermore, the author has a view of his or her readers and anticipates how they will respond to the story. Therefore, not only the standpoint of the author but also the standpoint of the reader (in the view of the author) may find indirect expression in the story.

The "implied author" of Mark communicates and recommends his norms and values to the reader by the way in which he narrates the disciples' story. Selective emphasis and control of evaluation of persons and events are indications of this communication with the reader. Selective emphasis establishes what we might call narrative hypotaxis, the subordination and superordination of narrative elements. Certain story elements are made to serve other elements, as the author focuses the reader's attention on what is important to the author.[13] For instance, in Mark certain aspects of the story are emphasized by repetition.[14] This includes repetition of elements in a single scene (Peter denies Jesus three times), repetition of statements in a sequence of scenes (Jesus repeatedly announces his coming passion), and narration of similar, though consecutive, events

the story suggests a set of norms and values in light of which action and character in the story should be judged. I believe that these features of "the rhetoric of fiction" can be found also in Mark's narrative.

11. The implied author may differ in significant ways from the author in everyday life, for one may write in order to be, for a time, a different person. The phrase "implied author" also calls attention to the fact that the position of the author must be inferred from the choices made in writing the story. Booth speaks of "the core of norms and choices [within a work] which I am calling the implied author" (ibid., 74).

12. Dan O. Via Jr. adopts the term "discourse level," as distinct from story level, to speak of this communication; see *Kerygma and Comedy in the New Testament: A Structuralist Approach to Hermeneutic* (Philadelphia: Fortress, 1975) 147.

13. The study of narrative "deep structure" should not draw our attention away from this narrative hypotaxis found in the so-called surface structure of the text. It is only through taking the latter into account that we can clarify the special way in which an author has used narrative structures to communicate with readers.

14. On the relation between repetition and emphasis see Tannehill, *The Sword of His Mouth* (1975; reprinted, Eugene, Ore.: Wipf & Stock, 2003) 40–41; see further 39–51 of the same book, where I discuss other significant aspects of repetition, with special reference to synoptic sayings. Some of these observations also apply to repetition in narrative.

(Jesus feeds a multitude twice, followed in both cases by a boat scene that reveals the disciples' lack of understanding). The use of repetition for emphasis is clear from the fact that the most detailed and emphatic instance is placed last, that is, the series forms a climax.[15] We will see below that the aspects of the story emphasized by repetition commonly express evaluation of the disciples' behavior.

A story may arouse expectation of an event and then report the realization or non-realization of our expectations. This not only emphasizes through repetition (our attention is drawn to the event before it happens and again as it happens) but also involves readers through their interest in the outcome of events. Readers may be involved in several different ways. There may be elements of the narrative that are puzzling, causing readers to look forward to further enlightenment. The reason for Jesus' commands to silence may constitute such a puzzle in the first half of Mark.[16] Or readers may anticipate several clear but mutually exclusive outcomes. Or readers may be fairly certain as to how the story will turn out but still be emotionally involved through fear or hope as they anticipate the outcome for important persons in the narrative. Jesus' announcements of his passion and his prediction of the disciples' behavior in 14:27–31 leave little uncertainty, but they can awaken fearful anticipation. Thus the selective use of prospect and retrospect in a story indicates emphasis by the "implied author." The material emphasized in this way is also likely to contain evaluation.

A further indication of emphasis is the selective use of dialogue and dramatic scenes. The use of dialogue in a dramatic scene involves the expansion of the amount of space in a writing given to a segment of time in the story, compared to the alternative possibility of presenting an event or series of events in a brief summary. Thus dialogue in a dramatic scene emphasizes, while summary narration of events gives them a subordinate position.[17] Of course, the author of Mark may have inherited many of the

---

15. This is the case in the three examples just mentioned. See 14:71 in relation to the preceding denials of Peter; 10:33–34 in relation to 8:31 and 9:31; and 8:14–21 in relation to 6:45–52.

16. See also Via, *Kerygma*, 154–55; he suggests that Mark develops and finally resolves the enigma of who Jesus is. However, this enigma, I believe, operates on two levels. When we compare what the story tells the reader with what the characters of the story know, we see that the reader is partially "on the inside." However, there are also enigma and surprise for the reader.

17. See Gérard Genette's discussion of "duration" in narrative in *Figures III*, Poétique (Paris: Seuil, 1972) 122–44. Genette also expands on a number of points mentioned above; see especially his discussion of order (including prospect and retrospect), frequency,

scenes in his Gospel from previous tradition and may have included some with little modification. Still, he chose to include this material and the emphases contained within it, whether he was fully conscious of what he was doing or not. These choices also reflect the "implied author."

Emphasis and evaluation are closely related, for much of what is emphasized in a story also has negative or positive value, and the emphasis helps to communicate the evaluation. Where the evaluating voice of the implied author is especially clear, we may speak of "reliable commentary." While such commentary may be expressed directly by the narrator, it is also found elsewhere in the narrative, for "the author is present in every speech given by any character who has had conferred upon him, in whatever manner, the badge of reliability."[18] In the Gospel of Mark it is obvious that Jesus wears the badge of reliability and authority. The most important evaluative commentary in Mark is given by Jesus. We are expected to judge the words and actions of others in light of the words and actions of Jesus. Our surest guide to the implied author's evaluation of the disciples is to follow the shifting relationship between Jesus and the disciples, noting where they are in concord and where they are not. The viewpoint of the implied author merges with that of Jesus in Mark, since the author has given him the role of chief commentator. If the evaluation of the disciples that emerges by tracing their relation to Jesus appears to be worked out with considerable care, as I believe it is, this evaluation reflects a major concern of the implied author. While the relationship between the disciples and Jesus is the primary basis for judgment of the disciples' behavior, the relations between the disciples and other figures of the story are also important. If the story suggests a similarity between the disciples and Jesus' opponents, this implies a negative judgment of the disciples. If certain minor characters in the narrative do what the disciples should but do not do, the contrast increases our sense of the disciples' failure. Noting the relations of similarity and contrast, or support and opposition, between the disciples and others in the narrative will help us to understand the disciples' story as shaped by the author.

The implied author's evaluation of the events and persons in this narrative is very important in the communication between author and reader. This evaluation, insofar as it is an accurate reflection of the implied author's perspective rather than a view that will later be rejected or modified, is being recommended to the reader. This indirect recommendation

---

the mimetic mode, and narrative levels.

18. Booth, *Rhetoric*, 18.

may reflect the author's perception of the reader's situation and needs. The author's communication with the readers is aided by the fact that, just as we constantly evaluate events and persons in everyday life, so we constantly evaluate the events and persons in stories. The author does his or her part by shaping and guiding our evaluation. Whatever we judge to be positive attracts us; whatever seems negative repels us. These forces of attraction and repulsion, controlled by evaluation embedded in the narrative, guide us in experimenting with life roles. A character role in a story to which we are attracted becomes a possibility for our own lives, perhaps only for a brief holiday during the reading of the story, perhaps in a more serious way leading to changes in our behavior and basic self-understanding. Noting the similarity between aspects of our own lives and negative aspects of story characters might also lead us to change. There is a natural connection between story and our experience of life, according to Stephen Crites, for human experience has a "narrative quality."[19] If experience is incipient narrative, it is not surprising that stories may react upon and "shape in the most profound way the inner story of experience."[20]

While any positive qualities of story characters will attract, a reader will identify most easily and immediately with characters who seem to share the reader's situation. Assuming that the majority of the first readers of the Gospel were Christians, they would relate most easily and immediately to characters in the story who respond positively to Jesus. The disciples, including the twelve, are the primary continuing characters who, at least at first, seem to respond in this way and so share the essential quality of the Christian reader's self-understanding.[21] I believe that the author of

19. Crites argues that "consciousness grasps its objects in an inherently temporal way" and memory retains a temporal order. Furthermore, "the inner form of any possible experience is determined by the union of . . . three distinct modalities": "the present of things past," "the present of things present," and "the present of things future," and "the tensed unity of these modalities requires narrative forms . . . for its expression." "The Narrative Quality of Experience," *JAAR* 39 (1971) 298, 301 [291–311].

20. Ibid., 304.

21. Karl-Georg Reploh's book *Markus: Lehrer der Gemeinde*, SBM 9 (Stuttgart: Katholisches Bibelwerk, 1969) is based on the correct insight that the disciples in Mark are representatives of the early church. However, Reploh, like other New Testament scholars, does not deal adequately with the narrative form of Mark. Furthermore, his selection of Markan material is too restricted. Especially striking is the omission of everything after 10:52. One cannot judge the meaning of a story without attention to its outcome. See also David J. Hawkin, "The Incomprehension of the Disciples in the Markan Redaction," *JBL* 91 (1972) 491–500. Hawkin rightly poses the question of "how the writer wishes the reader to relate to characters and groups within the story," especially to the disciples (493).

Mark anticipated this response by his readers. He composed his story so as to make use of this initial tendency to identify with the disciples in order to speak indirectly to the reader through the disciples' story. In doing so, he first reinforces the positive view of the disciples that he anticipates from his readers, thus strengthening the tendency to identify with them. Then he reveals the inadequacy of the disciples' response to Jesus, presents the disciples in conflict with Jesus on important issues, and finally shows the disciples as disastrous failures. The surprisingly negative development of the disciples' story requires readers to distance themselves from the disciples and their behavior. But something of the initial identification remains, for there are similarities between the problems of the disciples and problems that the first readers faced. This tension between identification and repulsion can lead sensitive readers beyond a naively positive view of themselves to self-criticism and repentance. The composition of Mark strongly suggests that the author, by the way in which he tells the disciples' story, intended to awaken his readers to their failures as disciples and call them to repentance. Allowing at first the comfortable assumption that Jesus and his disciples (and with them the Christian readers) are basically in concord, the story reveals points of essential conflict. The reader is left with a choice, a choice represented by the differing ways of Jesus and the disciples. In the light of what Jesus demands, this choice is not easy.

The view I am proposing conflicts with interpretations of Mark that assume that the disciples' difficulties arise from the fact that the passion and resurrection of Jesus, which are essential for true Christian faith, have not yet taken place. Since Christian readers of Mark can look back on the passion and resurrection, they do not share the disciples' problems. This, I think, is a misreading of Mark's story. Beginning in 8:31 Jesus clearly announces his coming passion and resurrection, and the author of Mark brings out the disciples' reaction with care. The passion of Jesus, in its Markan meaning, is not a solution to problems of discipleship but presents the problem in its sharpest form. Following the crucified Jesus means taking up the cross oneself (8:34). It also means becoming slave of all (10:44). These are not demands that disappear after Easter (see the prediction of suffering in 13:9–13), nor do they suddenly become easy to fulfill. Even in the first half of the Gospel the blindness of the disciples is associated with fear, lack of trust, and anxious self-concern (see 4:40–41; 6:49–52; 8:14–18), problems that do not disappear in the post-Easter church. Nor does the message of the resurrection guarantee a faithful response. The disciples heard this message from Jesus beginning at 8:31, yet failed to follow him, and an indication of further failure by Jesus' followers (16:8) comes immediately after the resurrection message at the tomb. The decision of the author to write a Gospel, including the story of the first disciples, rests on the assumption that there are essential similarities between the situation of these disciples and the situation of the early church, so that, in telling a story about the past, the author can also speak to his present.

The view I am proposing also conflicts with interpretations that regard the strikingly negative treatment of the disciples in Mark as an indication of polemic against a particular group in the church, a group from which the author sharply distinguishes himself and against which he is warning his readers. One version of this interpretation is carefully developed by Theodore J. Weeden.[22] Such a view cannot explain the positive aspects of the Markan portrayal of the disciples. In 1:16–20; 3:13–19; and 6:7–13 we learn that Jesus called members of the twelve and that the twelve were appointed by Jesus' own choice (stressed in 3:13) to share in his work and authority. If we assume a polemical situation, material pointing to the authority of the author's enemies and linking this authority to Jesus should be minimized or omitted. However, it is not. To say that it is Jesus as *theios anēr*, that is, the Jesus of Mark's opponents, who bestows his authority on the disciples simply enlarges the problem.[23] If Mark attempted to polemicize by first presenting his opponents' Jesus and then his own view of Jesus, both as parts of one continuous story, he surely failed. The unity of a story leads the reader to regard persons in it as unified characters. Change of character must be justified in the story. In this case the author of Mark would have to make unmistakably clear that Jesus himself has been converted to a different viewpoint and that what Jesus says about himself in 8:31ff. means the rejection of what he said and did earlier. The author does not do this.

Jesus' statement in 4:11–12 also conflicts with Weeden's thesis, and attributing these verses to tradition does not solve the problem,[24] for this is precisely the kind of tradition the author could not afford to include in a polemical situation. Furthermore, 14:27–28 and 16:7 indicate, through authoritative speakers (Jesus and the messenger at the tomb), the intention of restoring the broken relationship between Jesus and the disciples. Even if the reconciliation is temporarily frustrated (see 16:8), it remains the intention of Jesus (and the author). Weeden correctly notes the im-

---

22. See Weeden, *Mark: Traditions in Conflict.*
23. Ibid., 61.
24. Ibid., 141–42.

portance of Mark 13 as a clue to the post-Easter situation of the church as the author sees it.[25] However, he fails to note that the warnings and exhortations of Mark 13 are addressed to Peter, James, John, and Andrew, representatives, supposedly, of the enemy group. The setting that the author gives to this discourse assumes the identity or continuity of these four disciples with the church that must suffer and preach the gospel, of which Jesus speaks in Mark 13. Because Weeden's hypothesis of polemic against opponents does not seem to be adequate, we should consider further the hypothesis that the author has undertaken the more subtle task of speaking through story to his friends about the glory of their calling and the grave dangers of failure to which they are largely blind.

The implied author of Mark shapes a story that encourages readers to associate themselves with the disciples. This may begin with a simple identification, assumed by author and reader, of the disciples with Christians of the time of the writing. However, the relation between the disciples and the Christian reader does not remain simple. As the portrait of the disciples becomes clearly negative, the tendency to identify is countered by the necessity of negative evaluation. A tension develops between these two attitudes, with the reader caught in the middle. The degree to which the one attitude or the other is encouraged by the text varies in the different parts of the Gospel and from scene to scene within the parts. Initial identification is encouraged by positive evaluation of the disciples in the early part of Mark. Identification is encouraged later in the Gospel by the similarity between the problems faced by the disciples and the problems faced by the Gospel's first readers (and, perhaps, by later Christian readers also). But as the inadequacies of the disciples' response to Jesus become increasingly clear, readers must distance themselves from the disciples and begin to seek another way. The identification of readers with the disciples does not prevent this but contributes to the existential seriousness of the new search. The more clearly readers see that the disciples represent themselves, the more clearly the necessary rejection of the disciples' behavior becomes a negation of one's past self. The recognition of the disciples' failure and the search for an alternative way become a search for the new self who can follow Jesus faithfully as a disciple.

Wolfgang Iser's discussion of the role of "negation" in the novel offers a helpful parallel.

> Though the novel deals with social and historical norms, this does not mean that it simply reproduces contemporary values. . . . [In

---

25. Ibid., 71.

the novel norms] are set in a new context which changes their function, insofar as they no longer act as social regulations but as the subject of a discussion which, more often than not, ends in a questioning rather than a confirmation of their validity. This is frequently brought about by the varying degrees of negation with which the norms are set up in their fictional context—a negation which impels the reader to seek a positive counterbalance elsewhere than in the world immediately familiar to him. The challenge implicit in the negation is, of course, offered first and foremost to those whose familiar world is made up of the norms that have been negated. These, the readers of the novel, are then forced to take an active part in the composition of the novel's meaning, which revolves round a basic divergence from the familiar.[26]

For instance, a novel may present an appealing character, endowed with the qualities generally approved, who, in spite of or because of those qualities, comes to a bad end. The novel will often not state the alternative qualities or choices that would have led to a happier result. But the negativity in the story induces the reader to ponder what went wrong and imagine an alternative. Thus negation of the expected encourages "the reader's production of the meaning of the text,"[27] which requires the reader's active participation. It can also lead to a fresh perspective on one's past assumptions and values. The strong negative aspect of the disciples' story in Mark functions in a similar way, moving readers to ponder how those called by Jesus could go so far astray and what is required if they are to escape similar failure.

In important ways Jesus represents the positive alternative to the failure of the disciples. He not only calls the disciples to save their lives by losing them and to be servants, but he follows this way himself. Presenting the positive alternative within the story may seem to remove the necessity for the reader to imagine the "positive counterbalance," decreasing the reader's active role, so prized by Iser. However, closer study of the alternative to which the author points will show that it is far from a cut-and-dried answer to what is true and right. In 8:31–10:45, and again in 14:1–16:8, the central symbol of the death and resurrection of Jesus is related in successive scenes to different aspects of the life of the disciple. The repeated use of this symbol as a key element in dramatic scenes, with new and expanding meaning for the disciple, suggests that it is an "expanding

26. Iser, *The Implied Reader*, xii; see also 34, 37, 46, 118–19.
27. Ibid., 37.

symbol," with a depth of meaning not easily exhausted.[28] Furthermore, the continuing challenge of this expanding symbol to our basic assumptions about life comes to expression in the repeated use of paradox (8:35; 9:35; 10:43–44; see also 10:31).[29] Paradox, a conflict in language, reminds the reader that the positive alternative indicated by the author persistently conflicts with what people assume is right and reasonable. So the positive alternative remains a mystery and a challenge.

Mark's Story of the Disciples

We will now consider aspects of the Gospel's composition that indicate selective emphasis and guide the reader's response to the disciples. We must note the principal episodes in the disciples' story from the first to the last chapter of Mark, although the scope of the material will prevent detailed discussion. Our study will reveal a development presented with considerable care, indicating that we are dealing with a major concern of the author.

Immediately after Jesus begins his preaching, the author of Mark tells of the call of four disciples who will later take their place among the twelve (1:16–20). Jesus' command to follow him establishes a norm by which the reader can judge the behavior of the disciples. At this point the response fits the command. Later in the story Jesus will again call for followers (8:34), but the subsequent narrative (especially chap. 14) will demonstrate the disciples' failure. The positive relation between Jesus and the disciples is emphasized and developed in two further scenes in the early chapters of Mark that center on the intended role of Jesus' closest associates. In 3:13–19 we are told that Jesus selected twelve for a special relationship and responsibility. The twelve receive their position by Jesus' own choice (emphasized in 3:13). This position involves being "with" Jesus in close association and sharing in the work of preaching and exorcism that Jesus himself has been doing (compare 3:14–15 with 1:38–39). There is only one negative note, a reference to Judas' betrayal (3:19). The

---

28. See E. K. Brown, *Rhythm in the Novel* (Toronto: University of Toronto Press, 1950) 33–59. According to Brown, "the expanding symbol is repetition balanced by variation, and that variation is in progressively deepening disclosure" (57). "By the use of an expanding symbol, the novelist persuades and impels his readers towards two beliefs. First, that beyond the verge of what he can express, there is an area which can be glimpsed, never surveyed. Second, that this area has an order of its own which we should greatly care to know" (59).

29. On the significance of the form of Mark 8:35 and 10:43–44, see Tannehill, *Sword*, 98–107.

appointment of the twelve is obviously linked to 6:7–13 (see 6:30), where the twelve are actually sent out on the mission previously mentioned. They both preach and cast out demons, that is, they follow Jesus' instructions. Opposition is predicted, but there is no indication that this causes the twelve to fail in their mission. Thus the author of Mark distributes three connected scenes through the first six chapters of his Gospel, scenes that indicate, on the one hand, what Jesus commanded the twelve to do (establishing a norm by which they can be judged), and, on the other, the obedient response of the twelve. This series of three scenes presents the twelve positively. They have a special status and a special task, which, on one occasion at least, they fulfill. There is special emphasis on the close relation of the disciples with Jesus and the similarity of their role to his.[30]

This positive evaluation of the twelve in the early chapters of Mark is reinforced by other texts that refer to the disciples or "those around" Jesus. In 2:14–28 not only Jesus but the disciples face the criticism of the scribes and Pharisees, while Jesus defends both himself and them. In these controversies Jesus and the disciples stand together against the opposition of the scribes and Pharisees. (This is no longer so clearly the case in the controversy in 7:1–23, as 7:17–19 indicate.) In 3:20–35 the opposition of the scribes to Jesus is emphasized strongly and their attitude is associated with that of Jesus' family. This becomes the basis for some very positive statements about Jesus' followers. In 3:31–35 "those around" Jesus are contrasted with his natural family.[31] Those around Jesus are his true mother and brothers (another way of stressing close association with Jesus). The phrase "those around him" is then carried over to 4:10, and the twelve are explicitly associated with this group. In the statement of Jesus that follows, a sharp contrast is made between the disciples and the outsiders: The mystery of the kingdom is given to those around Jesus, but those outside do not see or understand. This is very positive evaluation of the disciples in authoritative commentary by Jesus, emphasized by contrast with the position of others. Whether the author wrote 4:11–12 himself or received these verses from previous tradition, they inevitably shape the view of the disciples that his writing presents. They must have some place within the purposes of the author if he was as concerned with his presentation of the disciples as he seems to be elsewhere. If the au-

---

30. A point correctly emphasized by Günther Schmahl, *Die Zwölf im Markusevangelium: Eine redaktionsgeschichtliche Untersuchung*, TTS 30 (Trier: Paulinus, 1974). However, Schmahl does not deal adequately with the negative aspect of the disciples' behavior.

31. On the significance of the rhetorical structure of this scene, see Tannehill, *Sword*, 165–71.

thor were engaged in polemic against a group of heretics represented by the disciples, these words would be counterproductive. They could and would be used by the opponents to support their own case. However, these words would be useful to the author if:

(1) he really believes that this is what Jesus intended and intends, that the mystery of the kingdom be revealed to the disciples and the church; and

(2) he is not conducting a polemical argument against recognized opponents but doing something more subtle: involving his readers in a story in which they will first recognize themselves and the positive qualities of their own self-image and then be led to self-criticism.[32]

In the material mentioned so far, the author goes out of his way to make the disciples attractive figures, both by stressing their close association with Jesus and by contrasting them sharply with negative groups. The first part of Mark's Gospel encourages readers to have high expectations for the disciples and associate themselves with them. If we think in terms of consistent but static doctrine, there may seem to be a conflict between this positive view of the disciples and other material in Mark. If we think in terms of narrative development, however, we have the common story technique of encouraging readers to contemplate one possibility so that they will feel more sharply the opposite development when it arrives. Jesus' authoritative statement about the disciples in 4:11–12 will serve as a norm by which the author will measure the disciples' failure (see 8:17–18).

When we look back at Mark 4 from the end of the Gospel, we can see that it already suggests the possibility of negative developments in the disciples' story. First, the hearing of the Word is presented as a problem. The Word does not always fall on good soil; it does not always bear fruit when it has once begun to grow. And Jesus speaks with urgency about the importance of hearing and about the revelation of the hidden. Second, in 4:13 Jesus appears to be critical of the disciples' lack of understanding. However, the explanation that follows allows the reader to assume that the problem has been cleared up, an assumption reinforced by closing the

---

32. Recognition of this positive self-image would be promoted by the fact that the contrast between the church's privilege of revelation and the blindness of the world was common in the early church, as we see from its presence in various parts of the New Testament. See Quesnell, *Mind,* 183–87.

scene with a general reference to private instruction (4:34). Third, Jesus' teaching in Mark 4 is followed by the story of the stilling of the storm, in which the disciples are criticized for their cowardice and lack of faith (4:40) and appear to be ignorant of Jesus' status (4:41). Still, the reader reading Mark for the first time would not yet guess that the disciples are involved in any major and continuing difficulty. The view of the disciples is basically positive through 6:30, although there have been some suggestions of difficulty. However, the foundation has been laid for a very negative judgment of the disciples if their behavior should conflict with Jesus' stated intentions for them.

The call of the four disciples (1:16–20), the choice of the twelve (3:13–19), and the mission of the twelve (6:7–13, 30) appear to be linked scenes that reinforce and develop a particular view of the twelve. This compositional technique of linking scenes by repeating (thereby emphasizing) and developing a set of motifs reappears in the three boat scenes in the first half of Mark. These three boat scenes, the stilling of the storm (4:35–41), the encounter with Jesus on the water (6:45–52), and the discussion in the boat (8:14–21), isolate Jesus and the disciples from the crowds by the setting of the scenes and highlight the attitudes of the disciples. The first two boat scenes are connected by the motifs of the disciples' difficulty with the sea, Jesus' miraculous power, and the disciples' fear and lack of understanding. The third is not a miracle story, but it is linked to the second by references in both to Jesus' feeding of a multitude, and it presents in a most emphatic way the disciples' failure to understand.

The second and third boat scenes follow closely the two feedings of the multitudes and refer back to them. Both feedings are preceded by a conversation between Jesus and the disciples. In 6:37 Jesus charges the disciples with the responsibility of feeding the crowd, but their reply shows that they see no way of fulfilling this responsibility. However, through Jesus the crowd is fed, and the disciples are given a subordinate role in the feeding. The feeding is followed by a boat scene in which the behavior of the disciples is clearly criticized. The fear and astonishment that the disciples show at their encounter with Jesus on the water is attributed in 6:52 to their failure to understand the feeding and to their hardened hearts (in evaluative commentary stated directly by the narrator). Then the cycle of events is repeated, emphasizing the theme of disciple blindness and bringing it to an effective climax. In 8:2–3 Jesus points out the need of the crowd to the disciples. It is not surprising that the disciples do not know what to do in the first feeding, but when the very same situation arises again (note that the author presents the feedings as two consecutive events, not two versions of the same event), the reaction of the disciples suggests a perverse blindness that must disturb the reader. The third boat scene (8:14–21) puts great emphasis on this perverse blindness of the disciples. After Jesus has twice fed a multitude, the disciples are pictured as anxious about their low supply of bread. Jesus castigates them for this, reminding them of the abundant supply of food left over from the feedings and, in the process, accusing them of the same blindness, deafness, and lack of understanding attributed to the outsiders in 4:11–12. The discussion begins with Jesus' warning against the leaven of the Pharisees and of Herod, a warning that the disciples are too preoccupied to heed. This scene functions as a climactic summary of preceding scenes. It is the climax of the boat scenes, bringing the theme of disciple blindness to emphatic expression. It refers to the feeding scenes, using these experiences as a basis for accusing the disciples. It recalls 4:11–12 (see 8:18) but shows that, contrary to Jesus' intention, the disciples share the blindness of the outsiders. They are heedless of the danger of sharing the blind opposition to God's messengers shown by the Pharisees and Herod (8:15), for, in fact, they already share their hardness of heart (see 6:52 and 8:17 with 3:5–6). A clear shift in the disciples' role has taken place. From a position with Jesus as his followers, the disciples have moved to a position that associates them with Jesus' enemies and the outsiders of 4:11–12.

As the author begins to present the disciples in strongly negative terms, some of the miracle stories become contrasting scenes. It is no accident that the final sequence of feeding and discussion in the boat, with Jesus' reproachful question concerning the disciples' inability to see and hear (8:18), is framed by stories of healing a deaf man and a blind man (7:31–37; 8:22–26). These two healing stories have a number of common features and phrases, so that the second one reminds us of the first. The healing of blind Bartimaeus in 10:46–52 is probably a third story in this series, for Bartimaeus follows Jesus on the way to the cross (10:52), a discipleship theme. The contrast between 8:22–26 and 8:18 is clearer than the connection between the former and Peter's confession in 8:27–29. These miracles highlight the deafness and blindness of the disciples by contrast and, at the same time, indirectly promise the reader that Jesus is able to create true discipleship in spite of the story of blindness and denial in which the reader is implicated.

The scene in 8:14–21 leaves the relation between Jesus and the disciples in a very unsatisfactory state, but, as long as the story goes on, there is hope for some resolution of the problem. The reader awaits such a resolution. Readers may not be entirely clear as to the nature of the disciples' problem, for the story has given various kinds of clues. On the one hand, the boat scenes have emphasized the disciples' fear, lack of trust, and anxious self-concern (4:40; 6:49–50; 8:14–16), associating these with a lack of understanding. On the other hand, the question of who Jesus is has been raised (4:41; see 6:14–16 and the identification of Jesus by demons). Perhaps the problem arises from the disciples' failure to identify Jesus correctly. Insofar as this is the problem, there is ironic distance between the reader and the disciples, for the reader knows what the disciples do not know. However, in 8:27ff. the reader discovers that the problem is not resolved when Peter makes a correct confession of faith (8:29). Jesus insists that something more must be said about himself and, as a direct corollary, about discipleship (8:31–38). Even this additional teaching does not solve the disciples' problem. For the role of suffering that Jesus chooses and the meaning of Jesus' role for his disciples (following in suffering, becoming servants) challenges and provokes the fear and anxious self-concern portrayed in the boat scenes.

In 8:31—10:45 there is clear evidence of careful composition, with close attention to the role of the disciples. Three passion announcements (8:31; 9:31; 10:33–34) become the basis of a major threefold pattern building up to a climax. Each of these passion announcements is followed by resistance (8:32–33) or behavior contrary to that of Jesus (9:33–34; 10:35–41) on the part of the disciples, followed in turn by Jesus' corrective teaching. This teaching points to Jesus' suffering as a model for Jesus' followers (especially at 8:34–35 and 10:45) and relates the approaching death of Jesus to two problems that probably reflect problems of the early church as perceived by the author: the possibility of persecution and martyrdom (8:34–38), and the desire for status and domination (9:33–37; 10:35–45). The passion announcements are accompanied by indications that the disciples are both afraid and without understanding (9:32; 10:32), recalling features of the boat scenes, but the disciples' anxious self-concern now takes specific shape as fear of suffering and desire for status. Both of these problems are clearly important to the implied author. The latter problem is carried over from the second to the third instance of the pattern, where it is addressed in a forceful climax (10:35–45). Placing this concern in final position in the pattern seems to give it the greatest emphasis.[33] However, the former concern is also supported by the larger

---

33. Anitra Bingham Kolenkow discusses Mark's emphasis on serving rather than seeking status; see "Beyond Miracles, Suffering and Eschatology," in *SBLSP 1973*, 2:155–202. It is worth noting that 10:35–40 combines the concerns of suffering and status. James and John are willing to suffer for status in the final glory.

composition of Mark. Not only is the teaching in 8:34–38 stressed by the voice from the cloud at the transfiguration ("Listen to him," 9:7), but this teaching picks up the previous theme of following (8:34) and provides a basis for evaluation of the disciples' behavior in chapter 14. The strong emphasis in Mark 14 on the disciples' failure to follow Jesus to suffering and death, as they had promised, shows that the concern expressed in 8:34–38 is also of major importance.

Jesus' teaching about discipleship is the last element in each of the three instances of the pattern discussed above. This aspect of the composition has the following effects:

(1) The teaching is emphasized through end position in the pattern and through contrast with the preceding actions of the disciples.

(2) Since no response of the disciples is narrated immediately after 10:45, there is still a possibility that the disciples will change their ways. The possibility of various responses not only holds open the outcome of the disciples' story but also allows readers to consider various responses for themselves. Of course, later actions of the disciples should be evaluated in the light of the authoritative commentary on discipleship in 8:31—10:45.

(3) Not only the authority of the teacher but also the emphasis and openness noted above allow this material to function as teaching to readers, not just teaching to the first disciples. This is also promoted by the generality of much of the teaching.

While the principal repetitive pattern in 8:31—10:45 gives special importance to the issues of suffering and desire for status, these are not the only causes of tension between Jesus and the disciples in this section. In various ways the disciples are put in a bad light, in connection with a number of specific problems. In 9:14–29 the disciples fail in the role of exorcists, to which the twelve were commissioned and which they had successfully performed (6:7, 13). In 9:37 Jesus instructs the disciples about the importance of receiving a child. In 10:13–16 they disobey this instruction and are rebuked by Jesus. (This is related to the theme of desire for status—see 9:35–37.) In 9:38–40 we learn of the disciples' attempt to end the work of an exorcist who "was not following us." Again their attitude proves to be contrary to that of Jesus. The story of the rich man is followed by a conversation between Jesus and the disciples about riches (10:23–31), which ends with a promise and a warning (10:29–31). While the promise evidently applies to the disciples, it has a critical edge to it. It pokes fun at the feeling that a great reward is due by speaking in extravagant terms of a present reward "with persecutions."[34] Thus in a variety of ways and in connection with a variety of specific issues the conflict between the desires, expectations, and actions of the disciples and the authoritative instruction of Jesus is shown to the reader. Readers must choose between the attitudes of Jesus and those of the disciples. It is clear how the choice should go according to the values of the author. But the difficulty of Jesus' demands reminds readers that in many ways they are like the disciples.

Chapter 13 is also important for the author's shaping of the disciples' story. This discourse of Jesus has a setting prior to Jesus' death and resurrection but deals with events that will transpire after the death and resurrection. Placing the discourse at this point in the narrative is a compositional choice by the author. Even if, for some reason, the author did not want to present this as a discourse of the risen Christ, he could easily have placed this material after the resurrection, either through presenting it in the narrator's voice (Now, before his death Jesus had said . . .) or in the voice of a story character (Peter said, "Remember what Jesus told us . . .").[35] However, this discourse is placed before the passion story, at least in part as preparation for the events in chapter 14.[36] It prepares for chapter 14 in two respects. On the one hand, Jesus' warnings refer to situations similar to those the disciples face in chapter 14. Jesus tells the disciples that they will face persecution and death and must endure to the end (13:9–13). He warns them (and the reader—see 13:37) that they must watch and not be caught asleep (13:33–37). However, as the story continues we learn that the disciples desert and deny Jesus rather than face death and that they fail to watch in Gethsemane. The disciples' failure is heightened by the preceding instruction. On the other hand, Jesus' discourse anticipates a continuing role for the disciples beyond the disaster of chapter 14. So the preparation is not entirely negative.

The importance attached to Judas' betrayal, the flight of the other disciples, and Peter's denial appears in the fact that Jesus predicts all three of these events. In the narrative these predictions serve both to emphasize and evaluate these events. They emphasize because the event is, in effect,

34. On the significance of Mark 10:29-30 in its setting, see Tannehill, *Sword*, 147–52.

35. On the significance of comparing order of narration to the chronological order of events in the study of narrative composition, see Genette, *Figures III*, 77–121.

36. The desire to end with 16:1-8 may have been another factor in the author's choice.

told more than once, the reader's attention being called to it before it actually happens in the sequence of events. This is coupled with strong negative evaluation. This is obvious in the remark about Judas in 14:21, and use of symbols of close relationship (table fellowship—14:18–20; kiss—14:44–45) heightens the sense of betrayal. The prediction of the scattering of the disciples and the denial by Peter also heightens the negative evaluation of these acts, for the disciples respond by rejecting Jesus' predictions and promising just the opposite (14:31). Thus the desertion and denial that follow are not only contrary to Jesus' stern call to follow him in suffering in 8:34–37, making the disciples liable to the judgment announced in 8:38. These acts are also contrary to an explicit promise by the disciples. When readers read these predictions, they know how the disciples' story will come out, for Jesus' predictions carry authority. But that does not lessen their emotional involvement. The emotions of tragedy are aroused as the reader witnesses the fatal promises being made and recognizes the approach of disaster.

The composition of the rest of chapter 14 fits what we now expect. In the Gethsemane scene the author emphasizes, through narrating the return of Jesus three times, the failure of the disciples to watch.[37] The desertion of Jesus by the fleeing disciples is reported in 14:50. The following flight of the naked young man probably dramatizes the shamefulness of the disciple's flight and satirizes the pretensions of Christians who claim to be ready for martyrdom.[38] The story continues by noting that Peter, who is now the last hope for faithful discipleship among Jesus' close associates, followed Jesus "from a distance" (14:54). The story of Jesus before the Jerusalem council is framed by the introductory reference to Peter's presence (14:54) and the following scene of denial, highlighting the contrast between Jesus' fearless disclosure (14:62), by which he is condemned, and Peter's denial. The construction of the denial narrative itself

---

37. The historical question of whether Jesus actually did return three times to find the disciples sleeping is irrelevant to my point. Even if he did, it is easy enough for a narrator to report similar but separate events in summary form (Jesus kept coming and finding . . . [Greek imperfect]). Drawing out this feature of the narrative by repeated narration results in emphasis. The same applies to the threefold narration of Peter's denial. See Genette, *Figures III*, 145–82.

38. This interpretation may be supported by the reference to the fine linen (σινδών) worn by the young man. Elsewhere in the New Testament the word is used only of the cloth in which Jesus was buried (see 15:46 and par.). If this detail is significant, it suggests that this man is so sure of his loyalty that he comes all dressed for death but suddenly changes his mind when death is a real prospect. His nakedness emphasizes the shamefulness of his flight.

encourages both sympathetic awareness of Peter's plight, as he struggles to escape the persistent accusations, and full recognition of the horrible thing that he is doing. The narrative goes into unnecessary detail, recording three separate denials and building to a climax with the third, which is accompanied by a curse (14:71). The composition of the story promotes both the reader's sympathetic involvement and an emphatically negative evaluation of Peter's act. Jesus' closest friends have completely failed to take up the cross and follow him.

In one sense the story of the disciples is over, for nothing further is recorded of the actions of the twelve, who have been the central figures in this story. The disciples' story has come to a disastrous conclusion, and the author has spared nothing in emphasizing the disaster. This ending sends reverberations back through the whole preceding story. Readers who were at first content to view the disciples as reflections of their own faith and who may have continued to hope for a happy ending to the disciples' story must now try to disentangle themselves from them, which will mean choosing a path contrary to their path.

The possibility of this other path is recognized within the story, for there is a sense in which the disciples' story is *not* over. There are features of the story that hold the future open. At 14:28 and 16:7 first Jesus and then the "young man" at the tomb announce a journey to Galilee and a meeting there between the risen Jesus and his faithless disciples. The relation between 14:27 and 28 indicates that this anticipated meeting can be a remedy (note "but" [ἀλλά]) for the scattering of the sheep and the loss of their shepherd; that is, this meeting can restore the relationship between Jesus and his disciples, in spite of desertion and denial. So the Gospel holds open the possibility that those who deserted Jesus will again become his followers, reinstating the relationship established by Jesus' call.[39] I say "possibility" because we are not told that the disciples have changed their ways and become true followers. In fact, the women's failure to follow the instructions of the resurrection messenger (16:7–8) gives an ambiguous quality to the ending of the Gospel. It is not clear how the story will develop from this point. The cowardly disobedience

---

39. It seems to me unlikely that 14:28 and 16:7 refer to a meeting at the parousia. The preparousia suffering of the church and its proclamation of the gospel (see 13:9–13) presuppose a restoration of the relationship between Jesus and his followers. The anticipated meeting can be postponed until the parousia only if we ignore its function of reconciling the scattered sheep with their shepherd and mitigate, as the author of Mark does not, the seriousness of the break between Jesus and the disciples that takes place in chapter 14. For other arguments against the parousia interpretation of these verses, see Robert H. Stein, "A Short Note on Mark xiv.28 and xvi.7," *NTS* 20 (1974) 445–52.

that characterized the disciples reappears in the behavior of the women. It has not been eliminated from the church by the resurrection. The failure of the women to convey the message may also suggest that the disciples are insufficiently aware of the need and possibility of a new beginning after disaster. So, on the one hand, a figure of authority clearly states that a meeting will take place (16:7), a meeting that carries with it the possibility of renewed discipleship. On the other hand, there are indications that this renewal is not a simple and automatic affair. A positive development is indicated but negative possibilities are also suggested. The Gospel is open-ended, for the outcome of the story depends on decisions that the church, including the reader, must still make.

The continuing story is developed most extensively in chapter 13, where Jesus, in a discourse addressed to Peter, James, John, and Andrew (three of these four have prominent roles in scenes emphasizing conflict between Jesus and the disciples), warns them, and the church, about the trials that they must face between the resurrection and parousia. The discourse assumes a restored relationship but also recognizes the continuing possibility of failure. Jesus speaks of the need to watch (13:33–37), although the disciples failed to watch in Gethsemane, and states that the disciples will be handed over to councils (13:9) just as Jesus was, although the disciples ran from this possibility in the passion story. The story is not over. It continues into the time of the early readers, and the author anticipates that each reader will decide how it comes out for him- or herself.

Finally, as the author emphasizes the disciples' failure he also points to a different possibility through very brief references to contrasting figures. These figures include:

- Bartimaeus, who follows Jesus on the way to the cross (10:52);
- the anointing woman, whose act appropriately recognizes the approaching passion (14:7–8);
- Simon of Cyrene, who must "take up" Jesus' cross (15:21);[40]
- the centurion at the cross, who makes the confession of faith that Peter refused to make (15:39); and
- Joseph of Arimathea, who cares for Jesus' burial as we would expect his closest friends and relatives to do.[41]

---

40. Eduard Schweizer notes that the verb is the same as in Jesus' call to take up the cross and follow in 8:34. See *The Good News according to Mark,* trans. Donald H. Madvig (Richmond, Va.: John Knox, 1970) 343.

41. The author takes the time to note that John the Baptist was buried by his disciples

These are figures who replace the disciples in the roles that they fail to fill. They appear in such brief flashes that they do not allow the reader to shift attention from Jesus and the disciples and become deeply involved with these other characters. But they do point to the way that contrasts with the disciples' failure.

Conclusion

I do not wish to imply that the disciples' story is the sole interest of the author of Mark. What we have discovered, however, does indicate that it has major importance within the larger story being told.

We have noticed various features of the narrative composition of Mark that seem to indicate selective emphasis and imply evaluation. We have seen how such composition shapes the narrative role of the disciples throughout the Gospel. We have noted the importance of relationships among characters, and shifts in those relationships, in the understanding of narrative roles. The changing relationship between the disciples and Jesus, moving from concord to expanding and intensifying conflict, has been a key element in this study. The role of the disciples is shaped by the composition of the author and reflects his concerns. The purpose of the author and the response that he anticipates from the reader begin to come clear when we consider the author's shaping of the disciples' role as indirect communication with the reader. The author assumes that there are essential similarities between the disciples and his anticipated readers, so that what he reveals about the disciples may become a revelation about the readers and so enable them to change.

(6:29). Is he suggesting a contrast with Jesus?

8

The Gospel *of* Mark *as* Narrative Christology

Important as the disciples are, Jesus is the central character in Mark's story. Approaching Mark from the same narrative perspective, this second essay on Mark seeks to expand on and balance the first by recognizing Jesus' central role. The importance of relating events to a character's "commission" is emphasized in this essay. As in the essay on the disciples in Mark, certain narrative patterns appear to be significant for shaping the impact of the story on its intended readers.

Jesus is the central figure in the Gospel of Mark, and the author is centrally concerned to present (or re-present) Jesus to the readers so that his significance for their lives becomes clear. The author does this in the form of a story. Since this is the case, we need to take seriously the narrative form of Mark in discussing this Gospel's presentation of Jesus Christ. In other words, we need ways of understanding and appreciating Mark as narrative Christology. But what should we look for? What aspects of the Gospel's narrative composition significantly shape its presentation of Jesus? Discerning some of the more important of these aspects is the task of this essay.

In the Gospel of Mark there is little description of the inner states of the story characters. Instead, characterization takes place through the narration of action. We learn who Jesus is through what he says and does in the context of the action of others. Therefore, the study of character (not in the sense of inner qualities but in the sense of defining characteristics as presented in the story) can only be approached through the study of plot. We must pay special attention to the main story lines that unify the Gospel, for it is not only the continuing centrality of Jesus that makes Mark a single story but also the fact that certain events can be understood as the realization or frustration of goals or tasks that are suggested early in the story. These goals or tasks (later I will use the word "commission") enable us to understand key developments as meaningful within the context of the story as a developing whole. We must also study features of composition that control the "rhetorical" dimension of the story. These features show that the story has been shaped in order to influence the readers in particular ways.

This essay is not primarily concerned with the use of Christological titles in Mark. Valuable work has already been done in this area, and I do not intend to repeat it. However, an understanding of the narrative composition of Mark may allow us to make some observations about the function of particular titles in relation to the developing narrative. For instance, the title "Son of God" does seem to have a special function in relation to Jesus' commission, as will be indicated below.

I prefer to speak of narrative composition rather than narrative structure because the latter term is associated with the methods of structuralism. While I have learned some things from structuralist analysis, this is not an essay in structuralism. Instead, I am following a path that began with the study of forceful and imaginative language in the synoptic sayings.[1] Careful study of the literary composition of the sayings, including their rhetorical and poetic features, enables the interpreter to clarify the kind of impact that particular sayings were designed to have on the hearer. Literary composition provides clues to the nature of the act of communication that the words are to make possible. It may provide clues to the speaker's purpose, the conception of the hearers and their needs, and the anticipations of response held by the speaker. It provides clues to the type of influence that the speaker wishes to exercise with regard to the hearer. And this influence may sometimes be at a deep level, challenging the hearer to radical change, so that it is appropriate to speak of a "depth rhetoric" whose goals and methods are partly akin to poetry.[2]

This approach can also be applied to the Gospels as narratives, if we find appropriate ways of analyzing narrative composition and understanding its significance as communication between writer and readers. Stories are shaped by authors, consciously or unconsciously, in order to influence readers in particular ways. The importance and danger of stories that exercise such influence becomes clear when we recognize that we understand our own lives and the lives of others by shaping them into stories, and the shapes of our life stories can be influenced by stories that we read or

---

1. See Tannehill, *The Sword of His Mouth* (1975; reprinted, Eugene, Ore.: Wipf & Stock, 2003).

2. Ibid., 18–19.

hear. This process is especially important because stories are uniquely able to reflect and give meaning to significant features of our experience.[3] My study of narrative composition in light of these concerns began with an essay on the disciples in Mark,[4] which sought to show the author's careful control of emphasis and evaluation, guiding the readers' judgments about the disciples, with possible repercussions for the readers' judgments about themselves. The present essay is an extension of that work, seeking to do greater justice to the fact that Jesus is the central character in the Gospel, through whom the Gospel's influence is most fully felt. This requires clarification of the roles of Jesus within the Markan narrative.

The original readers (or hearers, if we think in terms of a public reading) were, of course, people of the first century. Their problems and possible responses must be understood in terms of the first century world. Therefore, the approach taken here is not opposed to historical research. Its newness consists in the use of certain literary perspectives to sharpen our understanding of what is central to the story and of the way in which the story has been shaped in order to challenge the readers. This can give us a clearer view of the interaction between the author and his first readers. It can also deepen our understanding of what it would mean for a modern reader to read this Gospel well, with full appreciation of its power to challenge.

Mark 1:1—8:26

If we are to understand how the author of Mark wished to present Jesus Christ to his readers, we must apprehend the statements and events recorded there as parts of a unified narrative. Mark is a unified narrative because, in spite of clear division into episodes, there are connecting threads of purpose and development that bind the story together. These appear when we clarify the dominant commissions in the story.

In my usage, the term "commission" will have a meaning similar to the term "mandate" in recent structural analysis of narrative.[5] The latter term could be used, but since I will not be appropriating the full sys-

---

3. See Stephen Crites, "The Narrative Quality of Experience," *JAAR* 39 (1971) 291–311.

4. See Tannehill, "The Disciples in Mark: The Function of a Narrative Role," *JR* 57 (1977) 386–405. See chapter 7 above.

5. See Jean Calloud, *Structural Analysis of Narrative*, trans. Daniel Patte, SemSup (Philadelphia: Fortress, 1976) 17, 25, 27; and Daniel Patte, *What Is Structural Exegesis?* GBS (Philadelphia: Fortress, 1976) 37–44. The term "contract" is also used.

tem that goes with it, it may be better to keep terminology distinct. For my purposes, the most important observation is that a unified narrative sequence results from the communication of a commission to a person and the acceptance of this commission. The narrative sequence will then relate the fulfillment or non-fulfillment of the commission. The events of the narrative sequence are meaningful parts of the same sequence because they relate a movement toward the fulfillment of the commission or narrate encounters with obstacles that frustrate fulfillment. The commission provides an overarching purpose and goal that unifies the sequence and gives meaning to the parts. The sequence is over when the commission is fulfilled or is finally abandoned. The term "commission" is most appropriate when this purpose and goal are communicated from one person to another. This is not always indicated in the narrative. When it is not indicated, it may be better to speak simply of a "task." Such a task can have the same narrative function of determining the extent of a narrative sequence and bringing the events of that sequence into meaningful unity.

The Gospel of Mark is the story of the commission that Jesus received from God and of what Jesus has done (and will do) to fulfill his commission. We are probably to understand the baptism scene as the communication of this commission, for here we have a rare type of story, one in which God speaks directly to Jesus and declares who Jesus is (i.e., declares what his role is to be). Furthermore, the stories that follow show Jesus acting in ways that are meaningful in light of God's commission. It is true that the commission is not expressed as a series of instructions for action but simply by designating Jesus as "my beloved Son." However, action results: Jesus sets out on a mission.[6] If the words "You are my beloved Son" announce the commission that Jesus received from God, this should be taken into account in the interpretation of the meaning of this title in Mark. We will see that the special connection of the title Son of God with Jesus' commission from God is reinforced by later scenes in the Gospel.[7] Since this title does serve especially to announce Jesus' commission, its full meaning for the author can only be understood in light of the complete Markan narrative, for it is here that we are shown the content of the commission that Jesus received.

---

6. Even if we assume that the commission was given at some earlier time, the narrative function of the baptism scene would be the same: it is the point at which Jesus' commission from God is brought to the reader's attention so that the reader can understand the following events.

7. See below, 175–76, 186–87.

Although Jesus' commission is central in Mark, many other commissions and tasks are suggested. For each person who acts with purpose a commission or task can be assumed. Of course, many of the story characters in Mark appear only in a single episode, so it is not obvious that their commissions and tasks contribute to the unity of the Gospel as a whole. However, another commission and another task are indicated early in the Gospel and establish narrative sequences that persist until the passion story or beyond. In 1:16–20 Jesus calls four fishermen to follow him. This establishes the disciples' commission and begins a sequence of events that clarify this commission and tell the reader whether it is being fulfilled. This commission, as it is gradually clarified, will provide a norm by which the disciples' subsequent behavior can be judged. The narrative sequence that begins with the disciples' call is quite important in Mark. Furthermore, in 3:6 we are told that a group intends to destroy Jesus. This is an ongoing task in the Gospel narrative, for this intention reappears in 11:18, and Jewish leaders finally bring Jesus to the cross. These three commissions or tasks, then, have a scope that enables them to bind Mark together as a single narrative. As we shall see, each of these narrative sequences contains significant development, and the interaction among them is an important part of Mark's Gospel.

There is another task or purpose of even greater scope that stands in the background of the events that Mark narrates. The opening of Mark, with its Old Testament quotation indicating that God is sending his messenger, suggests that God also has a purpose and that God's purpose lies behind the central events of the story. It is to realize God's purpose and mission that Jesus is given his mission. From that point on, Jesus is viewed as the central actor in the fulfillment of God's purpose, and so attention centers upon him.[8]

In fulfilling his commission, Jesus assumes certain roles in relation to other persons in the narrative, and our understanding of Mark's narrative Christology will be advanced by considering these role relationships. In addition to Jesus' relation to God, from whom he receives his commission, four relationships seem most important because they involve either developing roles or prominent repeated roles. These are Jesus' relationships to his disciples, to the scribes, Pharisees, and Jerusalem leaders, to the supplicants who ask for healing, and to the demons. The narrative

---

8. Structural analysis would distinguish here between a correlated sequence that has become blocked (God's purpose as revealed in the Old Testament) and a topical sequence, involving a task accepted by Jesus, that has the function of making possible the fulfillment of God's purpose announced in Scripture; see Patte, *What Is Structural Exegesis?*, 37–38.

development of Mark's Christology begins to appear as we consider what Jesus does and who he is in relation to these important groups. We must give some attention to each of these four role relationships, but the former two, which involve significant developments affecting the story as a whole, will be studied more carefully, with attention focusing on these developments.

It is accurate to express Jesus' basic role as that of eschatological salvation bringer. In the more abstract language of narrative analysis, with religious connotations removed, we may speak of his basic role as that of ameliorator.[9] However, Jesus' narrative roles in Mark are more complex than this statement reveals. Jesus is not salvation bringer or ameliorator for all groups in the story, not, for instance, for the demons. And his saving action is often not simple and direct. To a surprising degree Jesus' action, rather than replacing the action of others, calls forth the action of others. Jesus becomes the ameliorator of others in that he incites them to become ameliorators for themselves and others. In other words, Jesus functions frequently as an influencer, one who moves others to action.[10] Jesus as influencer is closely related to Jesus as preacher and teacher. Nevertheless, there is some value in using the term influencer because: 1) this calls attention to the relation of what Jesus says to action within the story, to the successful or unsuccessful results of Jesus' words upon the narrated action; and 2) it opens the possibility that Jesus may exercise influence not only by what he says but by what he does and suffers.

The readers as well as persons in the story are objects of Jesus' influence. However, it is in relation to persons in the story that the author suggests the possible results of Jesus' influence.

The scenes at the beginning of Jesus' public ministry establish the basic role relationships that will be important in the Gospel. These scenes begin to clarify Jesus' commission, for what he has been commissioned to do is shown to us by what he actually does. The importance of Jesus as influencer is clear in the first two scenes, the announcement of the kingdom in Galilee (1:14–15) and the call of the first disciples (1:16–20). In the first of these Jesus seeks to move others to action by disclosing the opportunity to share in the kingdom's benefits. The recipients of these words are not specified, and the present participles suggest that the proclaiming and saying is repetitive. The influence is general. It is meant to encompass

---

9. See Claude Bremond, *Logique du récit*, Collection Poétique (Paris: Seuil, 1973) 282–85.

10. Bremond, ibid., 242–81, and "Le rôle d'influenceur," *Communications* 16 (1970) 60–69.

disciples, crowds, and readers. It takes place through disclosing the approach of God in ruling power. This scene relates the whole mission of Jesus to the coming of God's kingdom.

In 1:16–20 the intended relationship between Jesus and the disciples is established. Here, in light of the kingdom's coming, the first disciples are called to their continuing task. This scene is not complete in itself but is the beginning of a story line. The commission here given and accepted is gradually clarified in following scenes (see 3:13–19; 6:7–13; 8:34–38), and the author will give clear guidance to his readers in evaluating the disciples' behavior in relation to their commission.[11] The author emphasizes the parallel between Jesus' commission and the disciples' commission. The disciples should share in Jesus' mission and fate. They are meant to be co-ameliorators and co-influencers, subordinate to Jesus but sharing in his work.[12] In part, Jesus fulfills his commission by sharing it with others. The communication of a commission to the disciples allows another story line to unfold, which becomes the locus of important negative developments within the story of Jesus and a means by which the Christian reader's complacency is challenged.

In 1:21–28 we are told for the first time of an encounter between Jesus and an unclean spirit. Several aspects of this scene indicate a concern not only to institute Jesus' role in relation to the demons but also to relate this to other aspects of Jesus' commission. The unclean spirit asks, "Have you come to destroy us?" (note the plural: the question concerns Jesus' general role in relation to the demons), and the exorcisms that follow indicate that the answer is yes. In order to be the one who brings salvation to people, Jesus must be the destroyer of the powers that oppress them. But this exorcism story is also used to underline the authority of Jesus' teaching (1:22, 27), and Jesus' authoritative teaching is contrasted with that of the scribes. This points forward to the series of controversies in 2:1—3:6.

This series of controversies strongly suggests that the scribes and Pharisees are to be understood as opponents of Jesus as he seeks to fulfill his commission. The Jewish leaders in Mark do *intend* to oppose Jesus' work. However, the reader's initial impression that they will present the main obstacle to the fulfillment of Jesus' mission will prove false (see below, 178). As a reminder of this, I will refer to the Jewish objectors and

---

11. See Tannehill, "Disciples," 390–405 (in the present volume 140–59).

12. Note the parallel between the description of Jesus' ministry of preaching and exorcism in 1:38–39 and the task of the twelve as described in 3:14–15 and 6:12–13.

plotters in Mark as "opponents," using quotation marks. In the controversies in 2:1—3:6 Jesus again acts as influencer, for these stories emphasize Jesus' forceful words. The influence centers on key points in understanding Jesus' own role: his mission and authority to forgive sinners (2:10, 17), the eschatological joy and freedom for new action that he brings (2:19–22), the priority of human need over the sabbath commandment and Jesus' authority to set aside sabbath observance (2:27–28; 3:4–5). The effect of Jesus' forceful words is not limited to those who have raised objections; indeed, the (negative) reaction of the Pharisees is not made clear until 3:6. Jesus' influence is meant to reach the readers. Here the readers discover what was meant when they were told that Jesus taught with authority and not as the scribes.

The series of controversies ends in 3:6 with the statement that the Pharisees wished to destroy Jesus. This immediately raises the question of whether and how this intention will be realized. We now have three commissions or tasks operating in the text that are not restricted to single episodes but stretch across Mark's Gospel and come to resolution only with the passion story or beyond. These are the commission received by Jesus from God, the commission received by the disciples from Jesus, and the task of destroying Jesus that Jesus' "opponents" have undertaken for themselves. However, the last of these does not lead to immediate action. Although there are controversies following 3:6, the desire to destroy Jesus is not repeated until 11:18, and even then the "opponents" have great difficulty in finding a way to accomplish their purpose. The author introduces the death plot early in the narrative, but he wishes to develop the other narrative lines before continuing this one.

Between the report of the exorcism in 1:21–28 and the series of controversies in 2:1—3:6, the author reports two healings in response to requests (1:29–31, 40–45) and summarizes Jesus' healing and exorcising ministry (1:32–34). The relation of Jesus to supplicants is logically distinct from the relation of Jesus to the demons. Jesus helps the supplicant in response to a request, but he destroys or breaks the power of the demon. Hence, the relation of Jesus to supplicants institutes another role relationship. Nevertheless, these two relationships may appear in a single story, as when a father requests help for his demon-possessed son (9:14–27), and the author speaks of Jesus' healing and exorcising work together (1:34).[13]

---

13. A supplicant comes to Jesus with a clear intention to improve his own or another's lot. We may, therefore, say (to use Bremond's language) that the supplicant is an ameliorator and Jesus is the helper or (following Patte) that the supplicant is a subject with

Although the healing and exorcism stories make up an important part of Mark, they have a different status from material that emphasizes the disciples and those who try to oppose Jesus. The disciple and "opponent" material is part of developing narrative lines that come to a climax in the passion story. The healing and exorcism stories do not lead anywhere, for each is complete in itself. The need finds its resolution within a single episode. While the disciple and "opponent" material fits into progressive sequences that begin early in the Gospel and continue to its end, the healing and exorcism stories do not. They are not progressive but reiterative. Since they do not form a sequence leading toward the passion story, the narrative climax of the Gospel, they are subordinate to the material that does. Nevertheless, the repetition of similar stories emphasizes Jesus' roles as helper of supplicants and conqueror of demons. Furthermore, reiteration makes possible a different kind of development. Reiteration of a basic pattern allows and encourages variation of details. Points of emphasis can vary and various possibilities for filling the roles can be used. Thus the story of the Gerasene demoniac depicts a situation of desperate alienation with vivid detail, while the following story of the woman with a hemorrhage not only focuses on a woman instead of a man but also emphasizes her faith. Thus the reader's understanding of the possibilities inherent in a basic pattern of roles is enriched through providing a varied sampling of the same type of story.

Enrichment through reiteration with variation also takes place in Jesus' relation to "opponents" and to the disciples. In 2:1—3:6 we find a series of controversy scenes, each of which could be complete in itself. It is only 3:6 that makes a reiterative collection part of a progressive sequence. There are also patterns of similar scenes in the narratives about the disciples, such as the three boat scenes (4:35–41; 6:45–52; and 8:14–21), with their increasingly clear negative judgments, and the three passion predictions (8:31; 9:31; and 10:32–34), with the teaching that follows them. However, the patterns of disciple scenes also show climactic emphasis in the final scene of the pattern. Since similar action in similar situations gives us a sense of knowing a person's "character" (that is, his or her defining characteristics), the roles of Jesus in these reiterative scenes provide stable features for the picture of Jesus that the Gospel presents.

---

a mandate and Jesus is the helper. It is important, however, to note that rhetorically Jesus remains the dominant figure in the story. Jesus' act is presented as crucial to the realization of the goal. So the "helper" is not necessarily secondary in importance and interest in the "surface structure" of the story.

The importance of Jesus' relationship to each of the groups discussed is indicated by the fact that the author repeatedly reminds us of each relationship throughout the first half of the Gospel (to 8:26).[14] By 3:6 we have been introduced to the disciples, the demons, the supplicants, and Jesus' "opponents" with their plan to destroy him. Thus an important function of this first section of the Gospel is to establish the role relationships that are basic to the rest of the story. Scenes in which Jesus is related to each of these groups are repeated up through 8:26 in a rough pattern of rotation. In 3:7–12 the author returns to Jesus' ministry of healing and exorcism. This is followed by a scene in which the twelve are named and their task is specified, developing the narrative line that began with the call of the first disciples. Then there is a major controversy scene in 3:20–30. This rotation continues, although it is not always possible to classify the scenes simply and neatly. Combinations are useful to the author. Thus the controversy in 3:20–30 involves the scribes from Jerusalem, but it is a controversy about Jesus' exorcisms and contributes to our understanding of their meaning. The situation of Jesus' followers is indicated by suggesting contrast (see 4:11–12 after 3:21–35) or similarity (see 8:14–21 after 4:11–12 and 8:11–12) between them and the blind "opponents." However, none of the role relationships that have been discussed is allowed to disappear or recede in the first half of Mark. Through this rotation of scenes, developments are taking place. Although no action is taken to further the plan to destroy Jesus, successive scenes make clear the extent of the conflict and the points at issue. And significant development takes place in Jesus' relation to the disciples.

The relation of Jesus to the disciples passes through a development of considerable complexity. The author gives clear indications of how the disciples' behavior is to be evaluated at different stages of the narrative. The disciples' intended role is made clear by a series of three related scenes in the early part of Mark: the call of the first disciples (1:16–20), the choice of the twelve (3:13–19), and the sending out of the twelve (6:17–13). The nature of the disciples' commission is partly clarified in these scenes. It involves sharing in Jesus' work of preaching and exorcism. More generally, it means that they must "follow" or "come after" Jesus (1:17–18) and "be with" him (3:14). Jesus is the one who gives the disciples their commission and the one who continues to instruct them in its meaning. The author intends us to evaluate the disciples' behavior in light of what Jesus says and does. When the disciples are in harmony with

---

14. This is still true of 8:27—10:52, but to a lesser extent.

Jesus, the author intends them to be viewed with approval; when they are not, with disapproval. On this basis, the three scenes just mentioned give us a positive impression of the chief followers of Jesus (with the exception of 3:19). To this must be added the strong positive evaluation in 4:10–12. This initial positive evaluation has an important function: it encourages the natural tendency of Christian readers to identify with Jesus' followers in the story.[15]

A shift takes place, however, in the relation between the disciples and Jesus. Within the first half of Mark this is most clearly seen in the three boat scenes in which Jesus is alone with his disciples (4:35–41; 6:45–52; and 8:14–21). While the disciples' fear and lack of faith in the first of these scenes might appear to be a temporary lapse, the succeeding scenes suggest a consistent pattern of anxious self-concern is blinding the disciples to Jesus' power and mission. Thus the fulfillment of the disciples' commission is put in question. The anticipated and desired development has become blocked. This causes tension, and the reader naturally hopes for and expects some resolution of the problem in the rest of the narrative. It is now likely that the initial easy identification of the reader with the disciples has become a problem. The tendency to identify remains, but this now conflicts with the negative judgments that must be made about the disciples. While the disciples were called to "follow" Jesus and "be with" him, a chasm is beginning to open between Jesus and the disciples, which requires the reader to choose where he or she will stand. Perhaps the reader would like to stand with Jesus, rather than admitting a similarity with the blind and fearful disciples, but this will become increasingly difficult in the light of Jesus' demands. The implied criticism of the disciples threatens to become criticism of the reader.[16]

---

15. Those who, like Theodore J. Weeden, interpret the disciples as representatives of the writer's theological opponents face the difficulty of explaining why the first part of the Gospel emphasizes that the twelve have been specially chosen to share Jesus' work and have been given "the mystery of the Kingdom"; see Weeden, *Mark—Traditions in Conflict* (Philadelphia: Fortress, 1971) and Tannehill, "Disciples," 393–94 (in the present volume 145–46). It is possible that Jesus' relatives represent theological opponents (see 3:21, 31–35; 6:1–6), but the disciples should not be lumped together with the relatives (see John Dominic Crossan, "Empty Tomb and Absent Lord (Mark 16:1–8)," in *The Passion in Mark,* ed. Werner H. Kelber [Philadelphia: Fortress, 1976] 146), for the writer's attitude toward the disciples is much more complex.

16. For more complete discussion of the disciples in Mark and of methods by which the significance of this narrative role can be understood, see Tannehill, "Disciples," chapter 7 in the present volume.

Jesus, on occasion, is the protector of the disciples when they get into trouble (as in 2:18–22 and 2:23–28), but when the disciples show clear signs of failing to follow Jesus, Jesus increasingly becomes their corrector. He exercises powerful influence in order to call the disciples back to perceptive faith. This influence can be felt by the reader. We would also expect it to have an effect upon the disciples. The problem, however, is not easily overcome.

In all of this the author of Mark is telling the story of Jesus and of the commission that was given to him. The commission that Jesus received from God remains central and gives to the story its human and religious significance. But fulfilling this commission involves a struggle. Men have been called to share Jesus' work, but it is becoming doubtful whether they will fulfill the commission given them. "Opponents" not only criticize Jesus but wish to destroy him. Although nothing comes of this for the present, the intention can be revived and lead to action. The success of such an intention would seem to mean the failure of Jesus' work. Even in the miracle stories there seems to be some problem, for while Jesus demonstrates his power, the miracles are repeatedly accompanied by commands to silence, directed to the demons or to those healed. These commands to silence do not determine the actual course of events, for the author tells us that Jesus was not obeyed.[17] They do, however, express Jesus' intention. Jesus does not want to be known primarily on the basis of the miracles. Why this is so is not clear in the first half of the Gospel, but the emphasis placed on Jesus' disclosure in 8:31 suggests that Jesus cannot be proclaimed until the proclaimer comes to terms with Jesus' rejection and death. This does not mean that the miracles have no importance in the author's presentation of Jesus. They are emphasized through repetition and dramatic detail. Furthermore, through much of the Gospel, as Jesus' demand becomes increasingly strong and difficult for the disciples, it is primarily in the miracle stories that Jesus appears with grace and power to save, rather than with a condemning demand.

Mark 8:27—10:52

In 8:27—10:52, Jesus' role in relation to his disciples becomes the dominant concern. There are only two miracle stories in this section, and even they have discipleship themes attached to them (9:14–29—the disciples fail to heal the boy and want to know why; 10:46–52—Bartimaeus follows Jesus on the way to Jerusalem). Jesus responds to hostile questioning

17. See 1:44–45 and 7:36–37. I think 5:19–20 also demonstrates such disobedience.

in 10:1–9, but the principal references to the "opponents" in this section relate to the future. For Jesus speaks of his coming rejection and death in Jerusalem. So here we can expect to learn more about what Jesus means for the disciples (and for the church that they represent). This must be understood in light of the problem that has already appeared in the relationship between Jesus and the disciples. The strong but vague indications of the disciples' anxious self-concern and blindness in the previous section of the Gospel become concrete points of conflict between Jesus and the disciples.

Although the author regards Peter's confession as appropriate (see 1:1 and 14:61–62), so that the problem caused by the disciples' lack of perception might seem to be solved, the narrative sequence makes clear that a major problem remains. The confession is immediately followed by a new statement of Jesus' commission, declaring that Jesus must suffer, be rejected, be killed, and rise again, and this announcement is rejected by Peter. The repetition of this announcement in following chapters, the fear and conflict that it causes, and its close connection to the climactic events in Jerusalem show this to be the key element in 8:27—10:52.

As I indicated, this is a new statement of Jesus' commission. It announces a program of action that will be carried out in the rest of the narrative. Like the announcement in the baptism scene, it is to be understood as a commission from God, as the "must" of 8:31 suggests and as the transfiguration scene will confirm. It is remarkable that the Gospel delays the disclosure of Jesus' full commission. Information has been withheld from the readers. The readers have been allowed to form an understanding of the author's view of Jesus in which suffering and death have had no part.[18] But this was so that the suffering and death might be emphasized more strongly and placed in tension with the attitudes of the disciples and the church. There is no indication that the words of 8:31 contain new information for Jesus. This is new information, however, for the reader of Mark. Thus there is a certain surprise value to the announcement, which emphasizes it. Emphasis is also conveyed by the conflict that immediately arises through Peter's rejection of this statement, and by the repetitive pattern of three passion announcements (8:31; 9:31; and 10:33–34) connected with similar reactions from the disciples and similar corrective teaching by Jesus. Furthermore, this is a prospect or anticipa-

---

18. There is a hint in 2:20, but it is expressed vaguely. Most early readers of Mark probably knew that Jesus had been crucified, but there is still the question of how important this is for understanding Jesus and discipleship. Up until 8:31 one could assume that it was a temporary obstacle that made no difference in the long run.

tion of events still to come,[19] which provides a succinct summary of what is central in the story. A reader's natural interest in the outcome of the story focuses attention on this anticipation.

Jesus' commission from God at his baptism was quickly followed by the commission that the first disciples received from Jesus in their call. The new statement of Jesus' commission is quickly followed by a new statement of the disciples' commission. After Peter's objection to the passion announcement and Jesus' strong rebuke, Jesus speaks of what is required of anyone who "wishes to come after me" and of how one must "follow me" (8:34). Almost the same language was used in the call of the first disciples. Just as the work of the disciples was patterned after the work of Jesus in the first half of the Gospel, so now their commission is reformulated to conform to the new understanding of Jesus' commission. This is made clear not only in 8:34–38 but also in Jesus' teaching following the other passion announcements. The disciples must be willing to lose their lives as Jesus will lose his and like him become self-giving servants.[20] Jesus' role as influencer and corrector of reluctant and fearful disciples is dominant in 8:27—10:45. Each passion announcement is followed by an episode in which disciples reject what Jesus has said (8:32–33) or act in a way that conflicts with the path that Jesus has chosen (9:33–34; 10:35–41). This, in turn, is followed in each case by Jesus' corrective teaching. This teaching is formulated in forceful language. The full power of Jesus' verbal influence is used, and this power is reinforced by the threefold pattern of the narrative, coming to a climax in the extended scene in 10:32–45. The pattern ends at 10:45 with Jesus' teaching, leaving open the question of whether the disciples will finally accept this teaching and follow him. This teaching provides the standard by which the reader can judge the subsequent actions of the disciples in the passion story.

Jesus' commission comes from God and the commission that Jesus gives the disciples is also divinely authorized. Since there is a struggle between Jesus and the disciples over these commissions, it is not surprising that the author chooses to emphasize their divine origin. This is done in

19. One important aspect of the author's shaping of a work appears when we note the difference between the order in which events are recounted or evoked and the chronological order of the events themselves. The author may suggest the special significance of certain events through the use of prospect or retrospect; see Gérard Genette, *Figures III,* Poétique (Paris: Seuil, 1972) 77–121.

20. In 8:31—10:45 Jesus' call to accept suffering and to renounce the desire for status and domination is most strongly emphasized, but there are also other specific causes of tension between Jesus and the disciples; see Tannehill, "Disciples," 401–2 (in the present volume 154–55).

the transfiguration scene. The divine commission that Jesus received at his baptism is now disclosed to the disciples, using the same words: "my beloved Son." This underscores Jesus' divine authority for the disciples. The disciples, therefore, must "hear him" (9:7). While this may be an allusion to Deut 18:15, we must ask why the author places these words at this point in the narrative. They must have special reference to the words of Jesus in the immediate context, that is, to the teaching in 8:31 and 8:34—9:1 in which Jesus has just disclosed something new about his commission and the commission of his disciples.[21]

The baptism and transfiguration scenes show that the title Son of God is the preferred title in Mark when the author wishes to stress Jesus' commission from God. This will be confirmed by the confession of the centurion at the cross, which is a retrospective reflection upon Jesus' commission (see below 186–87). Thus in key scenes at the beginning, middle, and end of the Gospel the title Son of God has the special function of emphasizing Jesus' divine commission. Since this title is so closely associated with important scenes that report or confirm Jesus' commissioning, its meaning in Mark is influenced by the narrative that unfolds from that commissioning. That Jesus is Son of God means that he has been chosen and authorized by God to do what he is doing and thereby accomplish God's saving purpose. This is not to deny that current usage of the title in the surrounding world would influence its meaning, but the fine-tuning of the title's meaning takes place through the understanding of Jesus' commission that appears in the narrative as that commission is announced and fulfilled. It therefore encompasses Jesus' conquest of demons, healing of supplicants, call to the disciples, death in Jerusalem, etc.

The two scenes in Mark that speak of a voice from heaven or from a cloud (1:11 and 9:7) are both connected with Jesus' commission from God. It is unusual for the Gospels to depict God speaking or acting directly. There is, however, a point at which God cannot be represented by Jesus. That is where the author wishes to make clear, by dramatic action, that Jesus received his commission from God, as in the baptism and transfiguration scenes.

Within a narrative there may be points at which a major theme of the writing is succinctly expressed. We find such points in Jesus' teaching following the three passion predictions. This is particularly true of a group of sayings that are linked by form and meaning. Beginning with ὃς ἐάν

---

21. Note that the teaching of Jesus on the way down from the mountain reemphasizes the passion and resurrection announcement (9:9, 12).

(or ἄν) or εἴ τις, these sayings set forth a fundamental rule of life that applies both to Jesus and the disciples (see 8:35; 9:35; and 10:42–45). Rhetorically they are antithetical aphorisms. An antithetical aphorism is a brief but sweeping statement containing a sharp contrast that is emphasized by using antithetical terms.[22] The antithesis contained in each of these three sayings is sharpened to the point of paradox, for they assert a necessary connection between opposite terms. The attempt to save one's life will lead to the opposite; the goal of being first can only be achieved by its opposite. The clash of words in each of these antithetical aphorisms emphasizes the conflict between this vision of life and the normal view, in which people assume that they can directly achieve the goals that their anxious self-concern sets for them. These paradoxical words intend to shake the assumptions that normally control our thinking and planning.[23]

These words are part of Jesus' new statement of the disciples' commission. They also reflect, however, the commission that Jesus has accepted for himself. This is clear from the parallel drawn between Jesus' way and the way of the disciple in 8:34 and 10:45. Furthermore, the same paradox is dramatized in the mocking scenes of the passion story, where Jesus is presented as king while mocked by the soldiers (15:16–20) and as the savior who cannot save himself (15:31; note the connection with 8:35). The passion announcements make clear the external course of events and speak of the passion as rejection by the leaders of Israel. The inner meaning of Jesus' path for the one who follows it is suggested by the paradoxical sayings being discussed. Jesus, renouncing all concern for life and power, goes to the cross in service of others. Strangely, this death brings life. This is the meaning of the death of Jesus most strongly emphasized in Mark.[24]

---

22. For discussion of this rhetorical form and Gospel examples, see Tannehill, *Sword*, 88–101. Mark 10:42–45 is an expanded antithetical aphorism; see Tannehill, *Sword*, 102–7.

23. On the importance of not dissolving the paradox in interpretation, see Tannehill, *Sword*, 99–101.

24. Mark 10:45 is a climactic statement, but the reference to Jesus' death as a ransom for many is a subsidiary element in that statement. Jesus' death as ransom is used to explain the nature of Jesus' self-giving service—by his death as ransom he is giving himself in service—but it is the fact of his serving that is important to the forceful teaching in 10:42–45. The idea of Jesus' death as ransom does not appear elsewhere in Mark. Even 14:24 uses rather different language. On the other hand, the emphasis on self-renunciation is reinforced by the threefold pattern of sayings that we have been discussing.

Mark 11:1—16:8

Martin Kähler's famous footnote in which he speaks of the Gospels as "passion narratives with extended introductions" is both insightful and misleading when applied to Mark as narrative.[25] To speak of the first thirteen chapters as an introduction is inadequate, not only because of the wealth of material there but also because it is these chapters that establish and develop the commissions and task that come to a climax in the passion story. Mark is a single, unified story because of its progressive narrative lines. Events in the first thirteen chapters are necessary parts of the main lines of action, rather than being preliminary to them. The passion, however, is the natural point of emphasis within Mark because it is the climax of the three major narrative lines based on the commissions of Jesus and the disciples, and the task of the "opponents." Here these commissions and task lead to critical action, in which the commission is accepted or refused at high risk, and we discover the results. The three narrative lines are closely intertwined, we reach a high-point of tension, and we discover the ending with which the author chooses to leave us.

The intention of the "opponents," inactive since 3:6, is repeated in 11:18. From that point on it is kept alive by a series of controversies, together with repeated reference to the threatening presence of Jesus' enemies and their destructive intent (see especially 12:12 and 14:1). At the beginning of the series of controversies, the "opponents" are listed as "the chief priests and the scribes and the elders" (11:27). This group continues to be active at least through 12:13, and again in chapter 14. The list is the same as in Jesus' passion announcement in 8:31. Although Mark suggests that there is continuity between this group and Jesus' previous "opponents" (see the reference to scribes "from Jerusalem" in 3:22 and 7:1), the appearance of the specific group of which Jesus spoke suggests the possibility of the fulfillment of his prophecy. The "opponents'" intention, however, still leads nowhere, for they are frustrated by Jesus' powerful words (see 12:34) and the crowd's support of Jesus (11:18; 12:12, 37). It is only at 14:10–11 that a way is found to move forward with their plan. In chapters 11–12 Jesus appears to be beyond their power.

In Mark the high priests, scribes, and elders (and earlier the Pharisees) plot against Jesus and oppose him in controversy scenes, indicating that they view Jesus as an opponent of their essential purposes. However, while the author of Mark has firmly established the view that this group intends

---

25. Martin Kähler, *The So-Called Historical Jesus and the Historic, Biblical Christ*, trans. Carl E. Braaten (Philadelphia: Fortress, 1964) 80.

to oppose Jesus, he has also told us that Jesus has accepted a commission to be rejected and die in Jerusalem. This group has an essential role in fulfilling Jesus' commission. One of the interesting features of the plot of Mark is that the role relationships are not symmetrical. If Jesus is being opposed by the high priests, scribes, and elders, we would expect the relation to be reciprocal, so that Jesus must become opponent to his opponents, resisting their efforts in order to fulfill his commission. This is not the case, however, with the specific commission that Jesus announced in 8:31, for the group that intends to oppose Jesus has a necessary role in the fulfillment of this commission.[26] This not only points to the strangeness of the commission that Jesus has accepted. It also reflects an ambiguity that characterizes the passion story as a whole, not only on the level of role relationships but also on the level of the reader's response to the text. While the supporter of Jesus would naturally hope that Jesus will triumph over his enemies by escaping their plot, a hope repeatedly encouraged by the author,[27] Jesus himself has chosen a different way. Thus every step toward Jesus' death is likely to have both negative and positive value for the reader, as two ways of judging struggle within. There is a strong tendency for the reader to make the opposition symmetrical, but Jesus' words and actions repeatedly conflict with this.

The congruence of Jesus' commission with their own plans is not seen by those who intend to oppose him. The result is dramatic irony. The effect of the actions of the Jerusalem leaders conflicts with their purpose. They intend to bring Jesus and his mission to an end, but their actions have a place within Jesus' mission, and his work does not end. To be sure, rejection and death retain their strongly negative connotations in Mark. This appears most prominently in the struggle in Gethsemane and the word from the cross (15:34). In Gethsemane Jesus accepts the necessity of suffering; it is not good in itself. The way that Jesus goes is deeply unsettling, and this appears in the portrait of Jesus himself. But the author of Mark believes that the evil of death has been incorporated by Jesus into his victorious mission.

The irony of dramatic action that I have just mentioned could easily be missed. However, there is a series of scenes in the passion story that highlight the ironic relationship between Jesus and those who reject him.[28]

26. To be sure, the parable of the murderous tenants (12:1–12) assumes that the intended opposition deserves punishment.

27. See below 184–86.

28. Donald Juel calls irony "the most prominent literary feature of the passion story" in Mark; see *Messiah and Temple: The Trial of Jesus in the Gospel of Mark*, SBLDS 31

It seems to be important to the author of Mark that unwitting confessions of Jesus appear in the very acts by which he is rejected. The rejection and scorning of Jesus, prominent in the passion announcements in chapters 8–10, are dramatized in the passion story by scenes of mocking. These scenes are systematically placed, one following each of the main events after the arrest (the trial before the Jerusalem council, the trial before Pilate, the crucifixion). The last two of the three scenes are vivid and emphatic. All three are ironic and suggest to the reader important affirmations about Jesus. This is easily recognized in the second of the three scenes, in which Christ is mocked by the soldiers (15:16–20). The irony here actually has two levels. The soldiers act and speak ironically; outwardly they proclaim Jesus King of the Jews but actually they are rejecting his kingship. However, the reader is meant to take the soldiers' irony ironically—that is, as pointing to a hidden truth. This reading is supported by the repeated references to Jesus as Christ and king in the passion story.[29]

The other two mocking scenes also contain irony. In 14:65 Jesus is mistreated and commanded to prophesy. The mistreatment makes clear that the request is not meant seriously but is intended to degrade Jesus. But again ironic truth is suggested, for the reader knows that a whole series of prophecies by Jesus is coming to fulfillment in the passion story. The prophesied rejection by the chief priests, scribes, and elders has just taken place; the prophesied denial by Peter is about to take place. The reader is intended to recognize Jesus the prophet as he is mocked. The tendency in Mark's passion story to broaden and emphasize the mocking of Jesus appears in 15:29–32, for the mockers include not only the high priests and scribes but also the passersby and those crucified with Jesus. Again the words are ironic. The reference to the destruction and building of the temple may contain an affirmation about Jesus that the author accepts.[30] The command "Save yourself" is meant ironically, for the speaker

---

(Missoula, Mont.: Scholars, 1977) 47.

29. "Christ" is explained by "King of Israel" in 15:32. "Christ" is accepted by Jesus in 14:61–62 and used by the author in 1:1. Thus the context in Mark provides a guide for understanding the irony. It is often said that in irony the actual meaning is the opposite of what is expressed. The relation between expression and meaning, however, can be more subtle and complex. Wayne C. Booth speaks of the process of "reconstruction" required by irony; *A Rhetoric of Irony* (Chicago: University of Chicago Press, 1974) 10–12. Because of some incongruity the reader must reject the surface meaning and seek an alternative interpretation, which will to some degree be in conflict with the surface meaning.

30. This is the view of Juel, who says, "Jesus is the destroyer of the temple in a figurative and in an ironic sense: its destruction is a result of his death, brought about by those in charge of the temple worship"; *Messiah and Temple*, 206. See also John R. Donahue, *Are*

intends to highlight Jesus' powerlessness. The thought is continued by the statement in 15:31: "Others he saved, himself he cannot save." Although intended as mockery, this statement summarizes so well Jesus' story as told in Mark that it must be regarded as one of the points at which key elements of the total development come to expression. Jesus' power to heal and rescue has been demonstrated. But the rule proclaimed to the disciples in 8:35 applies to Jesus also: "Whoever seeks to save his life will lose it." Hence, "the Christ, the King of Israel" (again ironic confession) has power to save others but no power to save himself.

So the mocking scenes in Mark's passion story are Christological. They covertly proclaim Jesus as prophet, king, and powerful savior who does not use his power for himself. In each scene this is tied to the experience of rejection and death. The truth proclaimed by irony is that Jesus fills these roles as he suffers. Thus the paradoxical sayings that speak of life through death (8:35) and greatness through lowliness (9:35 and 10:42–45) become drama in the passion narrative.

Jesus has been the chief actor and speaker in Mark. At the arrest, however, he shifts to a passive role. He is the victim of the destructive action of others. To be sure, Jesus' commission is being fulfilled through these events, and Jesus' passivity expresses his basic acceptance of this commission. Although the action originates outside himself, Jesus is moving toward his goal, and this is called to the reader's attention by reminders of the passion announcements (see the Son of Man sayings in 14:21, 41) and by references or allusions to the fulfillment of Scripture.

More striking is the fact that Jesus becomes almost silent after the arrest. Perhaps this portrays Jesus' acceptance of his role of suffering. Jesus' powerful words, however, emphasized by their forceful style, have been the means by which Jesus has influenced others, and the role of influencer, moving others to action, has been important in Mark's portrait of Jesus. However, Jesus' words are, for the most part, no longer necessary. Jesus' teaching in 8:31—10:45 has already made clear the meaning of the passion events. This teaching included a call to follow Jesus to suffering and death (8:34–38). This call of Jesus is all the stronger because Jesus no longer speaks about accepting death and giving oneself in service but does these things himself. Here Jesus shifts from teacher to powerful paradigm. Thus the role of Jesus as influencer vis à vis the readers of the Gospel is

You the Christ? The Trial Narrative in the Gospel of Mark, SBLDS 10 (Missoula, Mont.: Scholars, 1973) 103–38.

probably increased rather than reduced as the author presents this passive, silent Jesus.

The teaching in 8:34–38 was given to the disciples, as well as others, and 8:31—10:45 showed a struggle taking place between Jesus and the disciples over the proper understanding of Jesus' and the disciples' commissions. At 10:45 the conflict is still unresolved. There is hope but no assurance that the disciples will see the light. The narrative line constituted by the disciples' commission is the third narrative line that comes to a climax in the passion story. In this case, however, the outcome is negative. In chapter 14 we find repeated and dramatic emphasis on the failure of the disciples to follow Jesus in suffering. The composition of the story highlights Judas' betrayal, the flight of the disciples, and Peter's denial by the fact that Jesus predicts each of these events. Thus the reader's attention is focused on these events before they happen in the narrative line.

Furthermore, the author guides his readers to a strongly negative evaluation of the disciples' behavior. In 14:31 the disciples reject Jesus' prophecy of their desertion and denial and explicitly promise faithfulness to death. So the actions that follow must be evaluated not only in light of Jesus' requirements in 8:34–38 but also as a clear betrayal of an explicit promise. We are also told of the disciples' repeated failure to watch in Gethsemane,[31] and Peter's denial is juxtaposed with Jesus' confession at his trial, highlighting the contrast, and is emphasized by repetition (Peter denies Jesus three times) with a strong climax (the last denial involves a curse). The disciples' story line stops at this point of failure. Christian readers must struggle with the fact that their heroes and representatives, those who share with them the call to follow Jesus, have failed the test. A clear choice is placed before the readers, represented by Jesus, on the one hand, and the faithless disciples, on the other. Choosing to stand with Jesus means accepting Jesus' words in 8:31—10:45 and living them out as Jesus does in the passion story.

The powerful effect of this is undermined if readers are allowed to fully distinguish themselves from the disciples, regarding them as heretics with whom the readers have nothing in common. It is important, then, that it is precisely the honored leaders of the church who have this role and that Mark's account initially presents them in a very positive light (see 1:16–20; 3:13–18; 4:10–12; and 6:7–13), helping the reader to view them as representatives of the church, its calling and privileges.

---

31. See Werner H. Kelber, "The Hour of the Son of Man and the Temptation of the Disciples (Mark 14:32–42)," in *The Passion in Mark*, ed. Werner H. Kelber (Philadelphia: Fortress, 1976) 47–60.

Furthermore, the author is not content to condemn the faithless disciples but clearly anticipates a possibility beyond failure. This can be seen in the passage that most clearly speaks of the post-resurrection situation, Mark 13. When Jesus says, "They will deliver you up to councils" and "You will stand before governors and kings for my sake" (13:9), he is speaking of what he endured and the disciples rejected in the passion story. Yet Jesus is speaking to Peter, James, John, and Andrew (13:3) about their future role. This does not mean that these once faithless disciples are securely faithful after the resurrection. They are also warned against being led astray. But this does show that the author of Mark believes in the power of Jesus' words and witness to create faithful disciples among the first followers and the church that they represent.

This anticipation of faithfulness in suffering is confirmed by Jesus' statement to James and John in 10:39. I also think that we should interpret 14:28 and 16:7 in light of this anticipated shift from failure to possible faithfulness. Jesus' statement in 14:28 must be understood in relation to the preceding verse. After speaking of the disciples as scattered sheep, Jesus says, "But (ἀλλά) after I have been raised . . . " This statement anticipates a shift in the disciples' situation as scattered sheep following the resurrection. Furthermore, the related message of a future meeting with Jesus in 16:7 is meant precisely for the disciples "and Peter," i.e., those who proved faithless in the preceding story. Thus the primary function of this meeting, as indicated by these verses, is to make possible the restoration of a relationship broken by the disciples' failure. To regard these verses as references to the parousia conflicts with this function and leaves unclear how Peter, James, John, and Andrew, who proved faithless at Jesus' passion, could be the ones who will suffer and preach the gospel, as indicated in Mark 13. To suppose that they could simply continue on as disciples as if nothing had happened mitigates the seriousness of the failure emphasized so strongly in Mark 14.[32]

Nevertheless, it is significant that the author stopped short of narrating the meeting of the risen Jesus with his disciples. Restoration of faithful discipleship is opened to the reader as gracious possibility, but it is not

---

32. For other arguments against the parousia interpretation of 14:28 and 16:7, see Robert H. Stein, "A Short Note on Mark xiv.28 and xvi.7," *NTS* 20 (1974) 445–52. To assert, as Crossan does ("Empty Tomb," 146), that Mark's empty tomb story was created to oppose the idea of resurrection appearances to Peter and the apostles requires us to declare the author of Mark to be inept. When the announcement of Jesus' resurrection is followed by a statement about Peter seeing him and this is conveyed in writing to a church that already told stories about the risen Jesus' appearance to Peter (1 Cor 15:5), the reader can hardly be blamed for taking it as a reference to a resurrection appearance.

narrated as accomplished fact. And it is a possibility that faces continuing obstacles from faithless people in the post-resurrection church (see 16:8).[33] Yet the words of Jesus have been trustworthy in the past, and the author wants us to believe that the words of Jesus in 14:28, repeated and clarified in 16:7, will also prove true in spite of fear and failure. The situation with which the Gospel ends is relevant to the author's audience. It is the situation between failure and possibility, a possibility not yet understood and believed. The author may know that some of the first disciples did respond to this possibility and became faithful followers of Jesus in suffering (see 10:39 and 13:9). But many of those to whom the Gospel speaks still stand between failure and unrealized possibility.

The drama of the passion story is heightened by unexpected developments in the role relationships. The opponents are both opponents and (in terms of Jesus' commission in 8:31) helpers. The disciples prove to be false helpers. Their failure, however, increases the impact of Mark's portrait of Jesus. Since Jesus' and the disciples' commissions are parallel, the disciples' failure makes them contrasting figures to Jesus. The choice is dramatized by showing both alternatives in action. The way of Jesus stands out starkly against the contrasting background of the disciples.

The passion story presents somewhat ambiguous evidence on the clarity of Jesus' vision and the firmness of his resolution as he approaches death. On the one hand, the passion predictions and the related sayings in 14:21, 41 and 49 lead us to believe that Jesus is perfectly clear as to his path and firmly resolved to take it. The Gethsemane scene and the cry from the cross give a different impression. These passages significantly deepen the portrait of Jesus, helping the reader to recognize the reality of Jesus' suffering and to share in it. Gethsemane is also a point of crisis in the Gospel's story of Jesus. For a moment the outcome hangs in the balance, and the previous impression of firm resolution could prove to be false. The struggle of Jesus, however, not only introduces suspense and helps the reader to recognize the reality of Jesus' suffering; it may also be relevant to situations that Mark's first readers would face. The three disciples play an important role in Mark's Gethsemane story, and the story, while indicating the disciples' failure, also indicates what they should do

---

33. If the women at the tomb include the mother of Jesus (compare 15:40, 47, and 16:1 with 6:3), and if the scenes that give a negative picture of Jesus' relatives (3:21, 31–35; 6:1–6) are criticizing a group in the writer's historical situation, 16:8 may be part of that criticism, indicating that Jesus' family, or the Jerusalem church, has become an obstacle to God's purpose for the disciples. In any case, it is the women, not the disciples, who cause the problem at this point.

in such a situation: watch and pray. Christians faced with suffering or death must face their own fears and come to terms with them. Otherwise their promises will carry no more weight than those of the disciples (see 14:31). The struggle of Jesus in Gethsemane, which the disciples were meant to share, would help such readers to identify with Jesus' way and to recognize the importance of their own spiritual struggle.

The author also has another way of leading his readers to recognize their selfish hopes and fears. Christian readers in Mark's church would, of course, expect the story to lead to Jesus' death because they had heard the story before. Nevertheless, one can imagine a different outcome. The author helps his readers imagine a different outcome by repeatedly suggesting the possibility that Jesus will escape. Such possibilities are appealing in light of the powerful desire for a way around the cross rather than through it. But the story continually calls the reader back from false hope to the reality of the crucifixion.

In Gethsemane Jesus suggests that it may not be necessary to die, since all things are possible for God (14:35–36).[34] This suggestion, however, involving a changed understanding of God's commission, is rejected, and Jesus remains committed to God's will as announced at 8:31. One avenue of escape is closed. At the arrest one person begins armed resistance (14:47). The comment of Jesus that follows is not a reprimand of this act but a protest of the manner in which he is being treated by the arresting party. Such a protest against injustice can easily lead to a call for resistance, and the preceding event suggests that some are ready to respond to such a call. But both resistance and protest are cut short by Jesus' final words: "But (this is happening) that the Scriptures may be fulfilled." The possibility of escape through resistance ends as Jesus submits.[35]

34. That all things are possible with God or for the believer is a repeated Markan theme, which heightens the plausibility of Jesus' request; see 9:23 and 10:27.

35. Here I follow the interpretation of Thomas Boomershine. See "Mark, the Storyteller: A Rhetorical-Critical Investigation of Mark's Passion and Resurrection Narrative" (Ph.D. diss., Union Theological Seminary, New York, 1974) 165–66. Boomershine argues, "The function of the final sentence in both speeches [14:36 and 14:48b–49] is to break unexpectedly the line of reasoning established in the rest of the speech. The use of the strongly adversative conjunction *alla* is one sign of the discontinuity of thought. . . . In the arrest speech, therefore, the final sentence has an adversative relationship to the first part of the speech. The possibility of resisting arrest is rejected in a climactic acceptance of God's will." Furthermore, "the function of the speech is inextricably tied to its structure and context. . . . Its context is determined by the hostile reaction to Jesus' arrest by one of those standing by. Jesus' initial response is in direct continuity with that action. The function of the speech is, therefore, to call forth a sympathetic reaction to expressions of hostility toward those who have arrested him and to raise the hope that Jesus may resist

In the trial before the Jerusalem council the author builds up suspense by repeatedly referring to attempts and failures to find testimony on which to condemn Jesus. The "opponents" of Jesus have run into trouble, for they have no legal case. Even the use of false witnesses does not produce the desired result. So it appears that Jesus will have to be released. But then the high priest asks Jesus, "Are you the Christ, the Son of the Blessed?" At this point Jesus need only remain silent, as he has been doing, and as he commanded the disciples to do when they recognized him as the Christ (8:30). But in seeming conflict with the whole Messianic secret theme, just at the most disadvantageous time, Jesus openly acknowledges his Messianic office. The result is his condemnation to death. Jesus himself provides the crucial testimony by which he is condemned. The possibility of escape by concealment is rejected.

At the trial before Pilate the crowd requests the release of one prisoner, as was customary. Pilate himself proposes that he release Jesus (15:9). The Gospel writer has repeatedly indicated that the crowd supports Jesus. That is the reason why the "opponents" have not been able to act. Now the crowd need only agree with Pilate's proposal. But the crowd chooses Barabbas and calls for Jesus' crucifixion. A clear possibility of release is suggested, but again it comes to nothing. Once more false hopes are aroused and then crushed.

Finally, the possibility of escape is again suggested when Jesus is on the cross. The mockers challenge Jesus to save himself by coming down from the cross (15:30–32). This, of course, is mockery, but the story, as it moves on, plays with the idea of a last minute, miraculous rescue. This can be seen in the response to Jesus' cry of forsakenness. The cry is misunderstood as a call to Elijah for rescue from the cross (15:35–36). The listeners wait with excitement to see if the rescuer will come. But Jesus dies without a rescuer.

Jesus has followed his path to the end, while a whole series of avenues of escape, representing most of the conceivable possibilities for Jesus and his followers, have been eliminated one by one. Hopes for a way around the cross for Jesus (and, by implication, for the believer) have been aroused sufficiently to be recognized and then have been crushed. This narrative pattern takes on meaning in light of the author's concern to purge the church of its desire for triumph without suffering.

---

arrest. Jesus' sudden acceptance of arrest . . . destroys that hope." Most of my further comments on false hopes for escape parallel points made by Boomershine.

The previous discussion suggests that the author intends this story of Jesus' acceptance of death for the sake of his mission to deeply color the readers' understanding of Jesus. This affects the significance of the titles applied to him in key scenes. The reservation of public announcement of Jesus' Messianic status until 14:61–62 makes the Sanhedrin trial a climactic Christological scene.[36] Three Christological titles that are of central importance in Mark are publicly appropriated by Jesus in his answer to the high priest. Jesus lays claim to the titles Christ, Son of the Blessed (that is, Son of God), and Son of Man as he goes to his death. Indeed, the public acknowledgment of his claim brings about his death. While previous use of the titles Christ and Son of God occur in private or are followed by commands to silence,[37] secrecy is no longer necessary when the titles are applied to the Christ of the passion, for then they are properly used. The narrative situation in which the titles are appropriated helps to define their meaning.

The centurion's confession at the cross (15:39) must be understood in light of the narrative line that comes to a climax in the passion. We have seen that the title Son of God has special importance in the scenes that establish or confirm Jesus' commission as a commission from God (see 1:11 and 9:7). That commission led Jesus to the cross. A principal function of the centurion's confession is to remind the reader that Jesus through his death has fulfilled God's commission. The recurrence of the title Son of God is appropriate for this purpose. This function also explains the phrasing of the centurion's confession: "*Truly* this man *was* God's Son." The past tense indicates that this is a retrospective statement. It is a comment on the story narrated to this point, declaring that Jesus has fulfilled the commission given to him by God. The use of "truly" fits with this, for the statement is an affirmation or confirmation of something previously stated in the commission scenes. Again it is apparent that the narrative development with its climax in the passion is important for understanding the meaning and function of Christological titles in important scenes in Mark.

---

36. See Donahue, *Are You the Christ?*, 88–95; Norman Perrin, "The High Priest's Question and Jesus' Answer (Mark 14:61–62)," in *The Passion in Mark*, ed. Werner H. Kelber (Philadelphia: Fortress, 1976) 80–95.

37. The voice at the baptism is a private communication to Jesus. The conversation in 5:7 may be private. In any case, it is followed by a restriction on communication in 5:19, which is disobeyed.

Conclusion

The study of Mark as narrative reveals more unity and art in this Gospel than is commonly recognized. These appear as we consider the narrative lines that flow from the commissions or tasks of major characters and groups in the Gospel. Our understanding of these matters is enriched by study of the role relationships among Jesus and others in the story, which sometimes involve reiterative enrichment and sometimes unexpected development.

The author guides the readers' response to the story by narrative patterns that control emphasis and the evaluation of events and characters. Among the compositional techniques considered in this study were the delayed disclosure of Jesus' and the disciples' full commissions, and the repeated use of irony, paradox, and enticement to false hope. In these and other ways the author communicates with the anticipated readers concerning their life situation by means of the story of Jesus. Studying Mark as narrative Christology provides a deeper understanding of the meaning and function of Mark's presentation of Jesus Christ.

9

READING IT WHOLE:
The Function of Mark 8:34–35 in Mark's Story

This essay fits with the two preceding essays on Mark because it, too, rests on a wholistic study of Mark as a narrative. In this essay, however, I seek to show that this approach can be illuminating even if one starts with a few verses in the middle of the Gospel. The significance of Mark 8:34–35 grows as we are able to relate Jesus' words to more and more of the Markan narrative. We discover that these verses have a key function in the narrative, which is not apparent if we consider them in isolation or fail to relate Jesus' words to the subsequent actions of Jesus and his disciples.

BOTH PROFESSORS AND PREACHERS fragment the Gospels. The preacher preaches on a pericope, an isolated scene or parable or saying, and usually assumes that there is no need to look further than this pericope and its immediate context in order to do responsible biblical preaching. Biblical scholarship seems to support this assumption. Since the Gospels were composed of units of tradition that originally circulated separately, the original parts seem more important than the subsequent whole. To be sure, the Gospel writers have been recognized as theological interpreters of the Gospel tradition. To some extent each of them has a unified theological perspective. However, unity of theological perspective is something different from the unity of story. We are only beginning to rediscover each Gospel as a story that, like any other story, is meant to be read as a whole.[1]

---

1. The following studies of Mark seek to understand it as a unitary story with the aid of perspectives from literary studies: Tannehill, "The Disciples in Mark: The Function of a Narrative Role," *JR* 57 (1977) 386–405; idem, *A Mirror for Disciples* (Nashville: Discipleship Resources, 1977); and idem, "The Gospel of Mark as Narrative Christology," *Semeia* 16 (1979) 57–95; Norman R. Petersen, *Literary Criticism for New Testament Critics*,

The preacher can profit from this rediscovery. When a story element is isolated from the story as a whole, it loses power and significance. The rediscovery of the relation of the story element to the total story may also be a discovery of power and significance previously unrecognized. This discovery about the text permits it to contribute more powerfully to the sermon.

I will not attempt to demonstrate how one might move from text to sermon, viewing the text in this way. I will simply illustrate the process of discovery as we begin to understand the text as a contributing part of the whole story. I begin with the question: What is the function of Mark 8:34–35 in Mark's story? If we can answer this question, we should discover that the significance of these verses expands as we are able to relate them to more and more of Mark's narrative. This does not work equally well with all passages in a Gospel, but with key passages such as this one it can be quite illuminating.

Antithetical Aphorisms and Passage Announcements

In Mark 8:34–35 we read:

> If anyone wants to come after me, let him deny himself and take up his cross and follow me. For whoever wants to save his life will destroy it, and whoever destroys his life for my sake and the gospel's will save it.[2]

For our present purposes it is important to note a few features of these words that will prove significant as we move on. First, both sentences begin in nearly the same way: either with "If anyone wants to," or with "Whoever wants to" (in Greek: εἴ τις θέλει plus infinitive, or ὅς ἐὰν θέλῃ plus infinitive). Second, 8:34 speaks of the requirements of discipleship, understood as *following* Jesus. Discipleship as following is defined by the way that Jesus chooses for himself. Since Jesus is now moving to-

---

GBS (Philadelphia: Fortress, 1978) 49–80; idem, "'Point of View' in Mark's Narrative," *Semeia* 12 (1978) 97–112; Werner H. Kelber, *Mark's Story of Jesus* (Philadelphia: Fortress, 1979); and David Rhoads, Joanna Dewey, and Donald Michie, *Mark as Story*, 2d ed. (Minneapolis: Fortress, 1998).

2. The active voice of ἀπόλλυμι can mean "destroy" as well as "lose," and the translation "lose," normally chosen for this text, may weaken the forcefulness of the original Greek. I have retained the masculine singular pronouns of the Greek text, but the general and indefinite reference of these sentences ("anyone," "whoever") suggest that a gender-inclusive translation is appropriate. This can be handled most easily by shifting to the plural: "Let them deny themselves," etc.

ward crucifixion (see 8:31), disciples are required to take up their crosses. Third, the saying about saving and destroying one's life is constructed from contrasting words combined in paradoxical fashion. This paradox is repeated in both halves of the sentence: the attempt to save one's life will destroy it; destroying one's life will save it. Elsewhere I have called this form of speech an antithetical aphorism.[3]

An antithetical aphorism is a brief and pointed saying that makes a strong, unqualified statement containing a sharp contrast. The contrast is expressed in a wordplay, using the same words in negative and positive form or using antithetical words. In Mark 8:35 the antithetical terms (save/destroy) express the conflict between Jesus' call and the human desire for security, a basic motive in our lives. The temptation for the interpreter is to reduce this paradox to a commonplace in order to make it seem reasonable. Then 8:35 seems to say that sacrifice now will bring a reward later, a statement that contains little surprise or tension. But the speaker's choice of words in 8:35 shows that he wishes to be paradoxical. He wishes to force his hearers to face the conflict between his requirement and the normal and reasonable concern to preserve one's life. If this antithetical aphorism is to have its intended power, it is necessary to feel (and help the congregation to feel) the grating conflict between these challenging words and normal assumptions of what is good and necessary.[4]

The sayings in 8:34–35 are supported by 8:36—9:1, for 8:34—9:1 form a chain of sayings with a common purpose: to show to disciples and prospective disciples that they must let loose of their lives, for discipleship is likely to lead to suffering and death.

As we begin to move beyond 8:34–35 to ask about the function of these words in the total narrative, we should note, first of all, that they follow Jesus' first announcement of his coming passion in 8:31 and Peter's rejection of this announcement, which calls forth Jesus' harsh rebuke. Furthermore, a similar sequence of events follows each of the three passion announcements that occur about a chapter apart in this section of Mark. Three times Jesus announces his coming passion (8:31; 9:31; 10:32–34). Three times the disciples show outright resistance or behave in ways con-

---

3. See Tannehill, *The Sword of His Mouth* (1975; reprinted, Eugene, Ore.: Wipf and Stock, 2003) 88–101. Some of the hermeneutical issues raised by this type of saying are discussed by William A. Beardslee, "Uses of the Proverb in the Synoptic Gospels," *Int* 24 (1970) 61–73; and idem, "Saving One's Life by Losing It," *JAAR* 47 (1979) 57–72.

4. For further discussion of Mark 8:34–35 see Tannehill, *Sword*, 98–101; and idem, *Mirror*, 67–70.

trary to the way of Jesus (8:32–33; 9:33–34; 10:35–41). Three times Jesus responds with corrective teaching (8:34—9:1; 9:35–37; 10:42–45).

Mark 8:34–35 is part of the corrective teaching in the first of these similar sequences of events. This much is commonly recognized in Markan studies today. However, we should also note that the pattern extends to the way in which the corrective teaching is formulated. In all three cases an antithetical aphorism has a key role in the corrective teaching, an antithetical aphorism that brings out the paradoxical difference between Jesus' way for himself and his disciples and common assumptions of how things work. Following the second passion announcement, the disciples are discussing who among them is the greatest. Jesus responds (beginning with the same phrase as in 8:34: εἴ τις θέλει plus infinitive), "If anyone wants to be first, he shall be last of all and servant of all" (9:35). Again we have an antithetical aphorism. First and last are linked together in paradoxical fashion.

Following the third passion announcement, James and John ask for positions of preference in the coming glory. This leads to the words of Jesus in 10:42–45, which are an expanded antithetical aphorism. First Jesus calls attention to the normal pattern of rule in the political world. The disciples must behave quite differently: "Whoever wants to become great among you [ὃς ἂν θέλῃ plus infinitive] shall be your servant, and whoever wants to be first among you shall be slave of all." Here the antithetical aphorism is doubled, the repetition adding emphasis, and the most emphatic formulation is used as a climax: "slave of all." Then a reference to Jesus' own servant role is attached: "For the Son of man also did not come to be served but to serve and to give his life as a ransom for many."[5] The servant role and death are linked in this verse, while previous announcements of Jesus' death have been followed by the call to give up one's life and become a servant. Furthermore, 10:43–45 corresponds to 8:34, the saying about taking up one's cross, because both passages emphasize the parallel between the way of Jesus and the way of the disciple. Thus at the beginning and at the end of the corrective teaching within the threefold pattern that I have discussed, the Gospel links the paradoxical demand of Jesus to Jesus' own choice of the cross. This parallel between Jesus' way and the intended way for disciples is important for understanding other parts of Mark.

The three antithetical aphorisms following the three passion announcements focus on two human concerns: security in face of death

---

5. On Mark 10:42–45, see Tannehill, *Sword*, 102–7.

(viz., saving one's life) and status or domination (viz., being first). These two basic concerns are challenged, for the call of Jesus conflicts with both. Note that Mark sees Jesus' death as presenting a fundamental challenge not only to our concern for safety but also to our concern for status and power.

The repeated passion announcements tell the readers in advance what will happen in Jerusalem. However, the repeated antithetical aphorisms are equally important in Mark's narrative. The passion announcements disclose the outward course of events. The antithetical aphorisms disclose the inner meaning of these events for the one who suffers and serves. Through their paradoxical promises, they emphasize the conflict of Jesus' way with fundamental human motivations.

The Function of Mark 8:34–35 in Mark's Story

I have discussed the relation of Mark 8:34–35 to a major section of the Gospel of Mark; now I must explore its place within the total story. The unity of the Markan narrative is clearer when we consider this common feature of stories: a commission or task, accepted by a story character, results in a unified narrative sequence as the narrator tells us how the character fulfills that commission or fails to fulfill it. The commission provides an overarching purpose or goal, and events of the plot take on meaning because they represent movement toward the goal or obstacles to its realization. Disconnected events do not form a story, but events that move toward or block the fulfillment of a major purpose do. The events of Mark form a unitary story in relation to the commission that Jesus received from God and the commission that the disciples received from Jesus. The story gradually discloses what these commissions require and shows Jesus accepting these requirements and the disciples rejecting them.[6]

Jesus first appears in the baptism scene, which also discloses to the reader Jesus' commission from God, as the voice from heaven says, "You are my beloved Son" (Mark 1:11). The brief statement at the baptism does not tell the readers what this special role will require of Jesus. The baptism scene makes clear that Jesus has a commission from God, thus beginning a story line, but the content of that commission—its implications for action—are only disclosed as Jesus begins to act and speak in fulfillment of his commission.

---

6. If we are reading Mark's story well, we will allow the story to define Jesus' and the disciples' commissions rather than imposing on the story our own preconceived notions of what those commissions were.

One of the first things that Jesus does is to call four fishermen to follow him. This begins another story line that features the disciples. The content of the disciples' commission is also incompletely disclosed. However, we are told that they are to come "after" Jesus, that is, "follow" him (1:17–18, 20). The commission of the disciples receives special attention in a series of three scenes, spaced at intervals just as the passion announcements and related material are spaced at intervals. These scenes are the call of the fishermen (1:16–20), the choice of the twelve (3:13–19), and the sending out of the twelve (6:7–13). In these scenes there are a number of indications that the disciples' commission is patterned after the commission of Jesus. They are to "be with" Jesus and to share in his work of preaching and exorcism. However, problems develop in the relation of the disciples to Jesus. These are brought out most clearly in a series of three boat scenes (4:35–41; 6:45–52; 8:13–21), climaxing in a scene in which Jesus berates the disciples for their lack of perception. A major obstacle to the fulfillment of the disciples' commission has appeared.

Peter's confession and Jesus' first announcement of the passion come soon after the third boat scene. The announcement of the passion is a new disclosure of Jesus' commission, of what he must do to fulfill his special role. And it is followed by a new statement of the disciples' commission, beginning with the verses with which we began, Mark 8:34–35. The function of the verses, then, is to provide a new disclosure of the disciples' commission, the commission that gives meaning to their whole story. Thus these verses have a key function in the story. They announce a program for action. They are meant to be lived out by the disciples in the rest of the narrative, just as Jesus lives out the announcement of the passion in the passion story. Just as previous scenes indicated that the disciples were to follow Jesus and do as Jesus was doing, so here they are called to follow him to the cross. The parallel between the way of Jesus and the way of the disciple is maintained.

By the time Jesus announces that he and the disciples must suffer and die, we are halfway through Mark's story. It is remarkable that these central aspects of the commissions of Jesus and the disciples have not been emphasized until this point.[7] Readers of Mark (here we must try to put ourselves in the position of the naïve reader, i.e., the reader who is reading Mark for the first time) have been allowed to form an impression of Jesus and the disciples without this crucial information. The emphasis on giving up one's life as a central requirement comes as a surprise. This

---

7. There are brief hints of Jesus' coming death in Mark 2:20 and 3:6.

heightens the contrast between the author's view and views of Jesus and the disciples in which this requirement is not central, thus helping to focus the decision that the author is presenting to the reader.

The author of Mark has shaped the story by emphasizing certain things through the threefold repetitive patterns that we have noted. An author can also exercise considerable control over the evaluation of characters and events within a story. Judgments of good and bad are influenced by certain norms or standards suggested within a story. These may be expressed through a character who is spokesperson for the author's values. A character who is given authority because he or she is presented as trustworthy and perceptive may be such a spokesperson. In the Gospel of Mark it is clear that Jesus is the central figure of authority. The author does not wish to cast doubt on Jesus' words but wishes to affirm them as true and important. Jesus and the author, then, speak with one voice, and the words and deeds of Jesus provide the norms in light of which the actions of other characters should be evaluated. This is particularly true for the disciples, who are called to follow Jesus. The author intends us to judge the behavior of the disciples by whether they are in harmony or conflict with the words and deeds of Jesus. Thus the call to take up one's cross and destroy one's own life in 8:34–35 is not only a new statement of the disciples' commission but also a new statement of the norm by which the disciples are to be judged. Once again we see that these verses have an important function in the total narrative: They state the norm by which the author expects us to judge the disciples' subsequent behavior.

Both the passion announcement in 8:31 and the call to follow by taking up one's cross in 8:34–35 point forward to the passion story. There we learn that Jesus fulfills his commission but the disciples utterly fail. Jesus is betrayed by one of his inner circle, and the other disciples desert him (14:17–21, 44–50). The disciples reject Jesus' statement that they will all fall away and promise that they will not deny him even if it means death (14:26–31). But they turn out to be faithless liars. Peter is the last hope. He is the only one who continues to follow after the arrest, but his following ends in the climactic scene of Peter's denial. The focus on Peter at the beginning and the end of the trial of Jesus before the Sanhedrin brings out the contrast between Peter's denial and Jesus' fearless confession (14:53–72), which leads to Jesus' death. The composition of Mark 14 does not play down the disciples' failure; it plays it up. Thus the judgment of the disciples that we reach when we compare their behavior to Jesus' words in 8:34–35 is confirmed by the strong emphasis on discipleship failure in Mark 14.

Jesus fulfills not only the commission to suffer and die, expressed in the passion announcements, but also the commission in 8:35. Jesus is the one who destroys his life and saves it. Although this verse appears in teaching to others, it applies to Jesus also. It is general in formulation ("Whoever will destroy his life"), and it follows a statement that links the disciples' way to the way of Jesus by calling on the disciples to follow Jesus by taking up a cross. "Whoever will destroy his life . . . will save it." This applies to the disciples because it first of all applies to Jesus.

The paradox of these words becomes drama in the passion story. There the tension that the saying expresses through using contrasting words becomes a dramatic tension in scenes of human conflict. This is especially true of the mocking scenes in the passion story. Once again, Markan emphasis is shown by the presence of three mocking scenes placed at intervals (14:65; 15:16–20, 29–32), in this case after each of the major events following Jesus' arrest (i.e., after the Sanhedrin trial, the Roman trial, and the crucifixion). The mocking scenes are related to the threefold pattern that dominates 8:31—10:45. The passion announcements that initiate that pattern refer not only to Jesus' death but to the rejection of Jesus, and to acts that show contempt for him (see 8:31; 10:33–34). This contemptuous rejection is most forcefully expressed in the mocking. Furthermore, the mocking scenes are ironic, and the ironic tension of these scenes corresponds to the paradoxical tension of the saying about destroying and saving one's life. The scenes are ironic because the words and acts of contempt reveal the truth about Jesus. He is mocked as prophet just as his words of prophecy are coming true. He is mocked as king, and he is the Christ, the king of Israel. He is mocked as temple destroyer and savior, and he is both.[8] What is more, he is prophet, king, and savior as he is condemned and dies. The irony of the mocking scenes preserves the paradox of the antithetical aphorisms in 8:35 and following, holding triumph in tension with degradation and death. And the mocking words at the cross, "Others he saved, himself he cannot save," recall the words of 8:35, "Whoever wants to save his life will destroy it."

The author of Mark has composed the story carefully, and 8:34–35 has a key place in that composition. The story was composed so that the readers would view these events in a particular way and respond to them in a particular way. In other words, the author had a message for the readers, a message that comes through the medium of a story about the

---

8. On Mark's negative attitude toward the temple, see Kelber, *Mark's Story of Jesus*, 57–70, 82–83.

past. This message cannot be reduced to simple statements without loss. It depends on a complex process of readers identifying with story characters. I think the author had fairly clear expectations as to how this process would work. The author anticipated that the Christian reader would identify with those called to follow Jesus, the disciples. This identification is encouraged by the positive portrait of the disciples in the early chapters of Mark, suggesting that the disciples best represent the faithful commitment to Jesus that Christian readers tend to see in themselves. For those who begin with this comfortable identification, the developing tension between Jesus and the disciples can produce an uncomfortable tension within the self. The readers discover that those called to follow Jesus are afflicted with a strange blindness, and when there seems to be a breakthrough with Peter's confession (8:29), the conflict reappears in sharper focus. The story moves on to a devastating climax for the disciples, a climax that leaves a glimmer of hope (see 14:28; 16:7) but records no accomplished resolution of the problem.[9] The resolution awaits a new decision to follow Jesus, one that must begin with the admission of past failure. Thus the story is a weapon for tearing apart and tearing open our comfortable assurance that we are adequate disciples. By involvement in a story we are made aware of the gap between what we are called to be and do, represented by Jesus' decisions, and what we actually are, represented by the disciples' false choices.

The contrast between the faithfulness of Jesus and the failure of the disciples leaves a clear decision for the reader. The same decision is posed by 8:35 and by the antithetical aphorisms that link being great and being servant. We might say that these sayings are the aphoristic statement of the passion, and the passion story is the dramatic portrayal of these sayings. The passion story enables the readers to live vicariously through the emotions, conflicts, and decisions implicit in these sayings, thereby preparing the readers for their own decisions.

Conclusion

Starting from two verses in the middle of Mark, we can gain an understanding of the contours and message of the whole story, which also en-

---

9. I accept 16:8 as the intended ending of Mark and regard 16:9–20, which is lacking in important early manuscripts, as a later addition by another author. On the significance of 14:28 and 16:7, a disputed point in Markan interpretation, see Tannehill, "Disciples," 403–4; and idem, "Narrative Christology," 82–84 (in the present volume 157–58, 182–83).

riches our understanding of the function and significance of these two verses.[10]

The preacher often feels that it is necessary to expand and dramatize the Gospel text in order to attract the interest of the congregation. This may be because we have robbed the text of interest by isolating it from the total story. Unless we are very careful, our attempts at dramatic expansion will import meanings foreign to the Gospel story and shift attention away from the issues that are central there. On the other hand, considering the story as a whole can increase our awareness of those central issues. Even within the confines of a sermon, the preacher can provide a sketch of aspects of the larger story necessary for full appreciation of the text.

In the case of Mark 8:34–35 it may be necessary to refer to:

- Jesus' commission of the disciples in the early chapters of Mark;
- the developing problem between Jesus and the disciples;
- the new announcement in 8:31 and the new understanding of discipleship that accompanies it;
- the climactic events of the passion to which 8:31, 34–35 point.

This will help the congregation relate to the story and its dramatic conflicts, from which central life issues emerge. This approach will contribute to preaching only if the preacher recognizes that each Gospel is in some respects unique (for example, the portrayal of the disciples in Mark is significantly different from that of Matthew and Luke) and understands how key parts of each Gospel fit into and contribute to the story as a whole. Past biblical scholarship has not been very helpful with this task. There is reason to hope that this situation is changing.

Addendum (2006)

This essay was written in a more peaceful time when we could not imagine that some religious people would volunteer to be suicide bombers. The words "Whoever destroys his life for my sake and the gospel's will save it" require us to face the possibility that some disciples of Jesus might actually have to die out of loyalty to their Lord. But now it is important to highlight the words "for my sake and the gospel's," which raise the question: For what purpose should one dare to give one's life? In a world that

---

10. The interpretation of Mark presented in this essay is discussed in greater detail in Tannehill, "Disciples"; and idem, "Narrative Christology" (in the present volume 135–87). The same approach to Mark as a unitary narrative is utilized in Tannehill, *Mirror*, a non-technical study of the disciples' story in Mark for local church use.

threatens to fall back into religious warfare, we must maintain a vision of the Reign of God that leads us toward peace. The disciple of Jesus must hold firmly to the link between love of God and love of neighbor (Mark 12:28–31) and the recognition that love of neighbor includes loving our enemies (Matt 5:43–48; Luke 6:27–36). Absent this link, love of God can lead to violent fanaticism. Because we are constantly tempted to meet violence with violence, those called to risk their lives "for my sake and the gospel's" must keep these additional words of Jesus in mind.

PART III
Paul's Gospel

10

Paul *as* Liberator *and* Oppressor:
Evaluating Diverse Views of 1 Corinthians

In an article entitled "Freedom and Responsibility in Scripture Interpretation" (now available in my essay collection The Shape of Luke's Story [Eugene, Ore.: Wipf & Stock, 2005] 271–85), I argued that we must recognize a considerable degree of textual "indeterminacy" in interpreting the Gospel of Luke. One reason for indeterminacy is our uncertainty in reconstructing social-historical contexts. There is similar uncertainty in reconstructing the situation that Paul addresses in 1 Corinthians. Different reconstructions of the situation can result in starkly contrasting evaluations of Paul's words to the Corinthians, as we see clearly in recent "political" and "feminist" interpretations. The possibility of such starkly different views has something to teach us about the work of interpretation.

PAULINE STUDIES ARE NO longer immune to the methodological ferment within biblical studies in general. New interpretations of Paul are appearing that may radically affect our evaluation of Paul and his work. In this article I will concentrate on two recent interpretations of Paul and 1 Corinthians that share a common concern—to demonstrate that New Testament studies can support movements of liberation from social oppression—yet result in quite different pictures of Paul. We can start by using the broad labels "political" and "feminist" for these two types of interpretation. Specifically, I will focus on the work of Richard A. Horsley and Neil Elliott, on the one hand, and Elisabeth Schüssler Fiorenza and Antoinette Clark Wire, on the other.

Although one may debate whether the two approaches are strictly incompatible, they are distinctly different, particularly in their evaluations of Paul's role for or against movements of liberation from social oppression. In the one case, Paul stands for liberation from the power of the Roman empire and the social structures that support it; in the other case, Paul is acting to limit the freedom of Corinthian women who have begun to claim their new freedom in Christ.

In this essay it is not my purpose to support one view against the other. Rather, I will point to some of the significant strengths of each. The underlying issue is how we should respond to two types of interpretation—both of them plausible but neither of them certain—that reach such different results. I will argue that both are valuable. As historical interpretations, neither of them (nor other competing interpretations) reaches the level of certainty, since our knowledge of Paul and his churches is limited to what we know from Paul's letters. Even so, they are valuable as hermeneutical exercises, demonstrating clearly how the same text can have different functions as the situation addressed changes, a lesson that continues to apply to the use of Scripture today. Specifically, they demonstrate how the same texts can either support or oppose the liberation of particular social groups, depending on how we understand Paul's interactions with other persons.

Introductory Issues

Conflicting readings may result from differing conceptions of the situation being addressed by Paul. The learned reader should be aware of options and the consequences of those options for understanding the impact of the Pauline text on the lives of people. Consideration of these options is likely to raise ethical issues for interpreters with strong ethical commitments. These ethical commitments might interfere with sound historical judgment. Awareness of this possibility should lead the interpreter to weigh argument and evidence carefully. One option may seem preferable because of the interpreter's commitments and values, but he or she must always ask whether a substantial case can be made for this option. "Substantial" is not the same as "air tight," for on the basis of available evidence it is unlikely that we can declare that all other options are impossible. Nevertheless, the scholarly interpreter must always carry the burden of providing substantial argument and evidence.

Our ethical commitments will influence the interpretive process, even though we usually do not acknowledge them in academic circles. These commitments need not interfere with balanced historical judgment. Indeed, along with our other commitments, we have an ethical obligation to the scholarly community to present a reasonable account of a historical text, one that can be examined by persons who do not share all our presuppositions. Ethical commitment does not release the scholar from the responsibility to present reasons for a particular interpretation of a historical text, which prevents us from turning the text into a simple mirror of our desires. Yet our interests and commitments appear in our interpretations, whether we acknowledge them or not.

If an interpreter appears to have a personal interest in the outcome or to be an advocate for a cause, some would be inclined to dismiss the results. Such suspicions are aroused by the two interpretations of Paul that I will discuss in this essay. Yet a fundamental interest of some kind must motivate our work. All of our work is "interested"; that is, there is some motivation behind it. Otherwise, we would not do it. The motivation may be religious or ethical, in a great variety of forms. It may be anti-religious—directed against religion in its historic and popular expressions. In so far as academic life has been professionalized, religious motivations may have weakened, but the result is not "disinterested" scholarship. Professional motivation takes over—the desire to advance one's standing in the profession through gaining an academic appointment, tenure, and recognition as an outstanding scholar. This motivation is just as likely to interfere with creative and sound scholarship as religious and ethical motivations. On the one hand, it can stifle creativity and critical thinking because of a fear of censure by those who presently hold the leading positions in one's field. On the other hand, it can lead to unfair criticism of previous work and exaggerated claims to uniqueness in an effort to present one's work as new and creative —"the latest thing." It can also lead to excessive attachment to one's own theory, which must be defended at all costs. All scholars need to be self-critical, not through denying their personal motivations but through awareness of the ways that these motivations may impinge on their scholarship, for good and ill. On ethical grounds one might argue, however, that a purely professional motive—the advancement of one's own career—is inferior to motives that aim at a larger good.

A consideration of the motives behind scholarship must also recognize the role of interpretive communities. In church history we can recognize that different denominations commonly represent interpretive communities, with different views of the significance of Scripture and the meaning of the Christian gospel. (This is a simplification, for denominations that maintain organizational unity over time may conceal considerable diversity and fluctuation in their roles as interpretive communities.)

Those who belong to these groups tend to interpret Scripture as the group does.

American biblical scholarship is influenced by interpretive communities of a different type. A proliferation of methodologies and interests has resulted in a diversity of seminars and work groups that meet over a series of years as part of the Society of Biblical Literature. These seminars and work groups both reflect and form interpretive communities within biblical scholarship. They represent distinct methodologies or distinct goals in scholarship. They are valuable because they promote intense and focused work and allow scholars with a common focus to stimulate each other. They also demonstrate how group interests guide scholarship. These groups promote the value of a particular method or goal. If they appear to be successful, they attract members to their group. Personal relationships develop. These relationships change attitudes about which ideas and which publications are worthy of attention. Members promote each other's careers. In particular, older members in the more respected academic positions become mentors to younger, less secure members because they share common interests. Thus, the interests of the group are promoted, perhaps at a loss to some equally worthy task and with the accompanying danger of developing an insular perspective. It has become increasingly difficult for members of different groups to engage in profitable dialogue. Some members who are institutionally less secure may hesitate to question the views of the influential leaders of the group.

Doing scholarship in the midst of multiple and conflicting interests is not an easy task, but these interests are the constant life context of our work. Good scholarship is promoted not by denying the existence of such motivating interests but by testing whether they lead to reasonable interpretations in light of textual and historical evidence. Furthermore, ignoring such interests divorces the scholarly vocation from our higher calling—living for the good. A life devoted to the good requires us to sort out and adhere to the best motivations. These can be compatible with good scholarship and good teaching, which become ways of fulfilling our life vocation of living for the good.

The way in which many academic essays are written disguises the actual function of these interests. Academic essays concentrate on the arguments and evidence for a particular interpretation. Frequently there is no explanation of why the interpreter is interested in presenting such an interpretation. If there is any explanation, it is commonly confined to brief remarks about the implications of the interpretation at the end of the essay, as if these implications arose through subsequent reflection on established conclusions. In actual research our interests and ethical commitments are frequently the stimulus to seek a new interpretation. They are present at the beginning of our work and lead to new acts of historical imagination, so that a hypothesis begins to take shape. The desire for a more satisfying interpretation—satisfying in light of our values and interests—is the origin of much of biblical and theological scholarship that is most significant for human life. The resulting new hypothesis must be tested through detailed study of textual and historical evidence. This study usually leads to modification of the hypothesis, sometimes in ways that defeat our original hopes, sometimes through the discovery of an even more attractive possibility. In the course of this work there is constant interaction between our motivating desires and the constraints of textual and historical evidence.

Current interpretation of the Pauline letters begins with the belief that they are situation-specific communications. Therefore, interpretation depends heavily on an understanding of the situation that Paul is addressing, although all specific information about this must be drawn from the Pauline letter itself. Recent development of a rhetorical perspective in Pauline studies, as represented, for instance, by Elisabeth Schüssler Fiorenza's recent work,[1] complicates an already difficult task.[2] Rhetoric views communication as persuasive action. Paul wants to persuade his audience, that is, to modify its thinking and acting. Our understanding of how Paul is seeking to influence his audience—the communicative force or human impact of Paul's words—depends on our understanding of the situation to which Paul is responding. These matters will, in turn, influence our evaluation of Paul. Was Paul doing the right thing in responding as he did? Although many scholars may want to avoid this question, it is a real and important question for those with ethical commitments. This question is especially forced upon us by recent feminist interpretation.

We are dependent on Paul's letters for our understanding of the situation in Paul's churches. However, definition of the church's problems requiring intervention is already a part of Paul's rhetoric. Definitions of situations are perspectival, and conflicts arise because perspectives differ. Speakers and writers try to persuade by getting others to see the situation from their perspective. It is likely that some of the Corinthians would deny that the problems Paul sees are real problems; they would contest

---

1. Elisabeth Schüssler Fiorenza, *Rhetoric and Ethic: The Politics of Biblical Studies* (Minneapolis: Fortress, 1999).

2. See especially Schüssler Fiorenza's discussion of the "rhetorical situation" in ibid., 108–9.

his understanding of their situation. Rather than assuming that we can infer the "actual" situation directly from Paul's words, we must recognize that there was no commonly accepted definition of the actual situation but only Paul's definition and various competing definitions that reflect motivations about which we can only guess.

If there was no common understanding of the situation, even by the original participants, and our knowledge is limited to inferences from Paul's letters, it is unlikely that we will be able to reach final conclusions about the situation in the Corinthian church. The proliferation of views in the history of scholarship is already testimony to the difficulty of the task,[3] although past scholarship has generally ignored the fact that we have access only to Paul's rhetorical perspective. Yet, as already noted, our understanding of the communicative force of Paul's words, their impact in the rhetorical situation, is dependent on our understanding of the situation. The result is a high degree of indeterminacy. This observation conflicts with the still prevailing assumption that there is one correct solution. The task of the scholar, then, is to prove that one's own solution is the correct one, thereby eliminating other possibilities. Our accomplishments are actually more modest, I believe. Although one interpretation may temporarily seem to rule (it may be attractive because it appears new, creative, and detailed), a rival is likely to appear or reappear. It is useful to discuss arguments and evidence for each position. Yet it is likely that the currently favored position will be only marginally better than the alternatives, which prevents us from eliminating them as possibilities, since no interpretation should assume that we are provided with full information. The large gaps in our knowledge will continue to permit various interpretations of the force of Paul's words.

This may appear to be a counsel of despair, especially for concerned church members who turn to biblical scholars to provide a true understanding of Paul's words so that their faith and life may be nourished. It would seem that no one can really say what is implied for believers today because no one can be sure of the purpose or likely effect of Paul's words in the original situation. I would suggest that the implications are actually more positive. In considering the significance of a biblical text for life today, it is always necessary to ask: Does this text apply to our situation? If so, to what aspects of our situation? Answers will depend on our understanding of the situation to which Paul's words are appropri-

---

3. For one attempt to explain the "Corinthian theology" through a critical examination of themes from previous scholarship, see Wolfgang Schrage, *Der erste Brief an die Korinther*, 2 vols., EKKNT 7/1–2 (Zürich: Benziger, 1991) 1:38–63.

ately addressed. The situation appropriately addressed may or may not be similar to the situation Paul actually addressed. That decision depends on whether Paul was acting appropriately. However, hypotheses concerning the original situation will help us to think about this issue, suggesting various possibilities that may have positive or negative effects for human life. It is useful to consider the various options because any one, or several, may illuminate our situation. Consideration of options may make us aware of possible negative effects, in certain situations, and encourage us to seek applications that will have positive effects.

We may find Paul's definition of the situation, as explained by various interpreters, to be the best guide for understanding how his words should relate to issues in our own time. However, we may decide that the tables have turned and now we need to listen to the voices of the Corinthian women prophets, who were problems for Paul but who have something to say to us.[4] We may even acknowledge the original historical context but decide that Paul's words in context are not appropriate guidance for us, perhaps because Paul's application is severely limited by the social practices of his time. Nevertheless, when placed in a new context, with a corresponding shift in their force, Paul's words become illuminating and powerful. We cannot predict with certainty how the illuminating word will be found.

By what criteria should such decisions be made? This is a question to which I cannot give an adequate answer. It would require probing our deepest religious and ethical commitments. I would note, however, that the double love commandment is presented in the New Testament not only as a guide to salvation (in Luke 10:25–28) but also as a hermeneutical principle for interpretation of Scripture,[5] for Matt 22:40 adds, "On these two commandments all the law and the prophets depend." Paul agrees in that he, too, presents the command to love neighbor as a hermeneutical principle, central to understanding the whole law (Rom 13:8–10; Gal 5:14). So I suggest that, following this fundamental scriptural principle, we give Scripture force in our lives in ways that consistently foster love of

4. See Antoinette Clark Wire, *The Corinthian Women Prophets: A Reconstruction through Paul's Rhetoric* (Minneapolis: Fortress, 1990).

5. I discussed this previously in my essay, "Freedom and Responsibility in Scripture Interpretation," in Tannehill, *The Shape of Luke's Story: Essays on Luke–Acts* (Eugene, Ore.: Wipf & Stock, 2005) 282–85 (orig. pub. 1998). See also Charles H. Cosgrove, *Appealing to Scripture in Moral Debate: Five Hermeneutical Rules* (Grand Rapids: Eerdmans, 2002) 158–61; idem, *Elusive Israel: The Puzzle of Election in Romans* (Louisville: Westminster John Knox, 1997) 43–44; and Ulrich Luz, *Matthew in History: Interpretation, Influence, and Effects* (Minneapolis: Fortress, 1994) 82–97.

God and neighbor. This critical principle applies to our use of Scripture but is also a self-critical principle for Scripture itself; there are some things in Scripture that cannot be positive guidance for us because they conflict with this scriptural principle. Of course, the double love commandment does not solve all our problems. Love is easily weakened to sentimentality. Furthermore, any implementation of love of neighbor depends on views of what is good for the neighbor, and there is much disagreement on this issue. Nevertheless, the double love commandment is a helpful criterion for deciding how Scripture should be used.

Now we need to consider the two recent perspectives on Paul and 1 Corinthians mentioned at the beginning of this essay, the "political" and the "feminist." They share a common concern: to integrate biblical scholarship with support of emancipatory social movements. Yet they reach quite different conclusions about Paul's attitude toward social emancipation. In general, they differ at the following key points:

1. Horsley and Elliott are inclined to find value in Paul's position (although Horsley is critical of Paul at certain points), but Schüssler Fiorenza and Wire listen for the voice of the Corinthians—especially the Corinthian women—behind Paul's words and attribute primary value to this alternate voice.

2. Horsley and Elliot are more inclined to base their understanding of the situation in Corinth on Paul's statements and evaluations, while Schüssler Fiorenza and Wire subject Paul's statements to a hermeneutic of suspicion and arrive at a contrasting understanding of what is happening.

3. Although both parties are concerned with the social status of the Corinthians, they use their conclusions differently. Wire believes that the Corinthians, especially the women, are persons of low social status who are being lifted up in Christ. Paul's social roots and religious experience are quite different.[6] Paul addresses the Corinthians in light of his own experience, which is largely alien to them. Horsley, too, believes that most Corinthians came from the lower classes, yet, in the competition for status typical of the time and place, some had begun to claim for themselves a high

---

6. Wire, *Corinthian Women Prophets*, 45; and, against Horsley, Wire, "Response: The Politics of the Assembly in Corinth," in *Paul and Politics: Ekklesia, Israel, Imperium, Interpretation*, ed. Richard A. Horsley (Harrisburg, Pa.: Trinity, 2000) 125–26 [124–29].

spiritual status.[7] In this context, Paul's strong criticism of the "puffed up" Corinthians may seem justified.

4. Both sets of interpreters probably share a broad commitment to the emancipation of oppressed social groups, including women, slaves, and the poor. Elliott and Horsley have introduced a new perspective, however, through their emphasis on the importance of the imperial cult and imperial propaganda, viewed as methods of social control. Unlike many interpreters, they believe that Paul's gospel has a political edge in opposition to this cult and propaganda.

Paul and the Corinthian Women Prophets

Elisabeth Schüssler Fiorenza continues to reflect in depth on the task of transforming biblical interpretation, as practiced in the past, into "emancipatory interpretation," a task that reflects her ethical commitment to the liberation of oppressed groups. Her reflections have evolved through a number of stages. I will focus on her recent summary of "seven interpretive strategies" in *Rhetoric and Ethic*.[8]

Rather than referring to patriarchy, Schüssler Fiorenza now speaks more broadly of "kyriarchal systems of domination" that appear both in the biblical text and in past interpretive practices. In order to carry out her vocation as a "public" or "trans-formative" intellectual[9]—one committed to liberative social change—she engages in "seven interpretive strategies." Beginning with a "hermeneutics of experience and social location" that makes the interpreter aware of the ways in which biblical texts, functioning within present religious and social contexts, have shaped the experience of victimized groups, she moves to an "analytic of domination"—an analysis of the ideological functions of texts in "legitimating the kyriarchal order"—and a "hermeneutics of suspicion" that "seeks to demystify structures of domination that are inscribed in the text and in contemporary contexts of interpretation." These tasks flow into a "hermeneutics of ethical and theological evaluation" that explores both "the cultural-religious

---

7. Horsley, *1 Corinthians*, ANTC (Nashville: Abingdon, 1998) 32, 38.

8. The following summary of Schüssler Fiorenza's hermeneutic is based on *Rhetoric and Ethic*, 48–54.

9. *Rhetoric and Ethic*, 81.

internalizations and legitimations of kyriarchy and . . . the values and visions that are inscribed as countercultural alternatives in biblical texts."[10]

This process is supported by a "hermeneutics of remembrance and re-construction" that "aims at making the subordinated and marginalized 'others' visible again and their repressed arguments and silences 'audible'." This hermeneutics "is fully conscious of the rhetoricity of its own re-constructions" and does not confuse them with "reality itself." It is inspired by a "hermeneutics of imagination" that "seeks to generate utopian visions . . . and to 'dream' a different world of justice and well-being." "Imagination," she explains, "enables us to fill in the gaps, empty spaces, and silences, and thereby to make sense out of the text." Imagination is as necessary to history and science as it is to art. The final goal and climax of the entire interpretive process is a "hermeneutics of transformation and action for change."[11]

I respect Schüssler Fiorenza's ethical commitments and her efforts to integrate those commitments with her profession as a biblical scholar. I also think that she is correct in emphasizing the importance of imagination in historical reconstruction. Recognizing the importance of imagination does not mean that biblical scholars can ignore textual and historical evidence. We still must accept the task of interpreting texts within a definable historical context. Yet the text and the historical context are seldom such "hard" evidence that they can be interpreted in only one way. Schüssler Fiorenza links her hermeneutics of imagination in historical reconstruction with the generation of a "dream" of a "different world of justice and well-being."[12] She does not ignore evidence in this task, but she seeks through her scholarship a nourishing and transforming vision that can be acted upon today, in spite of the structures of domination and rhetoric of oppression embedded in the biblical texts and their world. It may seem that there is a bias toward reconstruction of the early church as a utopian community, even if the biblical texts fall far short of Schüssler Fiorenza's standards. However, I do not see this as a fault, so long as her reconstruction is still a possibility when all relevant evidence has been examined, for there is an ethical purpose behind her work. Nevertheless,

---

10. Ibid., 48–51. The term "kyriarchal" (from the Greek κύριος, "lord") applies to any situation in which the more powerful (the *kyrios*) dominates and oppresses the less powerful. It would apply to the role of dominant males in ancient society, but elite women could also exercise kyriarchal power over male slaves or men of lower status.

11. Ibid., 51–54.

12. In spite of sharp negative statements about Paul and other biblical writers, Schüssler Fiorenza also hopes to find "biblical values and visions" that are liberative; ibid., 9, 45.

one cannot claim that her reconstructions eliminate other reconstructions that fill in the gaps differently through a different use of imagination. These alternatives might, in their own way, support a nourishing and transforming vision that provides a worthy guide to action today.

Antoinette Clark Wire's interpretation of 1 Corinthians, with a focus on the Corinthian women prophets, fits Schüssler Fiorenza's agenda. Wire seeks to reconstruct the religious experience of the Corinthian community, in which, she believes, the women prophets played an important role. She understands the women to be throwing off the restrictions imposed by society through claiming new freedom in Christ. She evaluates their thought and actions positively, with a correspondingly negative interpretation of Paul's efforts to restrain and correct them. Although there is a plausible basis for her emphasis on the Corinthian women prophets, as I will indicate below, Wire must use historical imagination to fill in what would otherwise be a murky picture. She does so by positing an alternative to the positions that Paul takes and describing the situation in ways that suggest that the women prophets' position was reasonable for them.[13] Thus, the women prophets "are able to tolerate more variety of opinion and practice than Paul."[14] They understand themselves to be "a new creation in God's image"[15] and seek to give full expression to this new reality. Paul fears that human glory will infringe on the glory of God, but the Corinthian women have a different view of God. "They do not see God on the defense, vindicating the divine glory by capital punishment, but on the offense, giving people gifts whose exercise glorifies both themselves and God."[16] The Corinthians regard eating sacrificial food as a "public witness . . . that the sacrificed meat will not harm them . . .

---

13. Wire provides supporting argument for her approach to 1 Corinthians. The subtitle of her book is *A Reconstruction through Paul's Rhetoric.* Paul seeks to be persuasive and therefore shapes his arguments to the audience (*Corinthian Women Prophets,* 3). Thus, "On whatever points Paul's persuasion is insistent and intense, showing he is not merely confirming their agreement but struggling for their assent, one can assume some different and opposite point of view in Corinth from the one Paul is stating" (ibid., 9). I agree that the intensity of Paul's words provides clues to the issues that he believes to be important in the Corinthian situation and, presumably, indicates that someone in Corinth was thinking or acting in a contrary way. This does not mean, however, that the Corinthian view was "opposite" in a precise way. There are likely to be a number of ways of interpreting the position that causes Paul's comment.

14. Ibid., 22.

15. Ibid., 126.

16. Ibid., 27.

because there is no God but one."[17] While Paul emphasizes the importance of restraint and listening in the assemblies, for the Corinthians it is important that many people "freely speak . . . expressing their own faith back and forth."[18]

Wire's interpretation of 1 Corinthians provides a good illustration of the way that historical reconstruction can radically change our understanding of the impact of a text in its historical context. For instance, a passage where Paul seems to be very careful to treat women and men equally (1 Cor 7:3–4) takes on a different meaning for Wire. She suggests that the women prophets were claiming authority over their own bodies so that they could abstain from sexual relations and dedicate themselves to prayer and prophecy. In spite of Paul's rhetoric of equality, then, he is intervening on the side of the men when he asserts that no married person has authority over his or her own body. Paul's intervention is the result of his fear that husbands will be led into extra-marital sexual relations because of their wives' withdrawal.[19]

Wire presents an interesting, detailed, and thought-provoking study of 1 Corinthians. Although she does not start with this passage, 1 Cor 11:2–16 provides a solid basis for saying that women prophets had a role in the Corinthian community. Rather than viewing this passage as an odd comment about a side issue, it is plausible to take it as a basis for reconstructing the Corinthian situation. The references to praying and prophesying in 1 Cor 11:4–5 provide a link to the further discussion of spiritual gifts, especially prophecy and tongues, in 1 Corinthians 12–14, and the issues of these chapters, in turn, can be linked to claims to "wisdom" and "knowledge" in 1 Cor 1:17—3:3; 3:18–20; and 8:1–2. Wire offers a variation on the view that the Corinthian "spirituals" celebrated their spiritual gifts, including divine wisdom, claimed freedom from social inhibitions, and felt that they enjoyed salvation in the present. There is this striking difference: Wire uses all of the indications of this behavior to describe the women prophets, and she, unlike most interpreters, presents these spirituals sympathetically. Discussion of the low status of most women in Corinthian society undergirds her sympathetic portrayal.[20] Wire's interpretation provides a useful correction of the tendency to dismiss the people Paul was addressing and devalue their religious experience.

17. Ibid., 103.
18. Ibid., 144.
19. Ibid., 82–83.
20. Ibid., 62–66.

Both Wire and Schüssler Fiorenza accept the command that women be silent in the assemblies (1 Cor 14:34–35) as an original part of 1 Corinthians.[21] Unlike many male interpreters, Wire and Schüssler Fiorenza are not inclined to defend Paul as a model of gender inclusiveness. Instead, they approach Paul with suspicion on gender issues. In spite of her extensive discussion of 1 Cor 14:34–35 in *The Corinthian Women Prophets,* Wire does not, in my opinion, give adequate attention to the seeming inconsistency between 14:34–35 and 11:2–16, where Paul regulates but does not prohibit women praying and prophesying. Against those who point to this inconsistency as a chief argument for declaring that 14:34–35 is a non-Pauline insertion, she makes the point that "[t]hey neglect the good possibility that Paul develops his argument as the letter proceeds, increasing restrictions on women's worship participation until he feels able to demand their silence."[22] But it is hard to understand how Paul could hope to be convincing if his position is not consistent.

Most of Wire's statements in *The Corinthian Women Prophets* are measured and cautious, with appropriate reference to the uncertainty of some of her proposals. The implications of her study for women, however, are strongly expressed in her short commentary on 1 Corinthians in *Searching the Scriptures,* where she states that the women prophets "are the group whose power he [Paul] is most persistently destabilizing,"[23] and she refers to "Paul's stranglehold move on these women's voices."[24] Similarly, Schüssler Fiorenza, in her response to the work of Richard Horsley, Neil Elliott, and others, stresses the importance of the "public health" aspect of her work, that is, her commitment to protect the public from the damage that the Pauline texts can do.[25]

Paul and Empire

A different view of Paul emerges when Neil Elliott and Richard Horsley consider Paul, placing him against a different background. They argue

---

21. See Elisabeth Schüssler Fiorenza, "1 Corinthians," in *The Harper-Collins Bible Commentary,* ed. James L. Mays (San Francisco: HarperSanFrancisco, 2000) 1090 [1074–93]; Wire, *Corinthian Women Prophets,* 149–58, 229–32.

22. Wire, "1 Corinthians," in *Searching the Scriptures,* vol. 2: *A Feminist Commentary,* ed. Elisabeth Schüssler Fiorenza (New York: Crossroad, 1994) 187 [153–95].

23. Wire, "1 Corinthians," 156.

24. Ibid., 188.

25. Schüssler Fiorenza, "Paul and the Politics of Interpretation," in *Paul and Politics,* ed. Horsley, 40–53 [40–57].

that proper assessment of Paul's gospel requires us to recognize the tension between it and the ideology of the Roman empire. Past interpretation has assumed, for the most part, that Paul is concerned with the salvation of individuals or with the church as a community, while showing little concern for political issues beyond the church. It may seem that Elliott and Horsley have a difficult case to make.

Neither Elliott nor Horsley believes that Paul was leading a rebellion or protest movement intended to cause the fall of the Roman empire. They do believe, however, that Paul was proclaiming an alternative king and kingdom destined, in God's plan, to replace the empire, and Paul was already forming an alternative society in anticipation of this change. Furthermore, Paul was more sharply conscious of the incompatibility of the two societies than has commonly been recognized.

In support of the view that Paul proclaimed a counter-imperial gospel, Horsley draws on the recent work of Roman historians who assert that the emperor cult was much more important than past New Testament scholarship has recognized, especially in Greece and Asia Minor, the areas of Paul's mature ministry.[26] Rome was able to control these areas of the empire with a remarkably small standing army and spare administrative structure. Control was maintained by the emperor cult and a patronage system with the emperor at the top. Local oligarchs were willing participants in this cult and patronage system, through which they received privileges. The emperor cult was an effective propaganda device supporting an ideology that helped unify the empire, an ideology projected by iconography, monumental buildings, public religious ceremonies, and persuasive rhetoric. Past religious scholarship ignored this reality because of the tendency to separate the religious from the political, while these structures are inherently religious *and* political.[27]

In this context, a gospel that proclaims a different κύριος who is served by an "international alternative society"[28] is not "politically innocuous."[29] In proclaiming his gospel, Paul uses terms that would be recognized, in the context of the emperor cult, as representing the honorific

---

26. Horsley, "General Introduction," in *Paul and Empire: Religion and Power in Roman Society*, ed. Richard A. Horsley (Harrisburg, Pa.: Trinity, 1997) 3–4 [1–8].

27. Horsley, "The Gospel of Imperial Salvation: Introduction," in *Paul and Empire*, 11–13 [9–24]; idem, "Rhetoric and Empire—and First Corinthians," in *Paul and Politics*, 75–78 [72–102].

28. Horsley, "General Introduction," 8.

29. Horsley, "Gospel of Imperial Salvation," 24.

attributes and benefits of Caesar;[30] and, in the Greek context, the term ἐκκλησία itself was primarily a political term, referring to the local assembly of citizens.[31]

Neil Elliott agrees with Horsley and provides further support by highlighting Paul's use of the terms "cross" (σταυρός) and "crucify" (σταυρόω). Paul does not simply refer to Jesus' death but speaks of the cross, and does so emphatically (e.g., Gal 3:1, 6:14; Phil 2:8; 1 Cor 1:17—2:2). Crucifixion was an instrument of public terrorism and social control, employed at that time by the Romans.[32] It would be imprudent to use such language if Paul wished to hide the fact that Jesus died a victim of the political violence of the Roman empire. Furthermore, in 1 Corinthians, following his provocative description of his message as "the word of the cross" concerning "Christ crucified" (1 Cor 1:18, 23; 2:2), Paul attributes Christ's crucifixion to "the rulers of this age" (2:8). The context shows that Paul is thinking in apocalyptic terms, and the reference to "rulers" should be understood by means of the apocalyptic passage in 1 Cor 15:24–26, which describes a coming transfer of "royal authority" (βασιλεία) through the destruction of "every rule and every authority and power." Elliott rejects the view that these are spiritual powers unconnected with political systems.[33] Rather, as in Daniel and other apocalypses, the threatening apocalyptic powers are manifest in earthly kingdoms that use the earthly instruments of "persecution" and "sword."[34]

Horsley also believes that Paul's apocalyptic is fundamentally "antiimperial" and emphasizes the importance of the apocalyptic perspective in 1 Corinthians.[35] Horsley finds "the fundamental counterimperial agenda of Judean apocalyptic" in "the underlying structuring components of Paul's arguments," most strikingly in 1 Corinthians 1–4 and 15, but elsewhere in 1 Corinthians as well.[36] Indeed, apocalyptic expectation repeatedly appears in the midst of Paul's detailed instructions (see 1 Cor 6:2; 7:29–31; 10:11; 11:26). It is Paul's task to help shape the Corinthian

---

30. See Dieter Georgi, "God Turned Upside Down," in *Paul and Empire*, 148–57; Helmut Koester, "Imperial Ideology and Paul's Eschatology in 1 Thessalonians," in *Paul and Empire*, 158–66.

31. Horsley, "General Introduction," 8.

32. Neil Elliott, *Liberating Paul: The Justice of God and the Politics of the Apostle* (Maryknoll, N.Y.: Orbis, 1994) 95–96.

33. Ibid., 109–31

34. See Rom 8:35–39 and Elliott, *Liberating Paul*, 122.

35. Horsley, "Rhetoric and Empire," 96–101.

36. Ibid., 98.

believers into an alternative society distinct from its social context. From this perspective the discipline Paul seeks to impose on the community—which may appear as oppressive limits on the community's freedom, from the perspective of Schüssler Fiorenza and Wire—is necessary in order to "maintain solidarity over against the dominant imperial society."[37] Thus, Paul wants the Corinthians to withdraw from the local court system (1 Cor 6:1–11), participate in the world with a consciousness that they are not really part of it (7:29–31), and avoid the religious observances that are part of the social fabric of Corinthian society (10:14–22).[38] According to Horsley, "In 1 Corinthians Paul was arguing with a religiosity of individual spiritual transcendence focused on personal devotion to and/or possession of heavenly Sophia, very similar to that articulated in" Wisdom 6–10 and Philo.[39] According to Elliott, Paul in 1 Corinthians is "challenging the ideology of privilege"[40] as he addresses the divisions between "the relatively lower status 'charter members' of the congregation and the more recent converts of Apollos whose wealth, power, and status have subtly introduced new standards and expectations for community life."[41] Horsley and Elliott clearly favor Paul when he is understood to be working against these dangerous tendencies in the Corinthian community. Here again we can see how reconstruction of the situation in the church fits with a particular evaluation of Paul's work.

Certain Pauline passages seem to conflict with the view that Paul preached an anti-imperial gospel. Foremost among these is Rom 13:1–7. To maintain the position of Elliott and Horsley, the grant of divine authority to rulers in Romans 13 must be reduced to a Pauline stratagem in dealing with a particular issue. According to Elliott, Paul's underlying concern is the safety of the Jewish community in Rome, whose delicate situation would worsen with civil unrest.[42] The view that Paul is com-

---

37. Ibid., 100; see Horsley, "1 Corinthians: A Case Study of Paul's Assembly as an Alternative Society," in *Paul and Empire*, 252 [242–52].

38. "Paul's prohibition of the Corinthians' eating of 'food sacrificed to idols' . . . cut the Corinthians off from participation in the fundamental forms of social relations in the dominant society. . . . Sacrifice was integral to . . . community life . . . at every social level from extended families to guilds and associations to citywide celebrations, including imperial festivals"; Horsley, "1 Corinthians: A Case Study," 247.

39. Horsley, "Rhetoric and Empire," 85; idem, *1 Corinthians*, 35–36, 51–56.

40. Elliott, *Liberating Paul*, 204–14.

41. Ibid., 205

42. Elliott, "Romans 13:1–7 in the Context of Imperial Propaganda," in *Paul and Empire*, 191–204.

mitted to a new society that removes the distinctions of the old may also be challenged on the basis of 1 Cor 7:17–24 and Paul's instructions to women in 11:2–16 and 14:34–35. To be sure, Elliott chides Schüssler Fiorenza and Wire for accepting 14:34–35 as Pauline,[43] and 7:17–24 may be instruction for the interim which, even in the interim, is not meant as a hard and fast rule.

Conclusion: The Hermeneutical Value of Diverse Theories about the Situation in Corinth

In founding and instructing the Corinthian church, was Paul a liberator or an oppressor? Possibly both, for the "feminist" and "political" interpretations of Paul's work, discussed above, tend to view Paul's work against different backgrounds, in the one case, the Roman empire as an ideological system, in the other case, the early church as a place of liberation for women. But tension remains between the two interpretations because a different evaluation of Paul results from the different factors that each group highlights, and they have different views of the situation in the Corinthian church. How should we respond to these diverse views?

After the provocative work of Schüssler Fiorenza and Wire, we can no longer begin study of the Corinthian correspondence with the assumption that Paul is correct and fair in all his judgments, while those he sought to correct, including the Corinthian women prophets, were necessarily in the wrong. But neither can we begin with the assumption that Wire's reconstruction of the situation in Corinth is the only plausible one and, by itself, yields a sufficient account of Paul's work. The view that Paul's gospel is, in important respects, "counter-imperial," and that this aspect of his convictions shapes his response to the Corinthians, is also plausible.

Feminist interpreters modify the traditional view of biblical authority. Wire states that we should no longer begin with the assumption that the biblical author's view is authoritative; rather, we should conceive the text's authority "more broadly as that of the full range of voices which speak through it,"[44] including the voices of women. Although some might want to replace Paul's authoritative voice with that of the Corinthian women prophets, I would advocate a more balanced view, which Wire also seems to support.

---

43. Elliott, *Liberating Paul*, 52–54.
44. Wire, "1 Corinthians," 157.

Wire rightly points to the close "relation of social experience and theological confession" in the religious life,[45] and she advances the interesting hypothesis that the differences between Paul and the Corinthian women prophets reflect their different social experience. Paul's encounter with Christ meant giving up social privileges; the Corinthian women began with a low status and few privileges but experienced exaltation in Christ.[46] Wire concludes, "Where conflicts with a religious tradition are understood in light of the different social experience of each party, it may be possible to move toward genuine mediation of the conflicts."[47] I take this to mean that neither of the two theologically-interpreted social experiences will be rejected. Furthermore, they will be set in dialogue with each other, as they were in the Corinthian situation, according to Wire, with the hope that deeper understanding and mutual acceptance may result. This may involve each party listening to and correcting the other. Taking multiple voices seriously means beginning with the assumption that both Paul and the Corinthians have something important to say but that the truth on each side must be understood and applied with due consideration for the insights and experience of the other party. Schüssler Fiorenza may also be open to this approach. In introducing her brief commentary on 1 Corinthians, she remarks, "The following commentary seeks to understand the debates in Corinth as legitimate discussions within the *ekklesia*. Paul is understood as only one partner, although in retrospect a very significant one, in the theological discourse of the early Christian missionary movement."[48]

Horsley recognizes the value of Schüssler Fiorenza and Wire's work in reconstructing multiple voices;[49] and he also recognizes that there will be multiple interpretations of Paul even by interpreters who share a liberationist concern. These diverse approaches, he says, are "to be valued rather than avoided."[50]

Some may view this openness as a counsel of despair: We are stuck with conflicting interpretations, and we may as well make the best of it. I have a more positive view of the situation. On the one hand, there is

---

45. Wire, *Corinthian Women Prophets*, 71.
46. Ibid., 63–69.
47. Ibid., 71.
48. Schüssler Fiorenza, "1 Corinthians," 1076.
49. Horsley, "Rhetoric and Empire," 85–86.
50. Horsley, "Introduction: Krister Stendahl's Challenge to Pauline Studies," in *Paul and Politics*, 15 [1–16].

value in scholarly attempts at historical reconstruction. Through this reconstructive work, seemingly bland and general statements may become telling remarks, words on target. We gain a sharper sense of their purpose and power. On the other hand, we must recognize that the voices of Paul's dialogue partners are muffled. Paul's letters indicate their presence, but the sounds are indistinct and subject to various interpretations. Therefore, historical reconstructions are necessarily interpretive experiments, some more convincing than others, but none likely to be so convincing as to eliminate all other possibilities (unless we foolishly succumb to fascination with the "latest thing" or attribute undue authority to the views of influential mentors). As Schüssler Fiorenza has said, historical reconstruction does not result in a "report of 'what actually happened'," for our reconstructions are always products of historical imagination that must fill in significant gaps.[51]

Therefore, it is appropriate to be tolerant of competing interpretations that have been developed with rigor (and even to consider whether undeveloped suggestions could be worked out with rigor), and it is appropriate to consider a number of options as we seek to read the text in historical context, recognizing that these remain possibilities, not certainties. Shifting perspectives on the situation will result in shifting views of the force of Paul's words and different evaluations of Paul's words and work.

This thought process is similar to the thinking required when we seek an appropriate application of Paul's words in our own time, and flexible historical imagination can contribute to our thinking about appropriate application. Since Paul's letters were written not to us but to churches far distant from us in time and space, it is always necessary to ask what situations today, if any, might be appropriately addressed by Paul's words (and with what adaptations). These decisions will be influenced by our faith commitments, theological understanding, and ethical values. Consideration of the multiple possibilities of understanding the original situation can play an ancillary role, making us more keenly aware of the ways that varying situations affect the force of Paul's words.

In my opinion, our preferences in interpreting the historical context of Paul's words should not strictly control our decisions about the appropriate application of those words today. It is quite possible to decide that a particular historical situation is most likely but that Paul's words in that context were damaging or dangerous. As a result, we may need to add warnings or seek an altogether different context where the results

---

51. Schüssler Fiorenza, *Rhetoric and Ethic*, 52.

will not be damaging. Members of Christian churches will apply Paul's words in various ways. It is important to think about the possible effects of these applications in various situations today. Acquaintance with the interpretive experiments of historical scholars can be a stimulus to this thought process. Multiple experiments in historical reconstruction will help us imagine the range of contexts in which Paul's words might have been written and gain a sense of the good and evil consequences, revealing useful applications we might not have considered, warning us of dangerous applications we might ignore, and suggesting necessary adaptations so that the words of Scripture might fulfill their purpose of promoting the love of God and neighbor.

We will, of course, make these judgments in light of our commitments and values, our varying visions of what is good. The four scholars studied in this essay are not to be faulted for operating in this way, for we are all obliged to follow the best that we know. Of course, our insight into the good is faulty and incomplete. We must remain open to learning more both from Scripture and from other sources. Paul rightly reminds us that we see only puzzling reflections in a distorting mirror (1 Cor 13:12) and will never achieve perfect knowledge in this life, for there is a truth beyond our truth to which finally we must yield.

11

PARTICIPATION *in* CHRIST:
A Central Theme in Pauline Soteriology

My first book-length publication was a revision of my Ph.D. dissertation, which was published with the title Dying and Rising with Christ: A Study in Pauline Theology, *BZNW 32 (Berlin: Töpelmann, 1967). In this volume I studied the passages in Paul's letters in which Paul refers to the believers' participation in Christ's death, resulting in a corresponding participation in Christ's life (both in the present and the future). I divided the passages into two main groups: those that presented dying with Christ as a past event that forms the basis of the new life, and those that refer to dying with Christ as an ongoing aspect of the new life, especially in Paul's experiences of suffering. I pointed out that there was a common pattern to the passages describing dying with Christ as a past event. The dying is a dying to the enslaving powers of the old dominion (sin, death, flesh, law), resulting in a transformed existence under a new lordship. This is a fundamental soteriological statement, a description of how the death and resurrection of Christ function redemptively. Here Paul goes beyond stating that Christ died "for us" to claim that we died with Christ, using participatory language—a type of language that may be puzzling to people today.*

The following essay revisits the topic by taking a broader look at Paul's soteriology, while still stressing the importance of Paul's participatory patterns of thought. I show that participation in Christ has an important role in Paul's argument for justification from faith (rather than being a separate and secondary theme), and I argue that the Son of God's identification with the human plight and the believer's identification with Christ through faith are important presuppositions of Paul's participatory language.

THERE HAS BEEN A revival of interest in Paul's participatory language in recent Pauline scholarship. Richard B. Hays, in the new introduction to the second edition of *The Faith of Jesus Christ*,¹ refers to "Participation in Christ as the Key to Pauline Soteriology" (the heading of a section of his essay).² Previously, Morna D. Hooker pursued a similar line of thought in essays on "interchange" in Christ.³ Anthony J. Tambasco argued that Paul's model of atonement involved a "participatory journey" with Christ, rather than viewing Christ as a penal substitute for sinful humanity.⁴ Terrance Callan has recently published *Dying and Rising with Christ: The Theology of Paul the Apostle*, in which he asserts that "union with Jesus in death and resurrection" is "Paul's most basic understanding of the way Jesus' death and resurrection save the human race from sin."⁵ Udo Schnelle, in a section heading, writes of "Transformation and Participation as the Basic Modes of Pauline Christology."⁶ And Douglas Campbell has argued for "pneumatologically participatory martyrological eschatology" (a mouthful that he regularly reduces to the acronym PPME) as the key to Paul's gospel. His argument for a participatory soteriology is accompanied by a sharp attack on the view that reconciliation with God requires a punitive death suffered by Christ to satisfy God's justice.⁷

I agree with the interpreters cited above that participation in Christ is a central aspect of Paul's soteriology, partly because the theme is widespread. (Here I am thinking not only of the phrase "in Christ" but also of the important motif of dying and rising with Christ and related motifs such as being baptized into Christ, being one body in Christ, putting on Christ, and "Christ in you.") Moreover, I claim it is central because more of Paul's soteriology can be explained from this perspective than from the alternatives. In particular, this theme of participation in Christ is prominent when Paul proclaims liberation from the enslaving powers of sin, death, flesh, and law and entry into a new redeeming obedience to a new Lord, a central and distinctive concern of Pauline theology. In many pre-

1. Subtitle: *The Narrative Substructure of Galatians 3:1—4:11* (Grand Rapids: Eerdmans, 2002).

2. Ibid., xxix.

3. See her two essays "Interchange in Christ" and "Interchange and Atonement," in *From Adam to Christ: Essays on Paul* (Cambridge: Cambridge University, 1990) 13–41.

4. *A Theology of Atonement and Paul's Vision of Christianity*, ZSNT (Collegeville: Liturgical, 1991) 61–81.

5. Callan, *Dying and Rising with Christ* (New York: Paulist, 2006) 91.

6. *Apostle Paul: His Life and Theology*, trans. M. Eugene Boring (Grand Rapids: Baker Academic, 2005) 410.

7. Douglas A. Campbell, *The Quest for Paul's Gospel* (London: T & T Clark International, 2005) 1–55, 146–77.

sentations of Paul, participation in Christ is viewed in isolation from, and therefore as an alternative to, other aspects of Pauline soteriology, such as justification from faith and Christ's death "for us." In my opinion this is a mistake that blinds us to the full significance of participation in Christ.

Paul proclaims that Christ died for us or for our sins, and he proclaims that we have died with Christ. These are not alternative and competing views of Christ's saving death. For Paul these affirmations fit together, as we see from Paul's logical inference in 2 Cor 5:14: "One died for all, therefore all died" (followed by a reference to the new life that results). This statement follows the pattern of dying and rising with Christ: participation in Christ's death leading to a new kind of life. But here Paul shows that, for him, this is a logical implication of—and perhaps Paul's distinctive explanation of—the affirmation that "one died for all."

In some passages Paul applies cultic language—the language of sacrifice and perhaps of "curse transmission" ritual[8]—to the death of Jesus. This language is largely opaque to us, and Paul does not explain it, unless he explains it in terms of participation in Christ's death, as in 2 Cor 5:14. In this same passage we find what may seem to be a classical statement of substitutionary atonement: "The one who did not know sin [God] made sin for us, in order that we might become God's righteousness in him" (2 Cor 5:21). Note, however, that this statement proclaims atonement for sin by means of an exchange of attributes between Christ and Christ's people. The same pattern of thought occurs without reference to an atoning death for sin in 2 Cor 8:9 ("For your sakes he became poor, although he was rich, in order that you might become rich by means of his poverty."), suggesting that the pattern of thought is broader and more basic than the idea of atonement for sin.[9] What are the presuppositions of this mode of thought? I suggest that it rests on a self-renouncing identification of the divine with humans in their need, enabling a reciprocal identification of needy humanity with God's Son, his death, and his victory over sin and death. I will argue that these acts of identification are important presuppositions of Paul's participatory soteriology.[10]

---

8. On curse transmission ritual see Gal 3:13 and Stephen Finlan, *The Background and Content of Paul's Cultic Atonement Metaphors*, Academia Biblica (Atlanta: Society of Biblical Literature, 2004) 73–121.

9. The focus in 2 Cor 8:9 is not on Christ's death but on his entry into the human world from the divine world, as in Phil 2:6–7. Human poverty here can refer to all the threatening limitations of human existence, not just the problem of sin.

10. Note that 2 Cor 5:21 says that we become "God's righteousness in him." "In him" balances "for us" in the first half of the sentence, following the same logical progression as

Paul's uses of cultic language to describe Jesus' death deserve attention, but this is a major task that I will not attempt here. I note in passing, however, the argument of Otfried Hofius that there is more continuity between the priestly sacrifice prescribed in Torah and Paul's thought than has usually been recognized.[11] The continuity is obscured by common misinterpretations of both priestly sacrifice and Paul. In both cases the death of the sacrificial victim is understood to include the death of the one for whom the sacrifice is made, according to Hofius. The victim represents and includes the one who benefits. The victim's death is the beneficiary's death, for the problem is not simply to remove sins as a stain external to the self but to gain a complete renewal of a self that has been corrupted within. Both priestly sacrifice and Paul's thought presuppose the identification of the beneficiary with the victim. Hofius' views, which are based in part on the work of Old Testament scholar Hartmut Gese,[12] help us to understand how Paul could pass so easily from Jesus' death as an atoning event to Jesus' death as an inclusive event. Whether this is the clear meaning of Old Testament sacrifice or its meaning is more ambiguous, the importance of participation in Christ for Paul suggests that he would interpret sacrificial language along these lines.

Stephen Finlan, in debate with E. P. Sanders, indicates that both participation (Sander's emphasis) and cultic imagery are important, "but the cultic action is logically prior; there could be no participation in Christ's atoning death if atonement had not first been accomplished in that death."[13] Atoning death, however, presupposes some kind of link between a particular death and other persons who somehow benefit. This link may be assumed for traditional cultic events, but it is not so easily assumed for the death of Jesus, which was not a cultic event in most people's eyes. It was not a ritual conducted by priests. It was the execution of a criminal on a cross. However, we can discern in Paul's letters certain presuppositions of his thought that establish for him the necessary link between Jesus and others. These presuppositions provide a basis for his striking images of participation.

Rom 8:3 provides an important clue as to what is missing if we assume that Jesus' death is somehow in itself an atoning event. "God,

in 2 Cor 5:14, where "died for all" is interpreted as "all died."

11. See "Sühne und Versöhnung: Zum paulinischen Verständnis des Kreuzestodes Jesu," in *Paulusstudien*, WUNT (Tübingen: J. C. B. Mohr, 1989) 33–49.

12. See "Die Sühne," in *Zur biblischen Theologie. Alttestamentliche Vorträge*, BEvT (Munich: Kaiser, 1977) 85–106.

13. *Paul's Cultic Atonement Metaphors*, 117.

having sent his own Son in likeness of flesh of sin and for sin [or "as a sin offering"],[14] condemned sin in the flesh." This verse reveals an important presupposition of Paul's gospel about Jesus' saving death. God has sent God's Son to participate in the human plight. The Son is sent "in likeness of flesh of sin," which makes possible effective action against sin and a new kind of life for believers. In other words, atonement for sin presupposes the prior divine action of sending God's Son to participate in the human situation, an act in which the Son identifies with humanity in its need. The reference to the Son as *God's own* Son emphasizes *God's* involvement in this through the sacrifice of someone precious to God the Father. Through the Son, God participates in the situation of human need. Note that this is not merely a general affirmation of divine intervention but an affirmation of the Son's identification with humanity in its situation of need, here characterized as "flesh of sin."

The phrase "likeness" or "form of flesh of sin" may seem to express a reservation about the Son's complete identification with the human situation, particularly when we recall Paul's claim in 2 Cor 5:21 that Christ "did not know sin," although God made him "sin for us." These observations should not mislead us. The logic of God's action against sin in Rom 8:3 depends on the Son's identification with humanity in its sinful state. This view is supported by the variant of the same pattern of thought in Gal 4:4–5, where the Son's participation in the human plight "under law" is linked by a purpose clause to redemption from that same plight: "God sent out his Son, born of woman, born under law, in order to redeem those under law."[15] Note that Gal 4:5 is linked to Paul's statement about the cross in 3:13 by use of the unusual word ἐξαγοράζω ("redeem"), which is not applied elsewhere in the New Testament to Christ's redeeming work. The link between these two verses is an important indication that the story of redemption through Christ includes more than the cross. It begins with the sending of God's Son to participate in the human plight, identifying with people in their situation of need.[16]

---

14. Some scholars wish to translate περὶ ἁμαρτίας with "as a sin offering"; others resist this view. For an argument in favor see N. T. Wright, "The Meaning of περὶ ἁμαρτίας in Romans 8.3," in *The Climax of the Covenant* (Minneapolis: Fortress, 1992) 220–25.

15. Eduard Schweizer argues that Gal 4:4–5, Rom 8:3–4, John 3:16–17, and 1 John 4:9 reflect "a traditional line of thought or even a formula" that existed "even before Paul." See *TDNT* 8:374–76.

16. On the relation of Gal 3:13–14 and 4:3–6 see Hays, *Faith of Jesus Christ*, 95–117; J. Louis Martyn, *Galatians*, AB (New York: Doubleday, 1997) 408.

Why, then, would Paul use the phrase "likeness" or "form of flesh of sin" in Rom 8:3 (with the Greek word ὁμοίωμα)? Our best clue is found in Phil 2:6–7, another passage that describes Christ's entry into the world to share the human plight, in this case through voluntary self-emptying. In this passage "being born in likeness of humans (ἐν ὁμοιώματι ἀνθρώπων γενόμενος)" parallels "taking the form of a slave (μορφὴν δούλου λαβών)" as descriptions of the state resulting from Christ's self-emptying. Both contrast with a previous state: "being in the form of God (ἐν μορφῇ θεοῦ ὑπάρχων)." Neither of these two "forms" of existence is a superficial appearance; both involve real participation in the divine or human state. The language of form or likeness creeps in because this unique being exists in two contrasting forms; his story involves a transformation. The same kind of thinking lies behind Paul's reference to God's Son being sent "in likeness of flesh of sin" in Rom 8:3. His existence had a different form, but now, to fulfill God's redeeming purpose, he must share the life of sinful humanity. If we wish to reconcile Rom 8:3 with 2 Cor 5:21, we must at least maintain what Fitzmyer maintains: the Son of God "came in a form like us in that he became a member of the sin-oriented human race; he experienced the effects of sin and suffered death, the result of sin."[17] This participation in the plight of sinful humans is the necessary presupposition for dealing with sin in human life.

To this point I have argued for the importance of the Son's participation in the human plight, a pattern of thought found in Rom 8:3 and in the related passage in Gal 4:4–5. Phil 2:7–8 also proclaims, as a central event in the sacred story, Christ's voluntary identification with the human plight through emptying himself and "taking the form of a slave." Similar ideas are found in 2 Cor 8:9. Christ voluntarily "became poor, although he was rich." His self-renunciation and identification with human poverty enables an exchange of attributes: riches are exchanged for poverty by Christ but his poverty produces riches for impoverished people. In other words, Christ's self-renouncing identification with humanity in its need enables humans to participate in the blessings that rightly characterize Jesus Christ as God's Son. A similar exchange of attributes is expressed in 2 Cor 5:21, where Paul says that Christ was made "sin for us in order that we might become God's righteousness in him."

Paul goes further. He not only asserts that we benefit through participating in certain attributes of Christ. He also asserts that we participate

---

17. Joseph A. Fitzmyer, *Romans*, AB (New York: Doubleday, 1993) 485.

in Christ personally[18] and in his saving acts, his death and resurrection. I am suggesting that these further dimensions of participation rest on the same presupposition, the self-renouncing identification of God's Son with humanity in its need, based on divine initiative. The participation is first of all divine participation in the human plight, which makes possible human participation in God's Son.

At this point we must explore the relation between participation in Christ and faith. We must begin by rejecting the view, common in traditional Protestant theology, that Rom 1–4, with its emphasis on justification from faith, is an adequate statement of Paul's soteriology. It is not, as we should recognize when we note that it is primarily from Rom 5:12 on that Paul writes of liberation from the hostile powers of sin, death, flesh, and law, and relates this liberation to the death and resurrection of Christ. Romans, by itself, easily misleads because the key terminology of δικαιόω, "justify," and πίστις, πιστεύω, "faith, have faith," almost disappears between Rom 5:12 and 8:29, leaving the impression that Paul has moved on to new topics, although he is actually deepening his soteriology while explaining its implications. We get a better view of the connection between justification from faith and participation in Christ from Galatians and Philippians. In core passages in both of these letters, while arguing fervently for justification from faith and not works of the law, Paul expresses his argument in terms of participation in Christ. In these passionate passages Paul grounds his assertion that justification is based on faith, not works of the law, on the reality and surpassing value of participation in Christ. These same passages suggest a neglected but important dimension to the meaning of faith for Paul.

In Galatians, after his initial statement of justification from faith in 2:16, Paul argues as follows: "For I through law died to law, in order that I might live to God. I have been crucified with Christ. And I no longer live, but Christ lives in me" (2:19–20). Here Christ's death is proclaimed as a freeing and transforming event that is effective because Paul is pulled into it and shares in it, resulting in a continuing participation in Christ, who is the new life-power in Paul. The next sentence provides important explanation. In Gal 2:20b Paul reformulates his statement that "Christ lives in me" and does so in part in order to relate his new life to the previously introduced (see 2:16) theme of faith: "And what I now live in flesh, I live by faith, the faith of the Son of God who loved me and gave himself

---

18. There may be a hint of this in 2 Cor 5:21. We share in God's righteousness "in him" (ἐν αὐτῷ).

over for me." This is the self-renouncing Son of God that we encountered in previous passages, the Son of God who renounced his own advantages in order to identify with humanity in its need, a renunciation carried to the point of death on a cross (Phil 2:8).

The phrase "the faith of the Son of God" contains a disputed genitive that is part of a larger controversy. Should "faith of the Son" be understood as an objective genitive or a subjective genitive? That is, does it mean "faith in the Son of God" (the preferred translation in RSV, NRSV, and NIV), or does it mean "the Son of God's faith" or "faithfulness," the faith or faithfulness that he demonstrated? (Πίστις can mean "faithfulness" or "fidelity" as well as "faith" or "trust.")[19] In recent decades scholars have presented strong arguments for translating "the Son of God's faith" or "faithfulness."[20] I basically agree that Paul is referring to Christ's faithfulness in Gal 2:20 and similar passages (Rom 3:22, 26; Gal 2:16; 3:22; Phil 3:9), with this proviso: Christ's faith (= his faithful obedience) is a founding event that opens a realm of faith in which others are invited to participate. Christ's faith is originating faith that is prior to and foundational for the faith of his people.[21] When his people put faith in Christ, they enter this new eschatological reality. They participate in Christ and share his faith.

"Faith of the Son of God" in Gal 2:20 refers back to the two references to πίστις (Ἰησοῦ) Χριστοῦ ("faith of Jesus Christ") in 2:16. There Paul also uses the verb πιστεύω in the following statement: "We put faith in Christ Jesus (εἰς Χριστὸν Ἰησοῦν ἐπιστεύσαμεν) in order that we might be justified from Christ's faith (ἐκ πίστεως Χριστοῦ)." Here Paul writes of faith as a human action directed toward Christ as object, but this is placed between two references to the πίστις Χριστοῦ, Christ's faith / faithfulness.

The same combination occurs two more times. Paul seems to have developed something close to a formula with two elements: the πίστις Χριστοῦ phrase accompanied by the verb πιστεύω, applied to believ-

19. "Faithfulness" is the first meaning listed in BDAG. Douglas Campbell argues that "faithfulness" is a commoner meaning of πίστις in Paul than is usually recognized. See *Quest for Paul's Gospel*, 185–86.

20. See Hays, *Faith of Jesus Christ*, 141–62, 272–97; Morna D. Hooker, "ΠΙΣΤΙΣ ΧΡΙΣΤΟΥ," *NTS* 35 (1989) 321–42; George Howard, "Faith of Christ," *ABD* 2:758–60; Sam K. Williams, "Again *Pistis Christou*," *CBQ* 49 (1987) 431–47.

21. See Gal 3:22–25 and Williams, "Again *Pistis*," 446: "When Paul speaks of *pistis Christou*, he has in mind that faith which is given its distinctive character by the absolute trust and unwavering obedience of Jesus, who created, in the last days, this mode of being human in the world."

ers. We find the combination not only in Gal 2:16 but also in Rom 3:22, and in Galatians Paul returns to this formulation a second time in Gal 3:22.

- Rom 3:22. δικαιοσύνη δὲ θεοῦ διὰ πίστεως Ἰησοῦ Χριστοῦ εἰς πάντας τοὺς πιστεύοντας. "God's righteousness through Jesus Christ's faith for all who have faith."
- Gal 2:16. ἡμεῖς εἰς Χριστὸν Ἰησοῦν ἐπιστεύσαμεν ἵνα δικαιωθῶμεν ἐκ πίστεως Χριστοῦ καὶ οὐκ ἐξ ἔργων νόμου. "We put faith in Christ Jesus in order that we might be justified from Christ's faith and not from works of law."
- Gal 3:22. ἵνα ἡ ἐπαγγελία ἐκ πίστεως Ἰησοῦ Χριστοῦ δοθῇ τοῖς πιστεύουσιν. "In order that the promise from Jesus Christ's faith might be given to those who have faith."

In each case πίστις (Ἰησοῦ) Χριστοῦ occurs in a prepositional phrase (with the prepositions διά or ἐκ) that indicates the source of justification, of God's revealed righteousness, and of the fulfilled promise.[22] While the double reference to faith in these passages could simply serve to emphasize Paul's theme of faith in Christ, as some defenders of the objective genitive have argued, it would be strange for the combination to occur three times unless both aspects of the double reference to faith have individual importance.

Furthermore, Gal 3:22, viewed in context, provides important evidence. In 3:16 Paul begins discussing the promises to Abraham and his one seed. Paul's insistence that the promises were given to only one offspring of Abraham will work for him only because of the participatory ideas with which he completes his thought. Those who belong to Christ are Abraham's offspring and heirs because they have put on Christ and are included in Christ, as Paul asserts in 3:26-29. Participation in Christ is essential to Paul's argument here that the promises apply to all who belong to Christ, including Gentiles.

The continuation of Paul's argument in Gal 3:23-25 is also important for understanding 3:22, with its combination of πίστις Χριστοῦ and the verb πιστεύω, applied to Christ's people. One of the points most convincing to those who maintain that πίστις Χριστοῦ means "faith in Christ" is the assertion that Paul nowhere clearly attributes faith to Christ. The fact that Paul refers to Christ's obedience (Rom 5:19; Phil

---

22. In Rom 3:26 and Phil 3:9 also, πίστις Χριστοῦ (or Ἰησοῦ) occurs in prepositional phrases with διά or ἐκ.

2:8) is insufficient.²³ However, Gal 3:22–25, in its most natural reading, equates the coming of Christ with the coming of faith. Verses 23–25 provide a clarification of the πίστις Ἰησοῦ Χριστοῦ phrase that precedes them (the articles with πίστις in 3:23, 25 are anaphoric). "Before the (aforementioned) faith came," Paul writes, and later, "When the faith came." A few verses earlier (3:19) he wrote, "Until the seed would come." He is referring to the same coming when he uses the same verb to speak of the coming of faith. This faith was "going to be revealed" (3:23) at a particular time (τὴν μέλλουσαν πίστιν ἀποκαλυφθῆναι), the time of the coming of Christ.²⁴ The references to something coming and being revealed put the emphasis on divine action for human redemption, not on the human response. Paul is not talking primarily about the faith of Christian believers, which, by itself, could not play the crucial role of releasing people from confinement under the law. He is talking about the coming of Christ, whose life and work are characterized by faith and in whom believers participate as dependent heirs of the promise to the one seed of Abraham.²⁵

In the three quoted passages in Romans and Galatians, Paul repeats a flexible formula that connects and coordinates πίστις Χριστοῦ with a responsive faith in Christ. By repetition of this combination, Paul emphasizes the interconnection between faith viewed from two perspectives. There is the πίστις Χριστοῦ and there is a derivative faith, which, as faith in Christ, connects one to Christ, the originator of eschatological faith.

Returning to Gal 2:20, we can see that these two perspectives on faith come together in an illuminating way in this verse. Paul says, "I live ἐν πίστει ("in faith, by faith"). This is the human, active part, the con-

---

23. See James D. G. Dunn, "Once More, ΠΙΣΤΙΣ ΧΡΙΣΤΟΥ," in *Pauline Theology*, vol. 4, ed. E. Elizabeth Johnson and David M. Hay, SBLSymS (Atlanta: Scholars, 1997) 77; Gordon D. Fee, *Paul's Letter to the Philippians*, NICNT (Grand Rapids: Eerdmans, 1995) 325, n. 44. Note, however, that in Rom 5:19 Christ's obedience is referred to in a prepositional phrase with διά similar to the phrases διὰ πίστεως (Ἰησοῦ) Χριστοῦ in Rom 3:22 and Phil 3:9. In all three cases Paul is affirming that human redemption is based on Christ's saving action.

24. Compare "the fullness of time" in Gal 4:4. Note also that Paul makes the same sort of contrast in 3:19 and 3:23–25: a temporary period of the law's function, ended by that which comes ("the seed," "faith").

25. Williams recognizes the importance of Gal 3:2–25 for the πίστις Χριστοῦ controversy. See "Again *Pistis*," 437–38. Another possible reference to Christ's faith is Rom 1:17. See Douglas A. Campbell, "Romans 1:17—A *Crux Interpretum* for the Πίστις Χριστοῦ Debate," *JBL* 113 (1994) 265–85.

tinuing existence that corresponds to Paul's statement about the past in 2:16: "We put faith in Christ Jesus." But Paul continues, "I live in faith that is of the Son of God," faith that originated with him and characterized him. It is Paul's faith (the faith in which "I live," Paul says), but it is a participation in the Son's faith. This way of viewing faith fits with the preceding assertion that "Christ lives in me." Thus Paul's participatory thinking includes his understanding of faith, and we find this mode of thinking at the heart of passages that proclaim justification from faith.[26]

The importance of participatory thinking in Paul's defense of righteousness from faith, in contrast to righteousness from works of the law, is also clear in Phil 3:2–11. The purpose of the passage is to reject the need for circumcision and the "righteousness in law" (3:6) that Paul previously claimed for himself. Paul approaches the issue autobiographically and introduces the language of participation in Christ in order to make his point, resulting in an intermingling of references to righteousness from law or through faith (vv. 6, 9) and strong statements about participation in Christ (vv. 8–9a, 10–11). The goal of Paul's life now is to "gain Christ and be found in him" (3:8–9). Being "found in" Christ is a present as well as a future reality, for Paul goes on to explain his meaning by referring to possession of "righteousness from God" and participation in Christ's sufferings, as well as Christ's resurrection power. Not only being "found in" Christ but also "knowledge of Christ" (3:8) implies intimate relationship that crosses the line to participation in Christ, for in v. 10 Paul shifts to the related infinitive (τοῦ γνῶναι αὐτόν; "to know him") and explains this knowledge in terms of sharing in Christ's sufferings and his resurrection power.

Phil 3:10–11 is an example of Paul's use of the motif of dying and rising with Christ. Paul's usage falls into two groups, passages that refer to dying with Christ as a past event by which believers were transferred from the old dominion ruled by hostile powers to the new dominion of Christ (Rom 6:1–11; 7:4–6; 2 Cor 5:14–15; Gal 2:19–20; 5:24–25; 6:14–15), and passages that refer to a continuing participation in Christ's suffering and dying, especially through Paul's apostolic sufferings (Rom 8:17; 2 Cor 1:3–9 [cf. 7:3]; 4:7–14; 13:4; Phil 3:10–11). The continuing participation in Christ's suffering maintains and reinforces the break with the old dominion that took place through the past dying with Christ. Phil 3:10–11 contains a chiasm with two similar references to participation in

---

26. Note also that in Gal 2:16–17 Paul rephrases by shifting from being "justified from Christ's faith" to being "justified in Christ" (ἐν Χριστῷ).

Christ's suffering and death surrounded by references to Christ's resurrection, first as a present power and then as a future hope. It is an impressive example of Pauline passages that describe Paul's continuing participation in Christ's death through his apostolic sufferings.[27]

In v. 10 Paul uses two terms that we have not noted before: κοινωνία ("participation, sharing") and συμμορφιζόμενος ("being conformed").[28] The latter word is related to the adjective σύμμορφος, which occurs in two passages that show the goal of conformity to Christ, namely, full participation in Christ's resurrection glory by being conformed to his image (Rom 8:29–30; Phil 3:20–21).[29] But Phil 3:10 indicates that the process begins with conformation to Christ's death.

The participation in Christ that is now the goal of Paul's existence requires and grants a new kind of righteousness in place of his former righteousness from law. The two are presented in concise contrast in 3:9. The one kind of righteousness is "from law," and it is "my" righteousness. (See the list in vv. 5–6, which includes both birth privileges and personal accomplishments; trusting those things means putting confidence "in flesh," v. 4).[30] The other kind is "from God" and διὰ πίστεως Χριστοῦ ("through Christ's faith" or "faithfulness"). Here we encounter the same question of how to translate the genitive, but the emphasis here on the transcendent source of this righteousness ("from God") and the contrast with human righteousness ("my" righteousness) support the view that Paul is not thinking of human action but rather of Christ's saving action when he writes of the righteousness through πίστις Χριστοῦ. This view is also supported by arguments for the same interpretation of the same phrase in Romans and Galatians. The second reference to faith at the end of v. 10 is sometimes viewed as a balancing reference to the responsive faith of Christ's people,[31] but the addition of the article, which is probably anaphoric, suggests that Paul means "the righteousness from God on

---

27. See Tannehill, *Dying and Rising with Christ: A Study in Pauline Theology*, BZNW (Berlin: Töpelmann, 1967; reprinted Eugene, OR: Wipf & Stock, 2006) 114–29.

28. Note the present participle of ongoing action.

29. This is a bit of evidence supporting Morna Hooker, who regards Irenaeus' statement, "Christ became what we are, in order that we might become what he is," as a fair summary of Paul's thought. See *From Adam to Christ*, 26.

30. James D. G. Dunn, an advocate of the "new perspective" on Paul, recognizes that Phil 3:5–6 provides evidence for Paul's rejection of both ethnic privilege and personal accomplishment. See "Philippians 3.2–14 and the New Perspective on Paul," in *The New Perspective on Paul*, WUNT (Tübingen: Mohr Siebeck, 2005) 474.

31. See Stephen E. Fowl, *Philippians* (Grand Rapids: Eerdmans, 2005) 154.

the basis of this faith" (= Christ's faith). Paul does, of course, affirm the importance of responsive faith, as we noted in the study of passages from Galatians and Romans, and as we can also attest from Philippians (1:29; 2:17).

Philippians 3:2-11 shows that having the righteousness that was manifested through Christ's faithful act for suffering humanity is an aspect of knowing Christ and being found "in him." It is a participatory righteousness, a righteousness that comes as a gift because it is first of all another's[32]—one who allows his people to share it by having their lives shaped by him.

In summary, our study of Pauline passages shows that we cannot draw a sharp line between Paul's participatory concepts and his juridical concepts, centering in the theme of justification,[33] for Paul argues for justification from faith with participatory language. What we discover from Galatians and Philippians should affect our reading of Romans. When Paul shifts to participatory language in Rom 5:12-21 and 6:1—7:6, speaking of dying and rising with Christ and describing Adam and Christ as supra-individual persons, he has not moved on from soteriology to a new topic but is deepening his soteriology, providing further insight into how redemption in Christ Jesus has taken place and explaining its implications.

Furthermore, concentration on Christ's atoning death by itself presents a truncated version of Paul's soteriology. There is more to the Christ-story, and the rest of the Christ-story helps to explain how Christ's death *can* be a death "for us" in Paul's eyes. In particular, we have noted the importance of the Son of God's identification with humanity in its need and a responsive identification of believers with God's Son.

These two acts of identification are important clues to the underlying presuppositions of Paul's participatory language. Participation in Christ, including the participation in Christ's death that frees people from slavery to sin, depends upon God's identification with humanity in its need, which takes place through the sending of God's Son to share

---

32. See 1 Cor 1:30: "Christ Jesus, who became wisdom for us . . . and righteousness." See also Rom 5:18, which indicates that Christ's righteousness (his "righteous deed") is effective in restoring all people to righteousness.

33. One of the two sets of concepts tends to be subordinated to the other by interpreters. E. P. Sanders puts it this way: "There should . . . be no doubt as to where the heart of Paul's theology lies. He is not primarily concerned with the juristic categories, although he works with them. The real bite of his theology lies in the participatory categories, *even though he himself did not distinguish them this way.*" *Paul and Palestinian Judaism* (Philadelphia: Fortress, 1977) 502. Emphasis by Sanders.

the human plight, an act of self-giving by God the Father and by God's Son. This divine act of identification is primary and makes available divine transforming power. But there is an answering act of identification, which is the believer's response of faith in Christ. Paul's faith-language overlaps with his participatory language, as we have seen. The Pauline passages we have studied should lead us to expand our understanding of faith. Faith in Christ for Paul is not only a trust-bond with Christ but also an act of identification with Christ, an identification that responds to and remains dependent on Christ's identification with needy humanity. This reciprocal identification goes some way in illuminating the dynamics behind the participatory language that appears in central statements of Paul's soteriology.

Appendix

Even if my readers grant that the language of participation in Christ is important in Paul's soteriology, they may harbor the conviction that this language is entirely foreign to our experience, so much so that it cannot be appropriated by us. I do not wish to ignore the gap between Paul's thought world and our own, but I add the following brief suggestions as a warning against a hasty dismissal of Paul's thought.

In recent decades theological scholars have emphasized that stories have fundamental importance for individual and group identity. Stanley Hauerwas, for instance, writes that "there are aspects of our experience that make story unavoidable." Indeed, "the mysterious thing that we call a self is best understood exactly as a story."[34] This story involves more than personal events, for we understand our personal stories as parts of larger stories. Sallie McFague TeSelle affirms that a life-story "is basic to *human* experience as such, to one's sense of identity," but then she adds, "We learn who we are through the stories we embrace as our own—the story of my life is structured by the larger stories (social, political, mythic) in which I understand my personal story to take place."[35] For the Christian believer, the Christ-story is this sort of fundamental, defining story.

---

34. Stanley Hauerwas, *Truthfulness and Tragedy: Further Investigations into Christian Ethics* (Notre Dame: University of Notre Dame, 1977) 78.

35. Sallie McFague TeSelle, "The Experience of Coming to Belief," *TToday* 32 (1975) 160. Emphasis by TeSelle. Similarly, Stephen Crites argues that human experience itself has a "narrative quality." Therefore, it is understandable that stories may "shape in the most profound way the inner story of experience." See "The Narrative Quality of Experience," *JAAR* 39 (1971) 304.

We can supplement these affirmations by referring to the psychological process of identification. Identification can be defined as a "psychological process whereby the subject assimilates an aspect, property or attribute of the other and is transformed, wholly or partially, after the model the other provides. It is by means of a series of identifications that the personality is constituted and specified."[36] This normally begins when the young child identifies with its parents, but identification continues to be a powerful process in later life. It is manifest in the behavior of sports fans at a football game or soccer match. Even though most fans may not be personally acquainted with any of the players on the field, they identify with their team. The team's victory is their victory; its defeat is their defeat. In situations of conflict in recent history, such as the tensions among Sunnis, Shiites, and Kurds in Iraq, we can see how strongly ethnic and religious identification influences the sense of personal identity and impacts behavior.

A single person's story may be the point of identification. For some people, especially some African-Americans, the life of Martin Luther King, Jr., has life-shaping significance. They not only honor him; they identify with him. Certain features of his life-story help to explain its powerful significance. Other African-Americans could recognize that he was like them, not only in appearance but also by sharing their plight—purposefully sharing their plight by demonstrating his solidarity with them at risk to himself. Yet he, unlike people before him, was able to break the oppressive powers of a segregated society. He did it not only for himself but also for others, even though it cost him his life. His identification with others in their need was a crucial step in a story that now enables others to identify with him. The story of Martin Luther King, Jr., both invites others to live in the freedom that he made possible and provides a guiding image of what their life is meant to be.

All analogies have limits, and Paul has a special vocabulary for expressing Christ's identification with a suffering world and the believer's identification with him. But Paul's language of participation in Christ is not entirely foreign to human experience today.

---

36. J. Laplanche and J.-B. Pontalis, *The Language of Psycho-Analysis,* trans. Donald Nicholson-Smith (New York: Norton, 1973) 205. My thanks to Dr. Fulgence Nyengele for help in understanding the psychological process of identification.